"An exploration of Islamic beliefs and history that aims to challenge American Islamophobia.... A clear, concise, and thoughtful introduction to Islam."

– *Kirkus Reviews*

"In his comprehensive, helpful debut, Slocum, an aircraft design engineer and former missionary, encourages Christians to establish friendly relationships with Muslims.... Effectively countering pernicious, misinformed narratives, this is an essential contribution to interfaith studies."

– *Publishers Weekly*

"Why Do They Hate Us? takes a stand against prejudice by advocating a different approach to not just tolerating Muslims, but getting to know them on a personal level.... It stands out from the crowd in offering a powerful blend of historical, political, and personal perspectives on a very complex issue..."

– D. Donovan, Senior Reviewer, *Midwest Book Review*

"Steve Slocum skillfully encourages us to reclaim our sight and rediscover the beautiful truth about our Muslim sisters and brothers: just like us, they are beloved image bearers of the Divine. This book is for the peacemakers, the haters, and everyone in between who long to see more clearly and who dare to believe that God inhabits uncommon friendships and, through them, is remaking the world."

– Jer Swigart, Co-Founder, The Global Immersion Project, Co-Author, *Mending the Divides: Creative Love in a Conflicted World*

"Steve Slocum's *Why Do They Hate Us?* offers readers a highly accessible introduction to Islam as a lived religion along with a helpful blueprint for how to build and maintain peace between Muslims and majority populations in the West. **In an era of rampant Islamophobia, Slocum's book is essential reading.**

– Todd H. Green, author of *The Fear of Islam: An Introduction to Islamophobia in the West*

WHY DO THEY HATE US?

MAKING PEACE WITH THE MUSLIM WORLD

WHY DO THEY HATE US?

MAKING PEACE WITH THE MUSLIM WORLD

STEVE SLOCUM

TOP READS PUBLISHING, LLC

VISTA, CA USA

First Edition

ISBN: 978-0-9986838-6-7 (paperback)
ISBN: 978-0-9986838-7-4 (ebook)

Library of Congress Control Number: 2018964027

Why Do They Hate Us? is published by:
Top Reads Publishing, LLC,
1035 E. Vista Way, Suite 205
Vista, CA 92084 USA

For information please direct emails to:
info@topreadspublishing.com

Cover design: Nathan Johnson
Book layout and typography: Teri Rider & Associates

Printed in the United States of America

DEDICATION

This book is dedicated to Suzanne, Andrew, Maria, and Faith, the family who accompanied me to Kazakhstan without a single complaint. They embraced the culture and the people with love and enthusiasm. And they suffered hardships and emotional wounds that altered their lives. I honor their unchosen, but willing sacrifices.

CONTENTS

LIST OF MAPS AND FIGURES

PREFACE

My exposure to the Muslim world began when I was a student at the University of Arizona in the late '70s. I remember Middle Eastern students flooding the campus and driving around in luxury cars, apparently endowed with limitless cash from selling oil to the United States. I was appalled when I saw them demonstrating during the Iran hostage crisis, brazenly displaying signs saying "death to Carter," taking full advantage of our freedoms to threaten death to our president.

As a newly converted Christian riding the wave of the Jesus-people movement of the hippie era, I took my exposure to Muslims as a challenge—to penetrate their community and convert them to Christianity. The first step was to get to know them so I could learn and understand their culture. Armed with this awareness, I could craft culturally relevant arguments and convince them Islam was wrong and that they should convert. Although my motivation was not pure, in the process of befriending them and learning their culture, I was greatly enriched.

My sense of intrigue for the culture of the Middle East Arabs continued to percolate over the years as I got married and raised my three children. I always found Arab students to invite over to the house for Thanksgiving dinner or some other holiday. I began researching opportunities to go to the Middle East as a Christian missionary. It took several years to convince my wife at the time, but we eventually packed all our things and headed to Kazakhstan with our three children. We lived there for five years. It was not exactly the Middle East, but it was a Muslim country and only a seven-and-a-half-hour flight from Kabul, and that was good enough for me.

While there were a handful of mosques in the major cities of Kazakhstan that had angry mullahs and orthodox teaching, the vast majority of city dwellers and villagers cared nothing for Islamic orthodoxy and were more concerned about staying healthy and having enough food to eat. As such, the actual religious practices followed were pre-Islamic: shamanistic in nature and folkish, involving rituals for healing and invoking the blessings of ancestors.

The Kazakhs, who describe themselves as "a humble people," take the practice of hospitality to the next level. Once, when visiting a Kazakh family for the first time, my family and I were treated with the customary generosity and given continuously replenished plates full of fatty mutton and succulent noodles. I was shocked to later find out we had consumed the last of this generous family's food. I felt ashamed for not being aware of the economic realities nor clued in enough to politely refuse without bringing shame upon the family.

We developed a deep love for our neighbors and friends. These dear souls generously shared what little they had and patiently guided us every step of the way. From buying bread on our very first day to tipping workers with bottles of vodka, they taught us how to survive. Never will I forget the kindness shown to us. I was an engineer with an advanced degree, finding myself wonderfully connected to Kazakh families who had been keeping herds of sheep as their primary livelihood for generations. I was deeply enriched and forever transformed.

My goal was to learn the language and culture so I could convince them to become believers in the Bible and followers of my version of the Christian teachings. I actually never quite got out of the mode of learning their language and culture in the five years I was there, and I never changed anyone's mind to become a believer in the Bible. It happened all on its own, as it did with many of the former Soviet bloc countries. Religion and spirituality had been the forbidden fruit during the seventy-year reign of the USSR, when communist atheism was the mandated religion. When this curtain of darkness was lifted, the people who lived under this oppression were joyfully discovering their spirituality and entering into a very real and lasting connection with something greater. It was a time of transformation and great joy for many people. I merely sat in the front row and watched it happen.

In the process, though I went to Kazakhstan to change people, I myself was transformed. By uprooting myself from the comfortable and the familiar, by choosing to honor the local people by learning their language, culture, and customs, I was able to get past the barrier of strangeness, of foreign-ness, and see that, although this group of humanity lived in an alternate reality from me, they were truly no different than me.

The wise whitebeards and elderly women struggled with aches and pains, complained about how today's youth don't appreciate the ancient customs, eventually passed on, and families mourned. Hardworking mothers and fathers slogged through the days, doing their best to get their children fed, clothed, educated, and launched into productive lives. The voices of teen boys grew deeper, while teen girls grew beautiful and shy, and boys and girls went from playing games to flirting and finding a life partner. Small children played, ate, and were the delight of their parents.

This was my transformation. The ethnicities and cultures I had an opportunity to experience while living in Kazakhstan are a small fraction of all those represented on this planet. And were I to repeat this experience in nearly any one of them, I would see the same humanity—births, joys, struggles, and departures.

And so, when one child dies, no matter if he is a Syrian refugee who didn't quite have the strength to make the journey, or the Turkish toddler who somehow escaped from the arms of her mother and was run over by a donkey cart, or the four young Palestinian boys who were killed by Israeli artillery while playing on the beach, my tears are the same as if I had seen it happen out in the streets from my own second-floor balcony. Each child who dies in some faraway place is not some "other" kind of creature. I know their parents are crying the same agonized tears I cried when I lost my son.

And so, we are truly one.

Since returning to the states in 1997 and reintegrating into my life here, I witnessed the horrible tragedy of 9/11 play out on my television screen. I watched the subsequent response of two invasions, with round-the-clock media portrayal of Islam as a religion of terror. After sixteen years of this message being pumped into Americans' heads, it is not surprising that we view any Muslim with suspicion, and are, in general, not in favor of providing assistance of any kind to Muslim refugees.

"Why Do They Hate Us?" is my labor of love to attempt to repay my debt to the wonderful people of Kazakhstan. In it I tell the story of the silenced Muslim mainstream.

My transformation experience in Kazakhstan provides the backdrop for the content of this book. It is by no means a comprehensive academic work, but rather a broad sketch of the geographical, historical, and political background along with personal stories. I hope you read it and find understanding.

Humbly,
Steve Slocum

INTRODUCTION

I've never been more terrified. Fear gripped my chest. I could feel it surround my rib cage and squeeze, along with a palpable physical sensation inside my chest cavity. My heart was racing, and sweaty palms gripped the steering wheel as my eyes strained to pierce the whiteout conditions. I was caught in the jaws of a vicious snowstorm dumping several feet of snow on the road over the treacherous pass just south of Ouray, Colorado. To make matters worse, my teenage daughter was sitting next to me in the passenger seat. We were on our way to the Durango airport after a spring break ski/snowboard trip to Telluride, Colorado. Having skied all week in sunny, bluebird conditions, we were dressed for our arrival in the sunny Southwest and driving a cheap rental sedan, which had seemed like a good idea at the time.

Snow was building up quickly as I tried to keep the car moving without touching the brakes. I leaned forward and got my face as close to the windshield as I could to get a better look at the taillights of the pickup truck some distance in front of me. My daughter didn't make a sound, but I know she saw the sheer drop off just outside the passenger window. I felt the front wheels lose traction while we rounded a hairpin turn, and I was forced to let my foot off the gas pedal. Regaining traction, I slightly accelerated onto a straight section with a steep upward slope on the passenger side and a steep drop on my side. The taillights of the pickup truck had now disappeared.

We rolled forward another hundred feet or so, and I no longer had any reference connecting my visual navigation system to the road. I suddenly realized all I saw was white. I was no longer able to distinguish sky from ground, up from down, or left from right. I had no idea where the road was in the three-dimensional space of endless white that had swallowed me up. It took about three seconds for the terror I was feeling to ramp up to the level of full panic. I remember shouting, "I can't see, I can't see!" and hearing my daughter scream.

My mental faculties barely functioning at this point, I instinctively slammed my foot on the brake, my panic overriding my awareness to only use the brakes with feather touch. I felt the car sliding, heard my daughter screaming, and I let out a long shout. And the car stopped.

As my heart began to stop pounding, my eyes were giving me no clues. I rolled my window down and stuck my head out to see if I could figure out what had just happened. I was so relieved to no longer be sliding that I didn't at first realize how close we had just come to disappearing until the summer thaw. I stared for a moment, confused by the mountainous pile of snow I had just plowed into. I slowly realized that we had narrowly missed being swept off the mountain by the massive avalanche now blocking about one hundred feet of the road in front of us. And I couldn't help wonder about the vehicle whose taillights I had been following. The highway department eventually showed up and guided the long line of cars that had begun to form back down the way we had come up. We were snowed in for several days.

Fear can overpower the bravest of us.

Terror is a tactic designed to trigger an irrational fear response in order to achieve political ends. My instinct to slam my foot onto the brakes while driving in a foot of snow was an irrational response to the terror I was feeling. And I contend that America, in response to the terror and trauma of the 9/11 attacks, has been in an ongoing state of fear toward Muslims. On a national level, we have responded with an all out "war on terror" across the ocean, including the invasion of Iraq, which had nothing to do with 9/11. The "war on terror" rages on in over a half-a-dozen countries, as of 2018. The fear has become so obvious and pervasive that a new term has been created: Islamophobia—the fear of Muslims.

Unresolved trauma often leads to the suppressing of associated emotional responses that are too powerful to face. So perhaps the fears related to our individual trauma from 9/11 remain on an unconscious level. I found this to be true for myself, until I did some recent international travel and those fears bubbled up into my consciousness.

I was killing time at my gate at the San Diego airport, lost in deep daydreams of adventures that lay ahead on my long-anticipated two-week trip to the Austrian Alps. My concentration was reluctantly extracted from a world of mountain chalets and alpine views to the sound of a strange language, yet somehow recognizable. As I unconsciously turned toward the sound, I saw a dark, bearded man, unmistakably Muslim, speaking what must have been Arabic into his cell phone. I heard words I recognized like *al-hamdulillah* (praise be to Allah) and *inshallah* (if Allah is willing). As I became aware of a creeping fear beginning to squeeze my chest, I found myself consciously wishing this man was not on my flight. The fear nagged me throughout the flight as I kept tabs on his whereabouts. We, of course, arrived at our destination without incident.

In April 2016, passengers on a Southwest flight were about to depart on a quick hop from Los Angeles to Oakland. They overheard a young man mention ISIS in his cell phone conversation and close the conversation with *inshallah*. According to the CNN report, within two minutes he was removed from the plane, undergoing searches and questioning. Subsequently, he was told by the airline, "Southwest will not fly you back," even though the FBI took no further action.[1] Unfortunately, this is not an isolated incident.

The psychological trauma produced by the spectacularly horrific 9/11 attacks has proven to be deep. How many of us can instantly recall the exact moment we received that phone call from a friend or loved one telling us something terrible had just happened and to turn on the TV?? The emotional damage caused by repeatedly watching those video clips of 737s full of passengers smashing into the sides of the World Trade Center towers cannot be overstated.

With Americans in the throes of post-traumatic stress, nine days after we watched the horrific collapse of the twin towers onto their own footprints, then president George W. Bush gave us the explanation our traumatized hearts were begging for in his address to a joint session of Congress. In his speech he posed a hypothetical question on behalf of all of us: "Americans are asking, 'why do they hate us?'" His wholly inaccurate answer powerfully reinforced our fear and set the stage for America's ongoing irrational response. He said: "...they hate our freedoms: our freedom of religion, our freedom of speech, our freedom to vote and assemble and disagree with each other."[2]

Now, over sixteen years after the 9/11 attacks, Islamophobia is at an all-time high, and the so-called war on terror is escalating uncontrollably. Islamic State groups are as resilient as dandelions, seemingly defeated and eliminated, yet only scattering to the winds of war and coming to life tenfold somewhere else. Meanwhile, hardly a week goes by without another news report of a disturbingly violent attack on random individuals in the West, both Muslim and non-Muslim, in reciprocating fashion.

Where is this runaway train car of violence and hatred going? With approximately 1.7 billion Muslims on the planet representing 25 percent of the world's total population, continued escalation and proliferation of wars and random attacks can only lead us to nightmarish outcomes.

Donald Trump's presidential campaign had a major anti-Muslim focus, and it is not a stretch to believe that this focus played a key role in his victory. As president, Trump has followed through with his campaign promise by issuing an executive order banning citizens from certain predominantly Muslim countries from traveling to the United States. He has also escalated military operations in Syria, Iraq, and Afghanistan, while promising the Saudi King a $110 billion arms deal and maintaining Israel's annual allotment of almost $4 billion in military aid. As of March 2018, the United States was involved in direct military or covert operations in at least six Muslim countries, yet, after three heads of state, Americans still do not have an accurate answer to the question, "Why do they hate us?" And fear marches on.

Several years ago I set out to find the answer to this question for myself. I wanted to understand the origins of Islam, its history – especially the part about becoming an empire, the present day teachings of Islam and practice of everyday Muslims, and I wanted to understand the connection with modern day extremism and terror. In my literature search, I found books that focused on the politics; I found books about the positive teachings of Islam, mostly written by Muslims; and the negative teachings, written by Christians; and I found books about Islam's storied history. But I didn't find a single book that connected all the dots and answered my question, from the perspective of a non-Muslim. *Why Do They Hate Us?* is that book.

The process of healing the psychological damage caused by severe trauma is complex and laborious, requiring great courage on the part of the victims. This process can be aided by introducing truth-based awareness of the circumstances surrounding the traumatic event. "Why Do They Hate Us?" seeks to help with this awareness by identifying who "they" are, and then painting an accurate portrait of the rest of Islam's 1.7 billion souls.

It is my hope that a better understanding of Islam's mainstream will help Americans take important steps in the healing of our collective and individual psyches. With a measure of healing and some awareness, we will be better equipped to make individual decisions and political policies that are not founded in fear.

May God give us courage.

INTRODUCTION NOTES

1. Carma Hassan and Catherine E. Soichet, "Arabic-Speaking Student Kicked Off Southwest Flight," *CNN* (April 18, 2016), https://www.cnn.com/2016/04/17/us/southwest-muslim-passenger-removed/index.html.

2. George W. Bush, "Text: President Bush Addresses the Nation," *Washington Post* (September 20, 2001), http://www.washingtonpost.com/wp-srv/nation/specials/attacked/transcripts/bushaddress_092001.html.

JIHAD AND SHARIA LAW ARE EVIL... RIGHT?

Islam's Roots in Social Justice

Terror is a weapon. The fear is real. 9/11 opened a gaping wound and left Americans feeling vulnerable. No longer was Islamic terror something that happened only in a crowded café in Tel Aviv. Since 9/11 we've lived with threat-advisory scales at airports and watched horrific news reports of mass beheadings in ISIS-held regions. It's no wonder that the fear of many Americans has grown in the years since 9/11.

Fear mongers exploit our fears for profit. Political opportunists fan the flames, brazenly using fear to expand their voter bases. And lies proliferate. A simple Ecosia[1] search on a phrase such as, "the Quran teaches killing," will turn up multiple websites that are full of anti-Islamic gibberish.

> It is the duty of every Muslim male to wage war against Infidels – not just by preaching and persuading, but by any means necessary and as the world has seen, by <u>extreme violence whenever possible.</u> It is one of the core beliefs of Islam.[2] [emphasis mine]

> Since Islam teaches that the entire world is to be subjected to its laws, we need to prepare ourselves to withstand <u>the</u>

future attacks motivated from the Quran that teaches killing in subjection of the unbelievers.[3] [emphasis mine]

Sharia is explicitly opposed to religious freedom, freedom of conscience and the free exchange of ideas. It is violent, openly bigoted toward non-Muslims, discriminatory, and unflinchingly sexist. Large sections deal with the practice of slavery.[4] [emphasis mine]

Dozens of action movies featuring Muslim terrorists such as *The Kingdom*, which depicts the suicide bombing of an American oil company compound in Saudi Arabia, have grossed hundreds of millions in box office sales in the United States—even before 9/11.

The award-winning TV series *24*, featuring Kiefer Sutherland as counter-terrorist agent Jack Bauer, premiered less than two months after 9/11 and continued for eight seasons, spanning 192 episodes. It became the longest running counterterrorism television drama in history.

Even the most moderate of cable news outlets, incentivized by viewer ratings, provides continuous coverage and analysis of each and every violent act of deranged terrorists. "Expert" commentary on the teaching of Islam is offered as an explanation.

The unsurprising effect of the universal portrayal of the typical Muslim as a demented fanatic has been to normalize radicalism—to conflate the acts of an extremist minority with those of a vast majority who are themselves often the victims of radical terrorism. By doing so, it is my contention that we have played directly into the hands of terrorist leaders by rendering impotent the most powerful force of Islam—its 1.5 billion mainstream moderates.

So let's take the spotlight off of the extremists and shine it on the ordinary Muslim. What is the bearded imam with the white cap and flowing robes teaching in the mosque that's in your city? Is he secretly teaching holy war against American infidels? And that mysterious woman wearing the hijab that you often see in the market—what about her? Is she biding her time until Sharia law is established?

With the truth about Islam shrouded in a mysterious fog, it's easy for such questions to formulate themselves in our minds. But the fresh sea breeze of awareness disperses the dark clouds of fear to reveal sunny, blue skies and crystal-clear visibility. The first thing we see is a helpless baby boy in the desert of Arabia, unaware of the fight for survival that lies ahead of him.

NO HELP FOR THE HELPLESS – MOHAMMED'S TRAGIC CHILDHOOD

The first Muslim was Mohammed. Before he had taken his first breath of desert air, the Hijaz had already dealt him its first blow. The Hijaz is the mountainous, desert region along the western coast of Saudi Arabia containing Islam's holiest cities. The year was 570 A. D. His father had succumbed to the unrelenting perils of caravan travel, where even the slightest mishap can be fatal, and died a young man, only days before the birth of his first child.

From the moment he was born without a father, Mohammed would be held captive by powerful, unarticulated cultural norms, even as a member of the most powerful tribe in Mecca, the Quraysh. Unless he could create his own fortune from nothing and establish a family, he was doomed to be an outsider—a loner, a castaway. As no man's heir, he had nothing to inherit. With no family status or inheritance, no father would give his daughter to Mohammed in marriage. It was far more likely that he would be reduced to a life of slavery.

Mecca is situated in a stagnant basin surrounded by volcanic hills. Smoke—from cooking fires and a smoldering mountain of manure on the edge of the city—hovered in the air. In the 100°F desert heat, life was almost unbearable. As in all ancient cities, the child and infant mortality rate was high. Infants had less than the flip-of-a-coin chance of surviving.

Any family in Mecca with the financial means to do so sent their infants to wet nurses among the Bedouin tribes on nearby desert oases. But the punishing cultural and economic realities took effect immediately for tiny Mohammed. Cultural norms required that Mohammed and his mother, Amina, be taken in by a male relative on her side. They would have been provided with food and shelter--nothing more. The wet nurses required payment for their services. Their families depended on this for survival. Now branded as a widow, Amina had no chance of securing a wet nurse, and it was looking like baby Mohammed would be taking the long odds in Mecca.

But coincidentally, one of the Bedouin mothers had also fallen on hard times and had been the only mother unable to secure a suckling on their group visit to Mecca. Perhaps she hoped that Amina would remarry and be able to pay after all, perhaps she simply didn't want to be the only one in the group without an infant to take back to the oasis. Either way, Mohammed's chances of survival went up dramatically when she collected him into her arms and joined her group for the return trip.

The city dwellers, known as sedentary Arabs, and the nomadic Bedouins needed each other. Just like the inhabitants of New York and Los Angeles depend on Iowa corn and Nebraska cattle, the people of Mecca depended on the Bedouins for the basics of life. But they didn't like each other. The Meccans considered the Bedouins unsophisticated hillbillies. The Bedouins disrespected the Meccans for abandoning the traditional life of the Arab to live in permanent dwellings in the city.

The Bedouins were similar to the indigenous groups of other continents. It was a centuries-old society organized by clans and tribes. There were no physical boundaries and no local or regional governments. Tribes shrunk and expanded, based on the collective good fortunes of their members. With limited desert resources as basic as water and grazing space—along with expanding flocks and herds—clashes between clans were common. And they were every bit as bitter as the Hatfields and the McCoys. Relations with other tribes and the social order within a tribe were managed by the sheikh. The sheikh was elected from among the tribal elders and did not serve as a ruler, but more as a judge. He had no authority to enforce his recommendations, which were made in consultation with the other tribal leaders.

Survival of the tribe in the harsh desert conditions depended on a cohesive social order. Anything questionable or under dispute was settled based on the group interest of the tribe. One of the key responsibilities of the sheikh was to look after the well-being of the weaker members such as widows and orphans. Characteristics such as patience, endurance, hospitality, and generosity were highly regarded.

In Mecca things were different. The fortunes of the Quraysh tribe and of the city itself were centered around an annual pilgrimage. It started out as a religious festival involving masses of people gathering around a small cinderblock enclosure covered in cloths dyed red and black, known as the Kaaba. Within the Kaaba were idols representing various deities. The crowds would encircle the Kaaba and walk around it seven times while chanting and worshipping.

Over time, the leader of the Quraysh, an innovative businessman named, Qusayy, managed to monopolize the organization and execution of the festival and ultimately took complete ownership of it. He next took steps to maximize attendance by including virtually all of the deities of the region in the religious rites, namely, in the circling of the idol-filled Kaaba. Worshipers from Arabia and the surrounding regions all made the yearly pilgrimage to Mecca.

Such a diverse gathering of clans and tribes was the perfect opportunity for trade, so the festival evolved to include a commercial fair. The Quraysh managed every aspect, including fees and taxes for entrance, care of livestock, housing, and all buying and selling of goods. The brilliant Qusayy had succeeded in creating a universal religious festival, which he then linked to a commercial fair, fully administered by the Quraysh. He thereby guaranteed their economic, religious, and political supremacy.

The Quraysh elite became obscenely wealthy. The inevitable outcome was an oligarchic system and a breakdown of the tribal ethic. Widows like Amina and orphans like Mohammed were no longer protected by a wise sheikh who was duty-bound to ensure the survival of all—even the weak. The wisdom of the sheikh gave way to a ruthless, survival-of-the-fittest culture. The unviable were often trapped in a cycle of coming up short, borrowing just to get by, being unable to repay, then eventually forced into a life of slavery to their debtor.

Mohammed's two-year reprieve among the Bedouins came to an end all too quickly and it was time to return the waddling toddlers to their mothers. But the breakdown of the social order would force another interesting twist for Mohammed. Traditionally, a widow would have been remarried not long after losing her husband. One of her husband's brothers would have stepped up and taken her as a wife, even if he was already married. Taking a second or third wife in these situations was considered a matter of family honor—a means of providing for the family of a deceased brother. And this would have allowed a widow and her children to be folded back into a normal family with all the associated benefits: provision, protection, and inheritance. The whole family shared in absorbing the financial burden of the loss. In Amina's case, even after two years, she was still on her own, causing some to speculate that she suffered from a chronic illness or had some other defect.

But, when it was time to hand Mohammed over to his mother, the Bedouin wet nurse surprised everyone by asking if she could keep Mohammed for a little longer. Perhaps it was a moment of compassion, or perhaps they were short a son for the task of tending flocks. Apart from the apocryphal stories of Mohammed's presence bringing abundance to the family, history offers no explanation. Amina, seeing no future for her son, consented. It was almost as if, in a moment of desperation, she had given Mohammed up for adoption. He would spend his formative years as a Bedouin.

As I consider Mohammed's early years living among tent-dwelling herders in the desert, I can't help recalling my own vivid experiences living in yurts among the mountain-dwelling nomads of Kazakhstan. Days are spent balancing the unpredictable forces of nature to eke out survival. Nights sometimes pass slowly, with only the felt coverings of their yurt separating a family from what lurks in the darkness outside.

For the Kazakhs, roaming about freely in the open spaces of the Tien Shan mountains or the Great Steppe—literally in Kazakh: "the great outside"—held profound meaning. The Kazakh word for heaven is simply "green." The image of a solitary yurt lost in the vastness of seemingly infinite grass-covered hills and mountains makes it easy to understand why.

A constant connection to the elements that sustain life—fresh mountain air, glacial streams, rich green grasses, the stars, the animal world, and familial love—produces a quality of life that is profound in its simplicity. Each day begins with the first one awake stepping through the small doorway into the chill air of the great outside. Family members sleep side by side like sardines, covered by blankets filled with wool batting. Almost like part of the family, the large flock of sheep and goats are penned up for the night just outside of the yurt, only a few feet away. The thick felt coverings of the yurt provide little attenuation to the sound of animals breathing, and the eerily human-sounding cough of a goat.

After each rises and steps out for a moment of privacy and a quick splash of icy water to the face, the family sits down to a simple breakfast of bread and tea, supplemented with milk, sugar, and jam. Afterward, the head of the family does a quick assessment of the flock and picks out any needing attention before sending them out for grazing with two or three of the boys. The boys take a stash of bread and dried curds and are not seen again until just before sunset. For drink, they take along animal-skin canteens filled with *kymyz*—fermented mare's milk. Each family possesses at least one mare used by the head of the household to check on the flocks and survey new areas for grazing.

Mother and daughters, and perhaps a grandmother and an aunt, work nonstop from dawn until well after dark. They start and maintain cooking fires, bake bread, pour an endless stream of tea for breakfast and lunch, milk animals, prepare the evening meal, and keep up with all the dishes and housecleaning—all with only the most primitive of supplies and ingredients. By the end of the day, they look exhausted. And there are no days off.

Before dark, dad and the boys slowly make their way back with the flocks. After the sometimes-comical chasing down of the last wayward sheep and closing the pen, all traipse back into the yurt, pull off their boots, and sit down, expecting to be fed. A hearty dish of boiled mutton with fatty broth and homemade noodles is served up, and the long evening of storytelling begins. After an exhausting day of flowing with the forces of nature, the wealth of internalized experiences is released around the warmth of a crackling fire in the coziness of a warm yurt. Those of us who have had enjoyed a family camping trip can perhaps recall the magical feeling around the campfire. For nomads, this experience is woven into the fabric of their daily existence.

During the dinner meal, the lighter chatter takes place. The boys brag of adventures of the day and the girls catch up on gossip. Eventually, a teenage daughter kneels to the floor at the end of the low table that is closest to the door and begins serving milky tea—an important part of the rites of hospitality that continue throughout the evening. She pours a spoonful of milk, some concentrated black tea, and hot water into a small bowl and hands it to the person on her right. This person then sends it all the way around to the head of the household, who is sitting on the floor at the opposite end of the table, in the place of honor. She does the same for everyone else at the table, and not long after everyone is served, the first sends his bowl back for a refill. The process is repeated countless times throughout the evening.

About the time that modern families turn on the television, the evening entertainment for the nomads begins. Nomadic cultures are steeped in all the facets of oral tradition—song, poetry, and storytelling. And the gifted spontaneously bring forth artistic creations in the media of language and song. As soon as they are old enough, kids participate, giggling and reciting simple poems. Both men and women take their turn uttering poetic verse or telling stories from the past. Everyday language is not used. A richer form emerges as they become mouthpieces of ancestral spirits. The complex and profound combination of phonetics, meter, rhyme, intonation, and meaning that flows from the mouth of the orators is captivating. I remember being spellbound, limited only to hearing and feeling. It wasn't until much later that I realized I was participating in an ancient tradition that few in the modern world have had the opportunity to experience.

During a pause, the family musician retrieves the two-stringed dombra and begins strumming in contemplative minor keys. The singer belts out a high-pitched song pregnant with extended, wailing notes at the end of each line—one of the haunting ballads about the trials faced by the Kazakh people. As the song goes on and fades into the background, faces become somber and eyes go glassy. Eventually, the children begin to drop off and the yurt grows silent as the ladies quietly go about the task of cleaning up after dinner. They are the last to crawl under the wool blankets and close their eyes.

Growing up among the Bedouin, Mohammed would have experienced a very similar life—with the exception of one key element.

Though not openly affectionate, Kazakhs greatly value the bonds of familial love. From the fat-faced toddler clinging to his mother throughout the day to the toothless grandma who groans every time she gets up from the floor, something more powerful than the frame and coverings of the yurt holds them all together. Each family member is unconsciously aware of their security within the genetic community defined by their yurt. So clear-cut is this definition that the Kazakhs use the name of a critical component of the yurt structure to symbolically define their family.

The gently sloping top surface of the circular yurt is supported by about twenty equally spaced wooden frames. Each frame begins at the vertical, exterior wall and extends toward the apex, where it is inserted into a wooden ring about three feet in diameter. This circular member, known as, the *shanyrak,* is every bit as symbolic as a wedding ring. As it ties all of the members of the yurt's ceiling structure together, so it represents the powerful connectedness of the family. Fathers and grandfathers proudly proclaim the blessings of God on their *shanyrak* in eloquent orations at festive gatherings for holidays and weddings.

Perhaps it was her recollections of seeing such a lifestyle among the Bedouin nomads that persuaded Amina to relinquish her son to be raised by strangers in the desert. Mohammed would spend his early years intimately connected with nature and observing the Bedouin traditions—he would be raised as a pure Arab.

With the substitution of the desert sand for the green grasses of the Kazakh summer pastures (and the addition of camels), Mohammed grew up in much the same way as the Kazakh children I would observe 1400 years later. As soon as he could walk he began accompanying his foster sister in the daily task of tending the flocks. By the time he was five, Mohammed was managing the flocks on his own, making a solid contribution to the family.

During the long days, Mohammed would learn the discipline of solitude as a child surrounded by the often terrifying forces of nature. During the evenings he would absorb the rich traditions of nomads. After the dinner meal, little Mohammed would drift off into dreamland to the sounds of prosaic stories and enchanting songs.

This was a society that recognized that if any member of the community suffered, all suffered.

But it wasn't only a connection with the natural world and the absorption of the oral tradition of the Arabs that he took away from his time among the Bedouins. The mores and values of their communal society were solidly embedded in his psyche. This was a society that recognized that if any member of the community suffered, all suffered. One that elevated, not the richest and most powerful, but the wisest and most generous. A community that provided for those rendered helpless by the often cruel judgments of nature and chance.

Even though little Mohammed was functionally included in the community and provided for, his identity as an outsider was reinforced. Among the Bedouin, he would never feel the unconscious comfort of a family community. While other sons and daughters were called by name, Mohammed was called by the title, the *Qurayshi*. And, the little *Qurayshi* was about to be dealt another severe psychological blow.

By the time Mohammed had reached the age of five, a Bedouin child had likely become available to do his job. The downside of Bedouin lifestyle is that the less fortunate household operated on a thin margin. At five years old, Mohammed was now just another mouth to feed. It was time to turn the *Qurayshi* back over to the Quraysh.

Since his birth, Mohammed had only lived with his mother for a few months. And his reunification with her would be short-lived. Amina must have been miserable living with her relatives in Mecca. Only months after her son was returned to her, she embarked on a desperate journey to the agricultural oasis of Yathrib, 200 miles to the north, in search of distant relatives who could perhaps take her and her son in. But her quest was unsuccessful. She either did not find any living relatives, or she was rejected by them. Not long after arriving they found themselves making the return trek to Mecca. Along the way, Mohammed would watch the mother he barely knew take her last breath as she succumbed to the elements—and to the cruelty of the Meccan societal order.

Six-year-old Mohammed was brought back to Mecca and passed to his feeble grandfather, who died less than two years later. Next in line was his uncle on his father's side, Abu Talib, who had been noticeably absent up until his point. Why had he not stepped up to marry, or at least care for Amina? Under his uncle's care, Mohammed would finally get a chance to begin carving out an identity for himself.

LOVE FOR THE UNLOVED – MOHAMMED'S CAREER AND MARRIAGE

Abu Talib was a wealthy merchant who maintained a large herd of camels used as beasts of burden for trade caravans. In addition to a continuous stream of smaller caravans into and out of Mecca, twice a year as many as 2,000 camels were assembled for lucrative trade excursions—one traveling as far as Damascus to the north, the other to Yemen in the south. Abu Talib put Mohammed to work caring for the camels. At first he was confined to the milk camels, critical for maintaining herd size. In this capacity, his early childhood education as a Bedouin herder would prove invaluable. He was more skilled with the stubborn beasts than his Qurayshi counterparts. After two years Mohammed began working with the traveling dromedaries—the castrated males-and Abu Talib started taking him along on the semi-annual trade expeditions. Mohammed's world was about to get a lot bigger.

It's one thing to observe the ways of strangers from the comforts of home. It's something else entirely to *be* the stranger in a faraway place with every sense screaming for a single familiar thing.

Mecca was a hub of international activity as the destination of the three-month-long religious festival and trade fair. Mohammed had already encountered merchants and pilgrims from faraway places. It's one thing to observe the ways of strangers from the comforts of home. It's something else entirely to *be* the stranger in a faraway place with every sense screaming for a single familiar thing. Mohammed's most interesting destination was undoubtedly the ancient city of Damascus. The Great Silk Road passed through Damascus, just sixty miles before coming to an end at the Mediterranean Sea. It was also the northern terminus of the caravan trade route from Mecca. Even at that time, Damascus was an ancient city. It had already been in existence for 1,600 years by the time Mohammed was born. It was under the control of the Byzantine Christian Empire at the time Mohammed would have first seen it. Prior to that, it had seen a handful of kingdoms and empires come and go.

From a cultural perspective, as the intersecting point of two of the world's great trade routes, Damascus would have vied for the title of "World's Most Exotic City." Along for the caravan ride, our teenage Arab herder would have heard the four tonal variations of Cantonese and exotic sounds from Persian stringed instruments. He would have seen the glorious architecture of the cathedral dedicated to John the Baptist and perhaps learned it had once been the temple of Jupiter. Among the merchants he would have encountered deep blue lapis lazuli from mines in Afghanistan, Buddhist texts etched on fragments of bark from the East, and colorful Indian spices. He would have watched the dancing of mystics, listened to conversations between Zoroastrians and Taoists, and seen the place where St. Paul had his revelation of Christ. His brain synapses must have been on fire. As the world would later find out, Mohammed was paying attention.

He was getting a top-notch education in world religions and culture with a minor in international commerce. Seeing that his nephew was intelligent and loyal, Abu Talib began keeping Mohammed by his side as he went about his affairs. Mohammed began to learn key economic principles such as how the supply of and demand for various commodities affected their market value. He learned to keep his eyes and ears open in order to gauge accurate price points for raw materials such as wool, leather, silver, and gold and the lucrative aromatics such as frankincense and myrrh.

He learned how to navigate local requirements to ensure safe passage of the massive caravan through the various territories between Yemen and Damascus: taxes, duties, customs, and protection money. Over the years at the side of Abu Talib, Mohammed became proficient in all aspects of the merchant caravan business, ultimately becoming Abu Talib's trusted lieutenant.

But Mohammed was not like the other merchants. In a business full of liars and cheats, Mohammed distinguished himself for being a man of his word. During my five years living in Kazakhstan, I shopped hundreds of times at bazaars full of merchants from afar. At first I was easy prey and fell for any trick. One of their favorites was the time-honored bait and switch routine. I walk up to the stall and see the beautiful apricots in the bucket and say I would like to buy a kilo of them. While I am counting out my money to the seller's partner, the first merchant quickly removes the top layer of plump apricots and dumps a kilo of bruised and pocked apricots into my bag, which I don't think to check. Eventually I learned to expect something from the bag of tricks with virtually every purchase.

Had it been Mohammed selling me apricots, I'm sure he would have shown me all of fruit he was putting into my bag and he would have charged me a fair price for it. And he would have earned my repeat business. In a trade where cheating is the norm, an honest man would be noticed. Mohammed's reputation as a man of integrity was so universally recognized that people started to refer to him as simply, "The Trustworthy One," or al-Amin, in Arabic.

Mohammed had come a long way from his beginnings as the unfortunate only child of a yet more unfortunate widow. By patient determination, he had worked his way up from being a recipient of the cultural welfare system to the position of right-hand man to a wealthy merchant. He was entrusted with the wealth of his uncle, which gave him further assurance that he now belonged.

By now Mohammed was well beyond the age of marriage for a normal Arab male. On the long caravan journeys, he was surrounded by men who missed their families and cheered themselves up by telling stories about them around late-night campfires. Mohammed felt only the cold darkness of being alone. His longing heart began to stir, and a scenario for creating his own family began to take shape in his mind. Feeling courageous because of his uncle's implicit trust in matters of business, Mohammed worked up the nerve to request the hand of Abu Talib's daughter.

Mohammed's request was as symbolic as it was personal. He wanted to belong. And he desired companionship and a family. Marriage between first cousins was common among all cultures of the sixth century. But Abu Talib's response made it clear that, just as he had no interest in taking on the burden of his brother's widow, he wouldn't be sharing his children's inheritance with her penniless son: He rejected Mohammed's request outright.

Mohammed was mercilessly brought back to the reality of who he was.

> In the name of God, the merciful to all, the Mercy Giver:
>
> I swear by the Late Afternoon, the human being is surely in a state of loss. Except for those who have believed and done good deeds and urged one another to Truth and urged one another to patience. (The Quran, surah 103)

If there was anything that Mohammed was good at, it was patience. From spending long days in the desert with flocks and herds at the age of four, to dreaming of a loving companion as a young man, Mohammed was a paragon of endurance.

He continued faithfully serving his uncle, but it would never be the same. Mohammed was now completely clear on his status, and his tentative hopes of being part of an ancestral circle seemed forever dashed.

But his qualifications and status did not go unnoticed. Another social outcast in the merchant caravan scene of Mecca began to take note. The enigmatic forty-year-old named Khadija was fifteen years Mohammed's senior, twice widowed, and childless. Although an aging widow in a man's world, her business skills and intriguing personality allowed her a place among the elite merchants of Mecca. She had inherited her second husband's share in the merchant cartel and was in need of a trustworthy agent. Well past the age of marriage and wealthy in her own right, Khadija was an independent woman who cared little about the constraints of Meccan social order. She offered Mohammed the position of senior agent representing her interests in the Damascus-bound caravan in the year 595 CE. Mohammed saw this as an opportunity to be out from under the control of his uncle and readily accepted.

The chemistry was undeniable. Sharing the common ground of profound loss and social status outside the mainstream, they connected deeply—two lonely souls at long last finding a counterpart. Upon Mohammed's return from the Damascus excursion with double the expected profits, Khadija rewarded him with a proposal for marriage. After two-and-a-half decades of being an outcast, Mohammed finally belonged.

The chemistry was undeniable. Sharing the common ground of profound loss and social status outside the mainstream, they connected deeply—two lonely souls at long last finding a counterpart.

Socially and economically, at the age of twenty-five, Mohammed had scratched and clawed his way into a respectable position in Meccan society. Having inherited nothing, he would now provide an inheritance to his four daughters by Khadija. Tragically, their son, Qasim, passed away before the age of two, leaving Mohammed without a male heir. But Mohammed had arrived.

For fifteen years, Mohammed, Khadija, and their children enjoyed wealth and prosperity. He had achieved his status without the benefit of a patriarchal figure and in spite of a childhood filled with loss. Mohammed was defiantly independent and needed no one. But even though he had overcome hopeless odds to position himself in the upper strata of society, The Trustworthy One was not satisfied. He was surrounded by a ruthless, oligarchic system that rewarded the haves, enslaved the have-nots, and made a mockery of the sacred pilgrimage. Mohammed had good reason to be disillusioned.

By this time, he had been exposed to Christianity, Judaism, and Zoroastrianism—all monotheistic religions. Jews had been emigrating from Palestine to Arabia since the days of the Roman Empire, and many Arabs converted to Judaism. Christianity is claimed in the New Testament to have found its way to Arabia via the apostles Peter and Paul, along with Thomas. Most Arabs practiced a form of polytheism.

Prior to the birth of Mohammed, the concept of an all-powerful, single, creator God had begun to emerge from the polytheistic mix. This God was known as *al-ilah*, or *Allah* in contracted form. But such a lofty God was not accessible; therefore, prayers for good health, riches, and safety from the deceptive spirits known as *jinn* were made to lesser gods.

The connection of Islam to Judaism goes back to the book of Genesis and plays a key role throughout the life of Mohammed.

For mediation between man and God, the spiritual poet—or soothsayer—was called upon. Known in Arabic as the *kahin*, these clairvoyants did not actually have access to God himself, but only to the jinn. They provided answers in the form of vaguely worded prose that was open to interpretation about matters such as finding a lost item of value, difficult decisions, and interpretation of dreams.

The connection of Islam to Judaism goes back to the book of Genesis and plays a key role throughout the life of Mohammed. Arabs and Jews trace their origins to half brothers of the same father, Abraham (or Ibrahim, as transliterated from the Arabic). In Mohammed's time, the Jews were part of the fabric of every day Arab life. The distinction between Arab converts to Judaism and those who had made their way to Arabia from Palestine in one of the various invasions was fuzzy, and both were considered Jews. Religious scholar, Reza Aslan, in his book, *No god but God*, describes the intermingling: "There were Jewish merchants, Jewish Bedouin, Jewish farmers, Jewish poets, and Jewish warriors throughout the Peninsula. Jewish men took Arab names and Jewish women wore Arab headdresses."[5]

The situation was similar with Christianity. Huge numbers of Arabs had converted to the way of Christ, and the city of Sanaa in Yemen was the site of a teeming Christian pilgrimage.

Mohammed was fully aware of the corruption of the opportunistic Quraysh leaders who had made themselves virtual kings of the Kaaba. He was the trustworthy one, and this did not sit well with him. In his own personal contemplations, Mohammed was gravitating toward the God concept of the Christians and Jews—the one known as Allah in the Arab pantheon.

He had had two decades to process the contradictions between the cohesive social structure of the Bedouin communities of his childhood and the predatory nature of Meccan society. He hated seeing the less fortunate being preyed upon and treated as outcasts. He was an empath, and he knew firsthand what it was to survive on the fringes. He saw the desperation in the eyes of the lame beggars and felt the pain of the child-slaves and wished something better for them. As an empath myself, I imagine him misty-eyed, pressing generous gifts into the palms of as many as he could, and feeling guilty that he could not help them all.

Perhaps it was the destitute widows begging for alms that touched the rawest nerve. The childhood memory of clinging to his mother as she slipped away into the next realm lingered in the dark places of his soul. Her expendability was not lost on him. As long as she was alive, Mohammed was destined to be the child of a desperate widow with little future besides begging or slavery. But after Amina's death, the social order placed Mohammed into the hands of patriarchal figures—first his grandfather, then his uncle. Under the patriarchal umbrella, Mohammed prospered. The value of a woman in Meccan society could not have been clearer to Mohammed's tender soul.

ISLAM IS BORN – MOHAMMED'S PROPHETIC CALLING

The visions began in 610 CE. Mohammed was forty years old. Disillusioned and contemplative, he often retreated to the mountains and caves surrounding Mecca for days at a time. On one of those dark desert nights, Mohammed had a heavenly visitation that would awaken his prophetic calling.

Mohammed's spiritual encounter was not a moment of ecstatic bliss. In subsequent descriptions to those close to him, he recalled feeling himself being squeezed by a powerful, unseen force. Three times the crushing pressure was repeated, and Mohammed was panic stricken, believing that an invisible creature was killing him. He fell to the ground terrified and thought to escape by hurling himself down the mountain. But in that moment, he heard a voice that identified itself as the angel Gabriel, who issued the command, "Recite!" Trembling, Mohammed asked, "What should I recite?" To which Gabriel responded with the first divine utterance to the newly commissioned prophet: "Recite in the name of your Lord who created, created the human being from a clinging substance. Recite, and your Lord is the most generous, Who taught by the pen. He taught the human being that which he knew not (The Quran 96:1–5)." And the archangel departed.

Mohammed was bewildered and shaken. As his head slowly began to clear, Gabriel's words were etched in his mind. He began to grasp what he was being commanded to do. And he wasn't happy about it. It had seemed like the fulfillment of an impossible dream to find himself married to a wonderful companion, the father of several children, and fully accepted as a member of society. He had worked hard to achieve his status. If the vision was real, he would be thrust out into the open as something like a soothsayer reciting mystical prose, and he feared the ridicule of the Quraysh. Mohammed wasn't even sure if it was real; he began to wonder if he was a madman. Distraught and disoriented, he climbed to the top of a precipice and again considered throwing himself off the mountain. Gabriel appeared again and restrained him.

Mohammed eventually pulled himself together enough to scramble back down the mountain and find his way back to the one person who could help him make some sense of this experience. When he found Khadija, he could only ask her to wrap a blanket around him and comfort him. Seeing that her husband was badly shaken, Khadija began to coax the story out of him. She knew her husband to be a hard-working man of integrity, serious and of sound mind. Seeing him in this state, it was obvious that her husband had had a profound experience. She gave Mohammed the comfort he needed by reminding him of his character and believing in him. She assured him that he was being rewarded with a divine encounter.

Khadija wisely sought the guidance of her deeply spiritual cousin, who had studied the Bible under Jews and Christians. Her cousin assured Mohammed that he had been called to be a prophet to the people.

With such reassurances, Mohammed slowly began to come to terms with his experience and accept the fact that he had been called by God. Mentally at least, he began to embrace his role as a spokesman for God. He believed he was ready. But nagging doubts about his sanity reemerged when two years passed without another word from the Most High. Mohammed had long since stopped managing Khadija's merchant business. He had begun spending many of his days and nights in contemplation and prayer in the same locale as the initial visitation.

Without warning or explanation, two years after the first experience, the revelations resumed. The early utterances were filled with reassurance:

> By the pen and all they write, you are not, by the grace of your Lord, a madman. And you will have a never ending reward. And you are a man of great moral character. You will see and they will see which of you is afflicted by madness. Your Lord knows best who has strayed from His path, and He knows. Then do not obey the unbelievers. They wish that you compromise, so they too can compromise (68:1–9).

There were words about the nature of God: "The Lord of the East and the West; there is no god but Him (73:9)," "He is the Source of all righteousness, and the source of all forgiveness (74:56)."

There were tender references to his childhood experiences:

> By the morning light and the night as it settles, your Lord did not abandon you, nor is He displeased. The life to come is better for you than this first life. And your Lord is sure to give you (so much), and you will be satisfied. Did He not find you orphaned, and shelter you? Did He not find you lost and guide you? Did He not find you impoverished and enrich you (93:1–8)?

Judgments were proclaimed upon those who took advantage of the less fortunate:

> It is you who are not generous with the orphans, you who devoured the inheritance (of others) with obvious greed, and you who passionately love wealth. No indeed! When the earth is crushed, pounded and crushed and your Lord comes with the angels, row after row, on that Day, Hell will be brought near. On that Day, and the human being will remember, but what good would that be to him then? He will say, 'I wish I had provided for this life to come. On that Day, none will punish as He punishes. And none will shackle as severely as He shackles (89:17–26).

There were revelations about heaven: "There will be Gardens of delight for those who are mindful of God (68:34)," and revelations about hell, "We have shackles and Hell and food that chokes and a painful punishment reserved for them, on the Day when the earth and the mountains tremble (73:11–13)."

The utterances focused on two themes: the goodness of God, and social justice as a response to God's goodness. Many believe that Mohammed focused on monotheism in his teaching regarding the nature of God, however Reza Aslan points out the broader message: The common understanding of the creator God was as an all-powerful yet distant force. Mohammed taught of a generous and benevolent God, intimately involved with his creation, who deserved heartfelt gratitude.[6] In the first revelation after Mohammed's initial visitation, we hear of a most generous God, who teaches man what man does not know (96:4). The title of chapter fifty-five is "The Merciful-to-All" and speaks of God creating man, teaching him and providing for him "fruits and date-palms in clusters and grains on flourishing stems and fragrant plants."

The only worthy response to such a compassionate and merciful Creator is a life of integrity and kindness. For example, in chapter 55:1–9:

> The Merciful-to-all taught the Quran, created man, taught him articulate speech. The sun and the moon run on precise calculations. The stars and the trees submit to Him. The skies He raised high and has established the balance, that you may not transgress in the balance, but weigh with justice, and do not violate the balance.

The mention of the balance referred to the scales used to weigh out grain or spices in the market, still used in the bazaars of Central Asia. A common trick for cheats and thieves was to use an underweight standard for one side of the balance, meaning that an underweight portion would be meted out on the other side to the buyer.

This passage directly connects an example from everyday life for a merchant to the description of God as a compassionate Creator. This is a common occurrence in the Quran, and it reveals the spiritual underpinning of Mohammed's reputation in the business world as The Trustworthy One. The Quran teaches of an inseparable connection between knowing of a compassionate God who is involved in our lives and a life lived with integrity and generosity towards those in need.

Orphans are mentioned in the Quran twenty-two times, usually included in a list of those one should help and do good unto, along with one's parents and kinfolk, the poor, wayfarers, beggars, and slaves.

A place in the heavenly gardens is reserved for the obedient and punishment is pronounced upon those who deny the "Lord's marvels," and who do not obey his commands. "Arise and warn!" he was commanded.

This was the early message of the Prophet, and it rang true in the hearts of his wife, his young cousin Ali, and a growing band of companions.

Still unsteady and not ready to accept his role, Mohammed remained quiet for a time. Eventually he began to share the convictions that had been percolating in his heart. Considering the psychological effect of Mohammed's childhood, understandably he was not brimming with confidence or charisma. He was an introvert. For some time, he shared his thoughts with only his closest relatives.

After Khadija and Ali, next in line to receive his message was his slave, Zayd, whom Mohammed hastily freed, followed by Abu Bakr, a fellow merchant and close friend of Mohammed. Abu Bakr had a rather exuberant personality and was unable to restrain himself from sharing Mohammed's profound new teaching with those around him, resulting in a small surge of new followers.

MOHAMMED COMES OUT – PERSECUTED BY THE QURAYSH

As the passionate yet introverted prophet, Mohammed shared his ideas with his early followers for some three years after receiving his first revelation. As he gained confidence, he began to emerge in public arenas to speak. As long as Mohammed quietly taught among his small band of followers, the Quraysh men of influence had no issues with him. But when Mohammed went public, the Quraysh leaders began to take note.

It was not his teaching of caring for those in need they found threatening, but his rigid proclamation that there is no god but Allah and that this idea had begun to get some traction among the masses. Mohammed's well-known character, along with his call for generosity towards the less fortunate, lent credibility to his proclamation regarding the nature of God.

The Quraysh had seen this before. Previously, a monotheistic group known as the *Hanif* had emerged from among the polytheists; the Quraysh were not taken by surprise and deftly managed the diversities of deities, along with warring tribes, to bring the populace en masse to Mecca.

But Mohammed was not playing the game. Put simply, the statement "There is no god but Allah" was clearly understood to mean that all the other deities were false. This was an open insult to their ancestral religion and was going to be a problem when it came to attracting worshipers of more than 300 gods to Mecca. The Quraysh began to view Mohammed as an existential threat and launched an aggressive campaign to silence him.

Mohammed was a member of the family, or "house," of the Hashim, of which Abu Talib was a leading chieftain. This was no small matter when it came to the law of retribution. As a deterrent to the escalation of violence, the law of retribution not only allowed but demanded life-for-life retaliation if a member of one's family was murdered. The Quraysh wouldn't touch Mohammed as long as he was under Abu Talib's guardian protection.

They tried every means at their disposal to cut Mohammed off from this umbrella of protection. When a direct appeal to Abu Talib failed, they launched a two-year economic boycott of the tribe, in hopes that other family members would prevail on Abu Talib to turn Mohammed over to them. When this also failed, they offered a direct bribe and even a substitute son to take Mohammed's place. Abu Talib refused to withdraw his protection, though he never accepted Mohammed's teaching. Mohammed agonized over the hardship he was bringing upon his faithful uncle.

With the Quraysh bearing down upon Mohammed and his family, his childhood friend—tragedy—struck again. Within a few short weeks, Mohammed lost his wife and companion of almost two decades, *and* the uncle who had been a father and protector to him. While still in the early stages of grief, he suddenly found himself exposed to an immediate threat of death. Mohammed had no choice but to flee.

Now in his fifties, Mohammed was barely able to escape Mecca with the help of Ali, who risked his own life by playing the role of Mohammed's decoy. His companions also slipped out of the city a few at a time. Those without the benefit of guardian protection suffered physical abuse and narrowly escaped with their lives. For now the Quraysh had the upper hand.

The community regrouped in a place hauntingly familiar to Mohammed: the agricultural oasis of Yathrib. His father's grave was in Yathrib and it was on a visit to Yathrib that his mother had succumbed to the power of the desert. Mysteriously, it was here that Mohammed and his small band of followers started over. Their message had been rejected by their own families and neighbors. Remarkably, in spite of the fact that Mohammed and his companions were fleeing in shame, it is at this very point in history that the Muslim calendar begins. Not at the time of Mohammed's ecstatic revelations, but at this point of defeat.

Something amazing was about to happen in Yathrib.

SHARIA LAW – JUSTICE FOR THE POOR AND THE WEAK

I was seventeen years old. Having just graduated from high school, I was now on campus at the University of Arizona studying mechanical engineering. It was 1973. I remember being captivated as I stood at Speaker's Corner outside of the student union listening to the street prophets preaching about Jesus. It wasn't long before I found myself in daily Bible studies and attending meetings at a nearby house church.

My heart burned with spiritual passion as I gathered with these committed believers and was challenged to a life of true discipleship. The words of Jesus were all that mattered: "Seek first the kingdom of God, and His righteousness, and all these things [earthly needs] will be given to you as well." (Matthew 6:33) "If anyone wishes to come after me, he must deny himself, take up his cross daily, and follow me." (Luke 9:23) "This is the greatest commandment, that you love the Lord your God with all your heart, all your soul, all your strength, and with all your mind." (Matthew 22:37). With these words burning inside of me, I turned away from all things worldly and became a *true follower*. I attended Bible school in Chicago, became a church leader and frequent speaker, and ultimately ended up as a missionary in Kazakhstan with my wife and three children.

To grasp what happened in Yathrib, it's important to understand what Mohammed's band of followers had given up. We have already seen the importance of family connections within a clan and tribe for the sake of economic status and protection. Those without such connections were vulnerable and often became slaves. Many of these committed disciples had abandoned their tribal connections to the most powerful tribe in Arabia, the Quraysh. Just like the disciples of Jesus, they had left everything and followed.

Even though they lived some thirteen centuries before me in the deserts of Arabia, I feel somehow connected to them. Like me, they had no idea what lied ahead. Leaving behind their livelihoods and their families, they were starting over in an entirely new place, knowing only that they believed in Mohammed. There was nothing theoretical about their forsaking of all to follow. They followed literally, as my family and I did when we went to Kazakhstan. In so doing, they created something entirely new.

In some ways this idealistic community was just another tribe or clan. However, it was not organized according to genealogy and birthright, but ideology. One simply needed to make the profession of faith, known as the *shahada*: "There is no God but Allah, and Mohammed is the messenger of God."

When this band of believers was forced from the comfort of their own homes and family connections in Mecca, they had to focus on their own survival as a community in a faraway place. And something incredible happened. Rather than pouring themselves into attempting to change the culture of Mecca, they simply lived out the principles that Mohammed was teaching. Thus, they took Mohammed's revolutionary teachings from theory to practice, laying the groundwork for what was to become Sharia law.

The importance of this special community in Yathrib (later renamed Medina, hereafter used interchangeably) cannot be overstated. Aslan, in *No god but God*, states:

> There exists an enduring mythology about Mohammed's time in the city that came to bear his name, a mythology that has defined the religion and politics of Islam for 1400 years. It is in Medina that the Muslim community was born, and where Mohammed's Arab social reform movement transformed into a universal religious ideology.
>
> "Mohammed in Medina" became the paradigm for the Arab empire expanded throughout the Middle East after the Prophet's death, and the standard that every Islamic kingdom and Sultanate struggled to meet during the Middle Ages. The Medina ideal inspired the various Islamic revivalist movements of the 18th and 19th centuries, all of which strove to return to the original values of Mohammed's unadulterated community as a means to wrest control of Muslim lands from colonial rule (though they had radically different ideas about how to define these original values). And with the demise of colonialism in the 20th century, it was the memory of Medina that launched the notion of the "Islamic state."
>
> Simply put, Medina is what Islam was meant to be.[7]

Medina is the kernel of the expression of Sharia law. Mohammed's movement was about sweeping social reform. It focused primarily on ensuring that the poor and weak did not become the prey of the rich, but also on integrity in business dealings. These matters were seen as the expression of true worship of the one true God. As this new social order began to develop, in many ways it was similar to the traditional tribal social order, in which a sheikh, in concert with other tribal elders, made sure the weakest members of the tribe were adequately provided for. But Mohammed's social order had several revolutionary concepts.

Mohammed's movement was about sweeping social reform. It focused primarily on ensuring that the poor and weak did not become the prey of the rich, but also on integrity in business dealings.

A key principle of the tribal order was known as "the Law of Retribution," which is nothing other than "an eye for an eye and a tooth for a tooth." This law was universally applied, with a kind of weighting factor based on the economic statuses of the offender and the one offended. A rich person offended by a poor person was entitled to a greater retribution than the offense, and vice versa. Mohammed brought two radical variations to the law of retribution.

First, the concept of forgiveness: "The retribution for a bad deed is one like it, but whoever forgives and makes peace will have his reward with God," (42:40). Forgiveness is a well-known Christian teaching, and its power is transforming. Only God himself can say how many wars could have been avoided, how many children could have been saved, what an entirely different planet this would be, had both Christians and Muslims merely observed this teaching common to both.

Secondly, over a millennium before it was stated in the United States Declaration of Independence: "We hold these truths to be self-evident, that all men are created equal," Mohammed eliminated any distinction based on wealth in the enforcement of the law of retribution—to the chagrin of the wealthier members of the community.

Usury—the practice of charging interest on loans—was strictly forbidden. Mohammed established an interest-free and tax-free banking system.

Mohammed's prophetic vision for compassionate community, in contrast to the heartless cruelty he witnessed daily in Mecca, are captured by Sadakat Kadri in his wonderful book, *Heaven on Earth: A Journey Through Sharia Law from the Deserts of Ancient Arabia to the Streets of the Modern Muslim World*:

> Whereas Meccans seem to have believed that life after death differed little from life before it, Mohammed began to warn that a great reckoning awaited everyone and that earthly deeds carried eternal consequences. In his telling, God was about to snuff out his stars and set seas boiling, and as creation shuddered to a close, trumpet blasts were going to wake all the dead there had ever been. There would then be a time at which commendable deeds would be weighed against sins—the Final Hour—and all the signs suggested that Meccans were in line for scorching winds, molten brass, and unquenchable hellfire.
>
> The apocalyptic vision was informed by solid moral arguments. The world into which Mohammed had been born was so stratified that clans did not even intermarry, while women were chattels and slaves bore a shameful status that lasted through generations. Vengeance was as valued as mercy was considered weak, and though the Meccans venerated three goddesses, the birth of an actual girl was so inauspicious that custom allowed for female infanticide. Against that backdrop, Mohammed had begun to claim that his followers were morally equal, regardless of sex or social standing, and to teach that clemency was no flaw but a virtue—so much so that compassion (al-Rahman) and mercy (al Rahim) were the first of God's many names. The killing of a single person was meanwhile tantamount to the murder of all humanity, and at the Hour of Judgment every baby girl ever slaughtered in Mecca would indict her parents from her grave but there was hope. Penitents might yet spend an eternal afterlife in cool gardens of endless delight.[8]

When we in the West hear the term Sharia law, we usually think of things like capital punishment by decapitation for blasphemers, chopping off of hands of thieves, or the stoning of an unfaithful wife. So we tend to be incredulous when the populaces of Muslim countries—including the women—seem to be in favor of it. Our perception comes from extremist groups such as ISIS or the Taliban, and not from Islam's mainstream. And we often hear non-Muslim "experts" quote verses from the Quran out of context in an attempt to prove that the Quran teaches the violent version of Sharia law. A careful look at the passages in question reveals a different story—that violence is far from the essence of Sharia law.

With reference to beheading, there are only two verses containing somewhat vague language thought to provide justification:

> 47:4 So, when you encounter the unbelievers (in battle), strike at their necks. Then, once they are defeated, bind them firmly. Then either release them by grace, or by ransom, until the war is over. God could have defeated them Himself if He had willed, but He wants to test some of you by means of others. As for those who are killed in the cause of God, he will not let their deeds go to waste.

> 8: 11 Your Lord revealed to the angels, "I am with you. Make the Believers stand firm; I will put terror into the hearts of the unbelievers. So strike above their necks and cut off their fingers."

It is important to remember that these verses were written during the period of persecution of Mohammed's followers by the Quraysh of Mecca, which will be covered in more detail in the following section covering *jihad*. The sayings are to be understood within the context of defensive struggle. They have nothing to do with civil law, and the conjured-up Western image of marching unbelievers (such as Christians) before bearded executioners for beheading. Although beheading was a standard form of capital punishment in both the Byzantine Christian Empire and the Arab world at the time, these two verses do not address any form of capital punishment, but rather refer to battle.

One particular list of punishments is highly cited in isolation as proof of Mohammed's extreme violent tendencies:

5:33 Those who wage war against God and His Messenger and strive to spread corruption on earth should be punished by death, crucifixion, the amputation of their hands and their feet, or should be entirely banished from (the face of) the earth. Such is their disgrace in this world...

It is misleading to attempt to assign meaning to this portion of a verse without considering the context. Looking at the complete context (5:27–34):

27 (Prophet) tell them the truth about the story of Adam's two son—how each of them offered a sacrifice, one sacrifice being accepted and the other being rejected. One said, "I will kill you!" The other replied, "God only accepts the sacrifice of those who are mindful of Him."
28 "even if you tried to kill me, I will not try to kill you. I fear God, the Lord of all the worlds."

29 "I would rather you bear the burden of my sins as well as yours. Then you will be destined for the fire. That is the destiny of the unjust."

30 His selfishness caused him to murder his brother. He killed him and became doomed.

31 God sent a raven to scratch the ground to show him how to cover his brother's body. He cried out, "How awful! Am I so helpless that I cannot do what this raven has done?" He then buried his brother and was filled with sorrow.

32 Because of this, We decreed to the Children of Israel that if anyone kills a human being, unless it is in punishment for murder or for spreading corruption on earth, it will be as though he had killed all of human beings. And, if anyone saves a life it will be as though he had saved the lives of all human beings. Our Messengers came to them with evidence of the truth. Yet, many of them continue to corrupt earth by their overindulgence.

33 Those who wage war against God and His Messenger and strive to spread corruption on earth should be punished by death, crucifixion, the amputation of their hands and their feet, or should be entirely banished from (the face of) the earth. Such is their disgrace in this world. In the Hereafter, a terrible punishment awaits them –

34 except for those who repent before you overpower them. You must bear in mind that God is forgiving and Merciful-to-all.

The first six verses (5:27–32) of this passage are plainly teaching that murder is wrong. God says the killing of one person is equivalent to the killing of all mankind, and the saving of one person as saving all mankind. Virtually every Muslim I have spoken with, as the conversation inevitably turns toward terrorism, quotes this verse to me, in context, denouncing terror as a violation of the teaching of the Quran.

Next, God states that he sent messengers to make sure that this concept of murder being wrong was understood. And yet "many of them continued to corrupt the earth by their over indulgence," referring back to the "children of Israel" and apparently referencing their long history of apostasy. In verse thirty-three, Mohammed applies this teaching against murder to his present day, referring to "those who wage war against God and his Messenger," clearly referring to the Quraysh.

Next, four degrees of punishment are prescribed, starting with capital punishment and ending with banishment, presumably linked to the level of injury caused. Crucifixion was common in that day and not a capital form of punishment. The recipient survived. It seems clear that the degrees of punishments are for varying degrees of crime. The most natural interpretation is that those who commit murder would face capital punishment, an injunction still practiced in the majority of the states of the US. Those who inflict lesser injuries would receive lesser punishment.

Finally, verse thirty-four is almost never included by those intent on proving that Mohammed taught killing in the name of Islam. Mohammed repeatedly emphasized the mercy of God and his willingness to forgive those who turned away from wrongdoing. In this case, even for the crime of murder, capital punishment was to be waived if the murderer repented.

I've spoken with dozens of Muslims in America. Each is feeling the sting of having their faith identified as a source of terror. They are careful to point out, citing this passage, that the Quran teaches nonviolence. I especially remember one conversation with Fatima, an Afghan filmmaking student. We were talking during some down time at a social event in a San Diego mosque. She bristled with anger and frustration that some were teaching that Islam commands the killing of infidels. She shared recollections of her grandfather teaching her, even during the Soviet massacres that took place in the 1980s, "No matter what the Soviet monsters do, we will not kill them in revenge."

Those who isolate the punishment of verse thirty-three from the description of the crime in the rest of the passage, and the opportunity for forgiveness, go beyond doing injustice to the passage or just missing the point. They actually *reverse* the true meaning of the passage.

A single verse is thought to command amputation for stealing:

> 5:38–39 As for the men and women who steal, cut off their hands as punishment for what they have done. It is a deterrent ordered by God. God is almighty and wise. As for him who repents after having done wrong, and makes amends, God will accept his repentance. God is most forgiving and most Merciful-to-all.

This verse is by no means unambiguous with reference to the penalty for stealing. The Arabic word translated "cut off" is also used in a general sense meaning "to cut." Some interpreters understand the command to be to about placing a cut on the hand of the guilty one, scarring them for life, making their history obvious to the merchants in the marketplaces. However, it seems the majority of Muslim scholars give preference to the amputation version; even now, this punishment is practiced in some places, including Saudi Arabia.

Again, with reference to adultery, the punishment is extracted from a single verse:

> 24:2 The (unmarried) woman or man found guilty of adultery, lash each one of them with 100 lashes, and do not let compassion for them prevent you from obeying God's law, if you believe in God and the Last Day. And let a group of the believers witness their punishment.

The practice of stoning an adulterous woman to death, as *is* taught in the Old Testament, is not present in the Quran.

It goes without saying that any form of violence as a form of punishment—lashes, lacerations, etc.—have no place in today's world.

Mohammed's commandments about the treatment of women are perhaps the most controversial and misapplied, from not long after his death until today. Having been married for over two decades to a woman who was fifteen years older than him and who, remarkably, carried her own weight among the leading men of Mecca, Mohammed had a unique perspective. As always, his primary concern was fairness. He considered men and women to be equal, yet understood their different roles. A significant portion of his following was women, so in matters of divorce, property ownership, and passing on of family inheritances, women were to be treated fairly. This was in stark contrast to the social order of not just all of Arabia but virtually the entire known world.

Although the Quran limits the number of wives a man may take to four, with the injunction that all must be treated equally, Mohammed himself had twelve wives, and the last was but a teenager. This also has been latched onto as another point of criticism of Mohammed. Obviously, the culture in seventh century Arabia was different than that of twenty-first century America. My purpose is not to justify Mohammed for having a teenage wife in middle age. When we consider the fact that the Virgin Mary was also a teenager when "the Spirit of the Lord overshadowed her," perhaps we can have a more open mind about how revelation adapts to culture.

With respect to the concept of having multiple wives, an important consideration is that many men had been lost in battle, leaving wives as widows and daughters as fatherless. Marriage brought with it the responsibility of providing for each wife, so this principle actually resulted in otherwise destitute women and girls having their daily needs met.

As for the punishment for adultery—one hundred lashes—note that, unlike in the Old Testament, there is no distinction made between the punishment of the man or the woman. Mohammed considered them morally equal.

I recently had a conversation on Facebook with a young man who had been raised as an Evangelical Christian. He made the following statement reflecting thoughts that are all too common, "...most prefer Sharia law and still are ok with extreme things like amputation for theft, stoning of adulterers, and the execution of apostates. All sanctioned in the Koran (sic)." As a former Evangelical myself, when I began my research I was expecting to find dozens of angry admonitions in the Quran to inflict all manner of violence upon anyone and everyone who doesn't follow Allah or commits some form of moral transgression.

I was shocked to learn that physical punishment is mentioned just five times in the entire Quran.

I was shocked to learn that physical punishment is mentioned just five times in the entire Quran. In contrast, a brief survey of the Torah (the first five books of the Bible) reveals a steady stream of admonitions to stone blasphemers, adulteresses, worshipers of other gods, or anyone who touched the mountain of God while He was on it. The vast majority of Mohammed's directives involve pure-hearted devotion to a merciful God as reflected by a life of integrity, respecting one's family, and, over and over again, helping those in need. The notion that Mohammed created a religion of violence is simply false. When compared to the pre-Islamic culture of Arabia and to the Christian Byzantine kingdom in which torture was commonplace, Islam was revolutionary for its strict regulations *against* violence.

Islam was revolutionary for its strict regulations *against* violence.

The concept of Sharia as approaching heaven on earth—a place where a just God cares for all equally and judges everyone fairly—is similar to the Christian concept of the coming millennial kingdom. It is the ever-elusive Muslim *and* Christian dream.

WINNING IN SELF-DEFENSE – THE MEANING OF JIHAD

Just after midnight in the early minutes of the new year of 2017, the lone gunman opened fire as he entered the Reina nightclub in Istanbul, Turkey. Indiscriminately shooting New Year's revelers, he lingered for seven minutes, calmly replacing spent ammunition cartridges. Thirty-nine people were murdered in cold blood that morning and dozens more were injured. Amazingly, the shooter escaped. ISIS claimed responsibility for the attack, calling it an act of revenge against Turkey, which had participated in bombing raids of ISIS-held areas of Syria.

Horrific acts such as this have become commonplace all over the world and are often claimed to be acts of holy war, or jihad, by the radicalized militants who commit them. Uninformed Western journalists readily reiterate this classification. Biblical fundamentalists chime in, quoting several of the alleged one hundred verses in the Quran that advocate violence for the sake of Islam.

But what did the Prophet teach and what was his example? Mohammed's story was about to transition from building a community to fighting for survival. How did this spiritual community focused on egalitarianism and social justice find itself engaged in armed conflict and the taking of lives? Is it really true that Mohammed became a warrior-prophet who taught his followers to attack all infidels? Did he really lead his warriors in dozens of conquests and battles to bring the world under the subjection of Islam?

The Muslims had emerged within a world of constant intertribal fighting—there was no question they would need to hold their own for basic survival. Interestingly, Yathrib was dominated by several clans of Arab Jews—Arabs who had converted to Judaism. In time, Bedouin Arab tribes settled there also, two of which brought their ongoing bloody feud with them. Mohammed was called into a secular role as civic leader and mediator between these two tribes, which provided him important exposure outside his community.

His secular role grew and he eventually named himself ruler of Yathrib in what is thought to be the first-ever written constitution. A key objective of Mohammed's in the formulation of this constitution was alignment of all of the tribes in the region for the purpose of defense. The community's multiplication in numbers and Mohammed's increasing fame had not gone unnoticed by the Quraysh of Mecca—they still had designs on eliminating him. It is essential to have this backdrop in place as we walk through Mohammed's very short history with tribal warfare.

As Mohammed's following in Yathrib grew to number in the thousands, he had attracted those from the lower economic strata with his emphasis on equality and social justice. With mouths to feed and caravan routes to Mecca passing by Yathrib, Mohammed began sending raiding parties to supplement the tribal income—he was a kind of Robin Hood of Arabia. According to Aslan, this was a "time-honored" practice among all tribes, and considered nothing out of the ordinary, as long as no one got hurt.[9]

However, because of Mohammed's history with the Quraysh, they were in no mood to sit by idly while he affected them economically. On one occasion in 624 CE, Mohammed got word of a particularly large caravan passing by from Palestine and recruited a group of more than 300 volunteers to raid it. Not everyone in Yathrib was supportive of their new Muslim neighbors and someone passed word of the planned raid to the Quraysh, who surprised Mohammed with a defense force a thousand strong.

Expecting only a bloodless round of productive banditry, Mohammed had no interest in attacking a force of a thousand soldiers with his band of 300 raiders. But neither did he back off and return to Yathrib. After a two-day standoff, small skirmishes turned into a full-scale battle, and when it was all over, the Quraysh defense force had somehow been routed. *This* was a game changer.

The Muslims had suddenly come into their own as a viable tribe. They had taken on the formidable Quraysh and emerged as the victors. This famous clash was known as the Battle of Badr.

The proud Quraysh had been badly embarrassed. Their ability to guarantee safe arrival of caravan merchandise to Mecca was now called into question. To maintain their dominance, it became necessary to eliminate this nuisance once and for all. The Quraysh chieftain bolstered his numbers by negotiating a coalition with several Bedouin tribes and marching on Yathrib with a fighting force of ten thousand. Being on the short side of ten-to-one odds this time, the Muslim army suffered a crushing defeat. Mohammed himself sustained a bloody head injury, leading many to believe he had been killed. Only this fact preserved Mohammed and his warriors from certain annihilation. When the cry of Mohammed's death sounded, the men fled in panic and the battle ended.

The bitter feud between the Quraysh and the Muslims went on for six years. And the Quranic revelations turned to the subject of combat:

> Fight in God's path against those who fight you, but do not be aggressors, for God does not love the aggressors. (If they start a fight) kill them wherever you find them, and expel them from where ever they expelled you. For oppression is worse than murder. Do not fight them in the Holy Sanctuary unless they fight you in it. If they fight you, kill them. That is the reward of the unbelievers. If they stop, God is forgiving and Merciful-to-all. Fight them until there is no more

> persecution and until all worship is devoted only to God. If
> they stop, there should be no aggression except towards the
> unjust (2:190–193).

This passage is packed with insight into the fundamental Islamic concept of war. More than an allowance for a man to defend himself and his family, this is a direct command to fight back with lethal force when attacked. The clear context is the ongoing struggle with the Quraysh. But, Allah, the merciful-to-all, makes two remarkable prohibitions: The Muslims should never be the aggressors and if the Quraysh stop fighting, then the Muslims should also stop. This is fighting in God's path—holy war.

According to Aslan, the term "holy war" was actually first coined by the Christian Crusaders, the warriors of the cross, "to give theological legitimacy to what was in reality a battle for land and trade routes."[10] In response to the Crusaders' invasion and occupation (1095–1291 CE), Islamic scholars adopted their own version of holy war, and it became associated with the Quranic use of the word jihad.

The Arabic word jihad, in its literal sense, simply refers to an intense struggle, or striving. It has no connotation of holiness or sacredness, and is used in many contexts not referring to war at all. In fact, according to the teaching of Islam, the internal struggle of living a life that is pleasing to God is considered the greater jihad, while the defense of one's family and community in battle is the lesser jihad.

In his book, *Islam: The Straight Path*, Director of the Center for Muslim-Christian Understanding at Georgetown University, John Esposito, points out that:

> Muhammad's use of warfare in general was alien neither
> to Arab custom nor to that of the Hebrew prophets. Both
> believed that God had sanctioned battle with the enemies
> of the Lord. Biblical stories about the exploits of kings and
> prophets such as Moses, Joshua, Elijah, Samuel, Jehu, Saul,
> and David recount the struggles of a community called by
> God and the permissibility, indeed requirement, to take up

arms when necessary against those who had defied God, and to fight "in the name of the Lord of hosts, the God of the armies of Israel." ... Similarly, in speaking of the Israelite conquests, Moses recalls: "And I commanded you at that time, saying, 'The Lord your God has given you this land to possess. You shall not fear them; for it is the Lord your God who fights for you.'" (*Deuteronomy* 3:18~22)[11]

What set the Muslims apart from the Hebrews, the Christians, and the Quraysh was the strict prohibition against initiating a conflict and the requirement to cease fighting the moment the enemy surrendered. While Israel was commanded to take the land from its inhabitants and "not leave alive anything that breathes," and the Christians in the time of Mohammed conquered most of the Middle East and large swaths of Europe and North Africa, Mohammed would teach, "The Truth is from your Lord. Whoever wills—let him believe; and whoever wills—let him deny the truth (18:29)." While Mohammed was alive, Islam spread by attraction. His followers were drawn to his character and chose to believe.

What set the Muslims apart from the Hebrews, the Christians, and the Quraysh was the strict prohibition against initiating a conflict and the requirement to cease fighting the moment the enemy surrendered.

The Quraysh marched on Medina one last time in an effort to eliminate their Muslim rivals. This time Mohammed decided that discretion was the better part of valor and employed a defensive strategy. In the time it took for the Meccan armies to arrive, the people of the city came together and dug a prohibitive trench around Medina. The Quraysh came prepared for a battle, not for a siege. After a short standoff known as the Battle of the Trench, they returned to Mecca in frustration.

Mohammed's next move would do more than frustrate the Quraysh. In a tactic that defied human logic, he boldly marched on Mecca—not as a warrior, but as a worshiper. He and a thousand of his followers showed up outside of Mecca without weapons in the same manner as all the other pilgrims. The Quraysh elite were perplexed and suspicious, but met with Mohammed outside of the city. What could they do? As the keepers of the Kaaba, how could they turn away these worshipers? They seized the opportunity to negotiate for an advantage.

In exchange for Mohammed's promise to end the caravan raids and immediately withdraw to Medina, the Quraysh agreed to a "cease-fire" and to allow him to return to Mecca the following year for the pilgrimage. Mohammed's followers were incensed that he agreed to these terms—especially his chief lieutenants, Umar and Abu Bakr. They were convinced that the tide had turned and felt that they now had the advantage. Why relinquish their current position for a future promise?

But the always patient prophet was true to the revelation and agreed to the cease-fire terms. He seemed to have a knowledge that was not of this world. He did return to Mecca a year later. Like Jesus riding on a donkey into Jerusalem to the cheers of the crowds, it was a triumphal entry. Here was Mohammed, born into this world without a father or an inheritance, who had clawed his way into the upper class, only to throw it all away in obedience to his prophetic call. After losing his wife and his uncle, and with them, his status, he was driven away in shame. But now here he was, with thousands of his followers, dressed in white and parading before his enemies. It was all too obvious to the people of Mecca who now had the upper hand. Without even realizing it, the Quraysh had just handed Mecca over to Mohammed—and all Arabia with it.

The Muslims returned to Medina, but before the pilgrimage of the following year, a skirmish broke out between two Bedouin tribes, one aligned with Mecca and the other with Mohammed. The tribe aligned with Mecca was seen as the aggressor, and lives were lost. It was a violation of the treaty. Mohammed declared the treaty null and void and once again marched on Mecca, this time with ten thousand men prepared for battle.

The Quraysh offered no resistance, and the people of Mecca received Mohammed with open arms. The most powerful tribe in Arabia had been laid low—not by superiority in battle, but by the power of Mohammed's character. Without striking a blow, Islam became the super-tribe of Arabia. All would soon confess that there was no god but Allah, and that Mohammed was his messenger.

Victorious and vindicated, it was now time for Mohammed to deal with the Quraysh once and for all: these ruthless opportunists who had rejected his prophetic message and sought to murder him when he was at his lowest point; these enemies who had forced him to flee from his home and start over with nothing; these murderers who had marched twice to Medina to kill him, his family, and his community; these infidels and unbelievers.

Islam was to be something different. It was to grow organically, not by means of overcoming one's enemy, but by the power of influence, energized by unwavering integrity and equal treatment for all.

According to the tribal protocol, Mohammed now had every right to execute the men of fighting age, enslave the women and children, and enrich himself with their goods and property. Mohammed's followers, many of whom had suffered much under the ruthless hand of the Quraysh, expected nothing less.

But in this profound moment, Mohammed would pronounce a judgment that would remove all doubt about whether Islam was birthed in violence. Perhaps he was tempted to exact revenge or to gloat in violent dominance. But he showed no signs of it. When he and his followers had worshiped at the Kaaba unarmed in the presence of the Quraysh, Mohammed had already demonstrated that his authority came from a higher source. Now the messenger of God, The Trustworthy One would prove once again that he feared not the weapons of man, but the power of God. Perhaps energized by the terror of being squeezed by an unseen angel, Mohammed pronounced a general amnesty on the Quraysh.

This was a decisive moment in the history of Islam. The rusty chains of the law of retribution—chains that had bound the tribes of Arabia to one another in violence for centuries—were shattered. Islam was to be something different. It was to grow organically, not by means of overcoming one's enemy, but by the power of influence, energized by unwavering integrity and equal treatment for all. Mohammed had made a powerful and undeniable statement: He was one who commanded authority by his presence, without the powerful human compulsion to eliminate one's enemies.

So when evangelical naysayers or radical imams quote Quranic verses out of context in their attempts to prove that Mohammed taught his followers to slaughter infidels, it is the <u>deeds</u> of the Prophet that prove them wrong—beyond all doubt.

After the declaration of amnesty, Mohammed wasted no time going to the Kaaba and destroying all of the idols except the statues of Jesus and Mary. The sacred pilgrimage to Mecca would now honor Allah alone, and pay respects to Allah's servants, the prophet Jesus and his mother.

In spite of the clear historical evidence affirming Mohammed's dedication to nonaggression, misunderstandings in today's world persist. At the center of this controversy are the terms "infidel," "unbeliever," and "idolater." For example, the Quran 9:5 says, "But once the sacred months are over, kill those idolaters wherever you find them, besiege them, ambush them and imprison them." In isolation, this verse seems to grant open season for Muslims to slaughter those whom they consider infidels. But who are the infidels? Jews and Christians? Mohammed never used the term "idolater" to refer to Jews or Christians—they worshiped the same God. On the contrary, the Quran is clear about affording them respect as "The People of the Book." And this mandate was followed for centuries.

From a historical perspective, Mohammed received all of the prophetic revelations pertaining to warfare precisely during the period of time when he was being persecuted by the Quraysh. And less than three years after taking Mecca, he was dead. There is little disagreement among scholars on the fact that the term "infidel" referred exclusively to the Quraysh. When we look at the complete context of the verse (9:5) it becomes clear that it is referring to a very specific incident:

> God and His Messenger repudiate the treaty made with the idolaters. "You are free to move around for four months, but you can never escape God, and God will disgrace all who deny the truth." On the day of the great pilgrimage, there will be a proclamation from God and His Messenger to all people: "God and His Messenger are released from all treaty obligations with the idolaters. If you repent, it will be for your own good, but if you persist, know that you can never escape God." Warn the unbelievers that they will have a painful punishment. As for those who have honored their treaty obligations, and have not assisted anyone against you, fulfill your agreement with them to the end of its term. God loves those who are mindful of the Him. But once the sacred months are over, kill those idolaters wherever you find them, besiege them, ambush them and imprison them. However, if they repent and pray, and pay the prescribed purifying alms, let them go on their way, for God is the Forgiver and the Mercy Giver (9:1–5).

The passage refers to the breaking of the treaty made with the Quraysh when Mohammed had marched on Mecca to worship at the Kaaba. To attempt to apply this passage to anything other than this specific incident is to misapply it. For comparison, 1 Samuel

15:3 from the Old Testament says, "Now go and smite Amalek, and utterly destroy all that they have, and spare them not; but slay both man and <u>woman, infant and suckling</u>, oxen and sheep, camel and ass (emphasis mine)." The application of this passage even in its original context is difficult enough to imagine. It certainly wouldn't be applied in any other context. Quranic injunctions allowing violence against infidels specifically and exclusively refer to the Muslims defending themselves against the aggression of the Quraysh.

A second persistent misconception is that Islam is inherently anti-Jewish. Mohammed's behavior towards the Jewish tribes of Yathrib is often cited as evidence. His relationship with the three dominant Jewish tribes in Yathrib was anything but cordial. When Mohammed and his followers showed up in Yathrib, the three Jewish tribes had been the primary players in the affairs of Yathrib. They were never quite sure what to do with Mohammed and kept him and his community at arm's length. As Mohammed gained strength and offered up his constitution as a means of binding the tribes together to protect them from attacks by the Quraysh, the Jewish tribes signed on reluctantly. They believed that eventually the Quraysh would restore their domination, but needed to hedge their bets with Mohammed.

As someone who had made a name for himself as a man of absolute integrity, Mohammed had no stomach for subterfuge, not to mention treachery.

As events played out, each of the Jewish tribes secretly helped the Quraysh in the major battles that took place in Yathrib—in spite of their oath to defend the coalition of tribes in Yathrib. As someone who had made a name for himself as a man of absolute integrity, Mohammed had no stomach for subterfuge, not to mention treachery. In the first two cases, at the Battle of Badr and the Battle of Uhud in which the Muslims suffered a crushing defeat, Mohammed was characteristically tolerant. The tribal code dictated severe consequences for defection—beheading of males and enslavement of women and children. Mohammed instead merely exiled the offending tribes, even allowing them to take most of their possessions with them. The tribes resettled on a not-too-distant oasis known as Khaybar.

But in the Battle of the Trench, the last remaining Jewish tribe, the Banu Qurayza, went so far as to provide weapons and supplies to the Quraysh to assist them in prolonging their siege of Yathrib. They had essentially joined the enemy forces—and Mohammed's line had been crossed. After pledging to support the community of Yathrib in defense of the Quraysh, the Banu Qurayza had virtually taken up arms against Mohammed.

"I am only a man like you, to whom has been revealed that your god is one God (18:110)." Mohammed was a man. Even he had his limits. The Banu Qurayza, by aligning themselves with the Quraysh, had forsaken their status as "The People of the Book" and aligned themselves with the "infidels."

Mohammed formally referred the case to arbitration by the sheikh of another major tribe. He knew that his own judgment would be clouded. This sheikh did not deviate from the tribal order— punishment by beheading was carried out without mercy.

The case of the Banu Qurayza is frequently cited in isolation to show that Mohammed was both barbaric and anti-Jewish. But when we consider the bigger picture of Mohammed's life, these conclusions don't hold water. We have already seen that Mohammed's first inclination was always forgiveness. In the cases of the first two Jewish tribes and the proclamation of a general amnesty for the Quraysh themselves, Mohammed has a proven record of erring on the side of tolerance and forgiveness—to his own harm. And even in the case of the Banu Qurayza, the Prophet recused himself. The judgment for beheading didn't come from him but from the sheikh.

Secondly, the harsh penalty on the Banu Qurayza tribe had nothing to do with them being Jewish, and everything to do with their treachery. The claim that Mohammed was anti-Jewish is a difficult argument to sustain, considering the fact that he validated all of the Hebrew prophets, from Adam and Noah through Moses and the long line of prophets that followed him, he adopted many of the Jewish dietary and purity requirements, and even encouraged his followers to marry Jews, as he himself did.

In the face of treachery and with the survival of his community at stake, Mohammed allowed the cultural norms to run their course. This by no means establishes him as homicidal or anti-Jewish.

Not long after his peaceful triumph in Mecca, Mohammed returned to Medina. He had no taste for city life, and the soul of Islam, the community, remained in Medina. Less than three years later, he died after a short illness.

History took a deep breath and paused.

Armed only with his revelations and his integrity, Mohammed faced down the rulers and cultural forces that had dominated the Arabian Desert for centuries. What would be the legacy of this humble orphan who had become the most powerful man in Arabia?

CHAPTER 1 NOTES

1. https://www.ecosia.org/.

2. *Islam: A Religion Based on Terrorism*, 2005–2016, http://www.targetofopportunity.com/islam.htm.

3. Matt Slick, "Islam, the Religion of Peace and Terrorism." *CARM: Christian Apologetics & Research Ministry* (n.d.), https://carm.org/islam-religion-peace-and-terrorism.

4. "Sharia (Islamic Law)," *The Religion of Peace*, 2002–2018, https://www.thereligionofpeace.com/pages/articles/sharia.aspx.

5. Reza Aslan, *No god but God* (New York: Random House Trade Paperbacks, 2011), 9.

6. Aslan, 40.

7. Aslan, 52.

8. Sadakat Kadri, *Heaven on Earth: A Journey Through Shari' a Law from the Deserts of Ancient Arabia to the Streets of the Modern Muslim World* (New York: Farrar, Straus, and Giroux, 2012), 22–23.

9. Aslan, 83.

10. Aslan, 81.

11. John L. Esposito, *Islam: The Straight Path* (New York/Oxford: Oxford University Press, 1998), 17.

Meteoric Rise, Ignominious Fall:

The Islamic Empire

As important as it is to understand the heart and soul of Mohammed, when we view his life we only observe the seed that produced today's Muslim world. Whether the tree would produce fruit representative of the seed beneath it would be the responsibility of the leaders to follow.

The first pillar of Islam is known as the *shahada*, the Muslim profession of faith: "There is no god but God, and Mohammed is the messenger of God." This declaration provides entrance into the Islamic faith. It was the second part of the shahada that would complicate the matter of producing a replacement.

Would this replacement also be the messenger of God? If not, would his role become that of answering the question, "What would Mohammed do?" How was the leader of Islam to be selected, and how would his authority be defined? Not unlike the disciples of Christ after the crucifixion, Islam's first adherents were completely unprepared for the death of their prophet and leader. Just as no one stepped forward as a replacement for a miracle-working Jesus, none of Mohammed's followers claimed to have a direct connection with Allah. Who would be chosen?

A PERFECT STORM – TWO EMPIRES FALL

In a moment of incalculable historical impact, the small group of Muslim leaders met secretly to choose a successor. It boiled down to two of the Prophet's earliest followers: Ali and Abu Bakr. Ali was Mohammed's cousin and first devotee. Abu Bakr was Mohammed's third follower and his exuberant colleague in the merchant world. Ali embodied the idealistic, mystical heart of Mohammed but was young at thirty years of age. Abu Bakr was seasoned, a great warrior, and a leader who commanded respect.

The recently-pardoned Quraysh leaders backed Abu Bakr as one of their own. But the bulk of Mohammed's original companions favored Ali, claiming that Mohammed had named him to be his successor on his last pilgrimage. Cloaked in secrecy, the committee convened in Mecca without any representation from Medina—not even Ali. They named Abu Bakr as *caliph*, a word that simply means "successor to the Prophet," and the Islamic caliphate was born.

The Medinan clans were outraged and rejected the decision. Ali responded with patience befitting the Prophet and recognized Abu Bakr. But it would take six months for his fellow Medinans to go along. There was talk of a violent overthrow.

Abu Bakr inherited a role that had not been defined to lead a movement that itself had no idea what it was or what it would become. At this moment in history, what did it really mean to be a Muslim?

In Medina, the community had developed a cadence of spiritual practice under the leadership of Mohammed. But what about in Mecca, where the Prophet's message had only recently been accepted, or in the oasis villages far away from both Mecca and Medina? It would not be until twenty years later that the prophetic utterances would be enshrined in the Quran. For the two years following Mohammed's takeover of Mecca, the annual three-month religious festival had continued. This allowed the tribes inhabiting the Arabian

Peninsula to be exposed to Islam. The majority accepted the teaching of the oneness of God and the equality of all people and, along with it, payment of an annual tax known as *zakat*. Under Mohammed's brief two-year tenure as leader, the Arabian Peninsula experienced a soft unification. However, except for the payment of the zakat tax and ridding the Kaaba of idols, life was not much different for most Arabs. This would change when Abu Bakr took the reins.

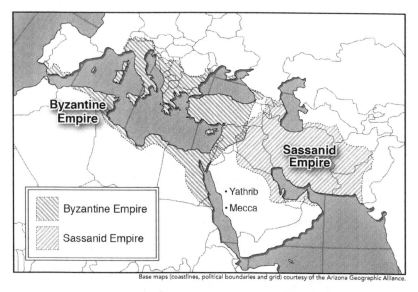

Base maps (coastlines, political boundaries and grid) courtesy of the Arizona Geographic Alliance.

Map 1 — The Inheritance of Abu Bakr ~ Two Major Empires Poised to Envelope Arabia

When Mohammed died, as was customary upon the death of a sheikh, many of the tribes located far from Mecca stopped paying the zakat tax. Also, Mohammed's teaching on social justice had apparently struck a chord and several other prophets and mystics had emerged throughout the Arabian Peninsula and garnered significant followings.

The ancient city of Sanaa, located near the southwestern elbow of the Arabian Peninsula, and today the capital of Yemen, had been the Mecca for Arab Christians. The coastal city of Aden, just south of Sanaa, was a key port city connecting the Arabian Peninsula with both Africa and India. Arabs from these cities were among the first to cut their ties.

Almost one and a half millennia later, I interviewed one of their ancestors. Mahmoud's family has been in Aden for uncounted generations. Perhaps his progenitors were Christians. When I heard his cheerful voice, I liked him instantly. Pleasant and gentle, and very upbeat, he was easy to talk to. We were meant to meet in the capital of Kazakhstan for the World Expo in 2017, but circumstances prevented our rendezvous, so we had a long telephone conversation instead. His story captured me. Mahmoud's father died of a heart attack when he was just a small boy. His mother, whose first husband had also died, was left on her own to care for her five children. Sound familiar? Mahmoud was the youngest. Needless to say, they were barely getting by. When Mahmoud spoke of his mother, it was with great pride. "She is my mother, and my father, and my friend," he said to me. And that explains why Mahmoud scrapes by on only a portion of the living stipend included in his scholarship to study in Prague, and sends as much as possible home to Yemen for his family.

Even though his mother was uneducated herself, she was very persistent about making sure that little Mahmoud got a good education. It got off to a rough start. By the time he was in fourth grade, he was struggling with basic literacy, hardly able to read or write in his own language of Arabic. His mother got involved. She found a way to hire a tutor and began to meet frequently with Mahmoud's teachers to make sure he was progressing. Her energy paid off. By the end of seventh grade, Mahmoud was the second-highest student in his class.

In 2010, for his senior year of high school, after qualifying in the top fifteen out of seven hundred applicants in English language ability, he was accepted into an exchange program to study in the United States. He tells of two experiences that remain embedded in his memory. First, one of his fellow students called him a terrorist to his face. When he asked one of his teachers what he should do about it, the teacher immediately wanted to know the name of the person who had made this accusation. Mahmoud decided to keep this to himself and responded by creating a presentation about the misunderstandings between the Middle East and America, which he presented to his class.

Mahmoud's second memorable experience was getting involved with volunteerism. During his year in the United States, he volunteered more than one hundred hours and was recognized for this by receiving the President's Volunteer Service Award. The volunteer spirit continued on in Mahmoud when he returned to Yemen in 2012, when he got involved with visiting orphanages, children with cancer in hospitals, and donating food and clothing to the poor.

Things would take a turn for the worse a couple of years later when, three semesters into a four-semester engineering program involving maintenance of oil equipment, Houthi rebels took over the city of Aden in the ongoing civil war in Yemen. In the attacks on Aden, Mahmoud's aunt was killed by mortar fire.

Lacking the gravitational attraction of Mohammed's character, Abu Bakr instinctively reverted to force as the means of keeping the super-tribe together.

Mahmoud subsequently applied for and was one of the five students from the entire country of Yemen accepted into a scholarship program at the prestigious Charles University in Prague, the Czech Republic. Mahmoud is in a three-year Czech language study program, after which he intends to study medicine, with the ultimate desire of becoming a surgeon. He also sees himself involved in leadership of interfaith dialogs and cultural exchange between the Middle East and the West.

It was among Arabs like Mahmoud's ancestors that Abu Bakr was about to set a dangerous precedent. In direct violation of Mohammed's teaching, he launched a military campaign to eliminate the rival prophets and force all tribes to pay the zakat tax, making no distinction between either group. Lacking the gravitational attraction of Mohammed's character, Abu Bakr instinctively reverted to force as the means of keeping the super-tribe together. In so doing, he set off the big bang that would produce a new universe.

The effect of the conquest of Arabia under Abu Bakr was to mobilize a growing Islamic military force that found itself bumping up against the margins of the two neighboring empires. What happened next would boggle the minds of historians and students of military strategy alike.

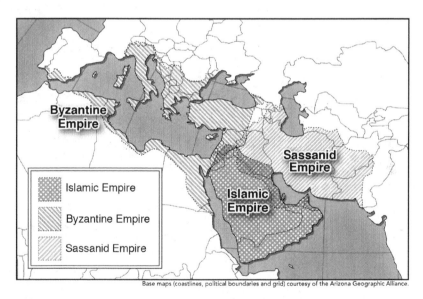

Base maps (coastlines, political boundaries and grid) courtesy of the Arizona Geographic Alliance.

Map 2 — The Formation of the Islamic Empire under Abu Bakr

Abu Bakr had a very brief stint as the head of the budding empire. After only two years as caliph, he died of an illness. Before his death, he again snubbed Ali and publicly named Umar, another mighty Qurayshi warrior, as his successor. The choice—and the process—did nothing to resolve the seething resentment of Ali and the contingent from Medina. But for the next ten years under Caliph Umar, Ali and his proponents would be occupied with other matters.

Call it a perfect storm. In the time of Mohammed, both the Christian Byzantine Empire of Europe and the Zoroastrian Sassanid Empire of Persia were expanding into the Arabian Peninsula and had claimed large portions of it. So when Abu Bakr conquered all of Arabia, he had already started to encroach into both kingdoms. Secondly, both empires had been engaged in a protracted war with one another and their military strength had been severely weakened. Nowhere was this more the case than at the farthest reaches of their empires, precisely where Muslim commanders were surging into the edges of the Arab world. Why stop at this village when there was another one just like it a little further on?

Before Umar's campaigns were complete, the Byzantine Empire had given up almost the entire Middle East and had retreated to the confines of modern-day Turkey. The Sassanid Empire was completely defeated in the East, and a front had been opened in North Africa extending all the way to Tripoli.

Could this be the same ragtag assembly of believers that had been chased out of Mecca a few years earlier and barely escaped with their lives?

Before becoming too critical of Islam as a religion of warfare, let's consider four critical points. First, both the Byzantine and Sassanid empires carried the religious banners of Christianity and Zoroastrianism respectively. David Nicolle, in his book *The Great Islamic Conquests*, wrote about the strategy of Heraclius, one of the most powerful Byzantine emperors. The emperor utilized propagandists to help him portray Byzantine wars in a very religious light, "using the most potent of Christian relics, the Wood of the Holy Cross, to inspire the fighting fervor of his troops."[1]

Nicolle goes on to point out that:

> ... the conversion of the peoples of what are now the
> heartlands of the Islamic world was a largely peaceful process
> and was separate from the Arabs' military conquest of these
> same areas. Indeed, the conversion largely resulted from the
> example set by the early Muslim Arabs themselves and the
> activities of preachers, missionaries and merchants. A desire
> for material, cultural and political advantage under the new
> regime also played a part.[2]

Secondly, just as the conquest of Arabia was contrary to the
teaching of Mohammed, so the expansion of the Islamic Empire
had nothing to do with the social reform Mohammed had begun
and everything to do with Qurayshi tribal power. I am convinced
that had Mohammed still been alive, or had Ali been selected as
his successor, the wars and conquests would not have taken place.
Mohammed had risen above the culture and created something new.
Abu Bakr and Umar, without their own direct spiritual connection
or Mohammed to regulate them, reverted to the ancient tribal ways.

Thirdly, Islam had hardly begun to define itself before it found
itself covering all of the Middle East. By the time the Quran was
formally transcribed, duplicated, distributed, and taught, the territory
conquered by the armies of Islam had nearly reached its maximum
extent. It's a tough sell to claim the teaching of the Quran drove the
Islamic conquest since the takeover was virtually complete before the
Quran was available. The theological underpinnings of the Islamic
faith were lagging behind the tidal wave of imperial expansion.

Finally, those peoples on the edges of the great kingdoms were
generally not wholehearted subjects of the kingdom in power, nor
genuine believers in the religions these kingdoms brought with them.
When conquered, terms of subjugation were imposed involving some
aspect of the incoming religion, payment of taxes to the conquering
kingdom, and conscription into their fighting forces. These were
merely incredibly invested spectators in the realm of war in the cosmos.

During my study of Islam while training for my missionary service in the Muslim world, I was taught by Christian teachers that the spread of Islam took place by conquest and by threat of death: "Convert or die." When I told my Algerian friend Mustafa about this, I saw his face fall. I could see that this had affected him deeply. More than incredulous, he was genuinely hurt. If there is a single message that I hope every reader takes away from this book, it is that 1.5 billion mainstream Muslims are people of peace. They have no interest in your forceful conversion to Islam.

Would Islam find a way to reinterpret the message of God to justify its imperial conquest? Theological interpretations primarily explained the rapid expansion as the blessing of God and proof of the truth of Islam. But from a purely strategic perspective, when Mohammed declared a general amnesty of the Quraysh after his takeover of Mecca, he set the table for them to reestablish their preeminence after his death. The result was an eminently powerful Quraysh tribe—infused with the teachings of Mohammed.

In a time when there were no national boundaries, tribal (and imperial) growth was a viral phenomenon. A tribe was driven to expand territorially to consume as many clans as it was capable of. The super-tribe created by Mohammed and hijacked by the Quraysh was simply following the natural order of things. Islam as a religious ideology was just going along for the ride.

The teaching of Mohammed had a profound effect on how peoples would be governed. Umar ruled not with the iron fist of a conqueror, but with kindness and fairness. Umar made it a special focus to make no distinction between Arab and other ethnic groups; all were welcomed into the Muslim community with full privileges. He also gave orders not to change existing governmental systems or impact local customs and practices.

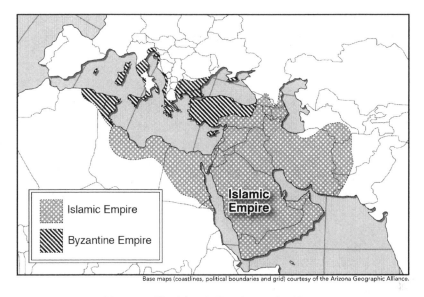

Base maps (coastlines, political boundaries and grid) courtesy of the Arizona Geographic Alliance.

Map 3 — The Islamic Empire under Umar

The mighty Umar was stabbed by a disgruntled Persian slave in Medina, ironically, nowhere near the ever-distant battlefronts. With his death, the empire of Islam was about to take another leap away from the heavenly ideals of the Prophet. The caliphs were being drawn into a descending orbit by the black hole of wealth and power.

HIJACKED! THE DYNASTIC TAKEOVER OF THE ISLAMIC EMPIRE

When Umar realized he was about to die, he convened a group of six candidates and charged them with selecting the next caliph from among themselves—and he gave them three days to do it. It was a halfhearted attempt to satisfy protocol and keep Ali in the mix. Five of the six were wealthy members of clans from the Quraysh tribe, and the sixth was Ali. The five had risen to wealth as a result of the massive influx of taxation revenue pouring into Medina from the ever-growing list of subjugated peoples. Ali was excluded from this abundance and made ends meet as a gardener.

The next three days played out like the final episode of *Survivor*. On the last day, Ali and the other finalist were presented with a trick question: "If selected, will you lead according to the examples of the first two caliphs?" Ali never wavered: "I will follow God and the example of the Prophet." For his truthfulness, the role of caliph was, for the third time, transferred to another Qurayshi, a septuagenarian by the name of Uthman, a member of the powerful Umayyad clan.

Abu Bakr and Umar had been highly respected leaders from among Mohammed's companions, so Ali and his proponents tolerated the obvious snub. But the selection of Uthman was now seen for what it was—a dynastic takeover and return to preeminence of the Quraysh elite.

Uthman wasted no time. He replaced nearly all of the governors of conquered provinces with members of his immediate family. The governors, known as *amirs*, had originally been appointed by Abu Bakr and Umar. They had been deliberately selected from leaders outside of their own clans to avoid any appearance of favoritism.

Next, if there was still any doubt as to his intentions, Uthman began raiding the reservoir of zakat tax revenues and making lavish distributions to family members. At the same time, Uthman ridiculously named himself *Caliphat Allah*— The Successor to God. He sought to reinforce this proclamation by canonizing the Quran. He accumulated the extant written renderings of Mohammed's revelations and compiled them into a complete manuscript. He burned any variants that didn't make it into his final cut.

His new title notwithstanding, it was obvious to all what was happening. The list of his detractors kept growing: replaced amirs, Mohammed's companions, rival clans in Medina, Ali's supporters, even the committee chairman who had selected him. After ten years of corruption, the seething rebellion boiled over. A delegation from Egypt traveled all the way to Medina to present their grievances and things got out of hand. The Successor to God was murdered.

The empire was now in a state of crisis.

After waiting patiently for two decades, Ali now found himself in the unenviable position of being the leading candidate for caliph. Unenviable because, although he had nothing to do with Uthman's assassination, it would be impossible to disassociate himself from it. Acceptance of Ali's caliphate was far from unanimous. The Umayyad clan had grown wealthy as the recipients of Uthman's unbridled nepotism, and they were not about to take his assassination lying down.

Having grown up under the tutelage of the Prophet, Ali did his best to smooth things over with minimal violence and liberal forgiveness. But he was unable to avoid a multi-faction civil war. Ali's brief tenure played out like a Greek tragedy. One of his own allies ultimately murdered him, angry that he had accepted truce terms rather than finishing off the rebel forces.

With Ali out of the way, there was nothing left to impede the powerful Umayyad clan. Their hijack of Mohammed's social reform movement was complete. They ruled in dynastic fashion for almost a century.

But just when it looked like Mohammed's only legacy would be a fractured empire, the spirit of Islam began to stir and come to life anew.

ISLAM DEFINES ITSELF – THE EVOLUTION OF SHARIA LAW

By the time the dust had settled, in 730 CE Islam's political empire extended all the way to India in the East and Spain in the West. A large swath cut across North Africa and it included territories as far north as Kazakhstan and the Caucasus. After over 100 years of potent military conquest, the empire finally reached its limits.

Leaders throughout the empire started to focus more on sustaining rather than expanding their domain. It became clear that spiritual direction was not going to come from the Umayyad monarchs, who were lost in the excesses of absolute power. Who would take the mantle of spiritual leadership? Now a hundred years after the death of its Prophet, could Islam in its original form be rediscovered and deployed throughout a multicultural empire?

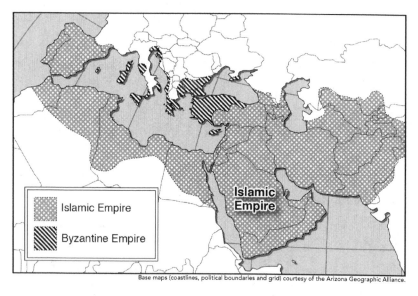

Base maps (coastlines, political boundaries and grid) courtesy of the Arizona Geographic Alliance.

Map 4 — The Islamic Empire at Its Maximum Size

The Ulama — The Scholars of Islam

The spiritual hunger to remain connected to the messenger of God was a powerful driving force. Over a hundred years later, how could Mohammed's followers reproduce the beloved community of Medina? And how could they deploy this socio-religious pattern throughout the empire? First, they must precisely define it. And this gave birth to a new societal class—the Islamic scholar. These eighth century researchers explored the intricacies of Arabic linguistics, pored over the Quran, and attempted to concretize the traditions of the early community, preserved in a collection of writings known as the *hadith*. As groups of these scholars began to find one another throughout the empire, momentum for the formulation of an Islamic theology began to build. Schools for religious study were opened, attracting the brightest Muslim devotees.

By the close of the Umayyad dynasty, the beginnings of religious authority had emerged. At the highest level was a council known as the *ulama*, literally meaning *"scholars or learned ones."* Although they had no secular authority, they were the final word when it came to Islamic theology—and its practice in the community (*Sharia*). Multiple *ulama* councils existed throughout the empire, each with their own flavor of Islam, often affected by local customs.

The next step was deployment throughout the hundreds of villages and cities now governed by the Islamic Caliphate. The motivation was not to enforce the personal practice of Islam, but to infuse local governments with Islamic precepts regarding social justice. Appointed local judges who had previously relied on personal judgment, Arab or local customs, and the Quran now had access to a codified *Sharia Law* in day-to-day civic matters such as business disputes or disagreements about family inheritances.

Christians and Jews

What happened when the armies of Islam conquered the Christian cities of Byzantium? Even after Damascus was named the capital of the Islamic Empire, the vast majority of the Syrian population remained Christian. According to David Nicolle, there, and in other conquered territories, "Jews and Christians were allowed to worship in public, to maintain their own religious buildings and to have their own religious organizations."[3] Christians and Jews were given the official title of "Protected Peoples." Jews, and Christians who deviated from the Byzantine brand of Christianity, enjoyed considerably better treatment under the Muslim rulers than under the Christian kings.

Sufism

Not Christian or Jew or Muslim, not Hindu
Buddhist, sufi, or zen. Not any religion

or cultural system. I am not from the East
or the West, not out of the ocean or up

from the ground, not natural or ethereal, not
composed of elements at all. I do not exist,

am not an entity in this world or in the next,
did not descend from Adam and Eve or any

origin story. My place is placeless, a trace
of the traceless. Neither body or soul.

I belong to the beloved, have seen the two
worlds as one and that one call to and know,

first, last, outer, inner, only that
breath breathing human being. (Jalal ad-Din Mohammed Rumi) .
(Essential Rumi)[4]

At the same time the ulama were studying the Quran to
find their way back to Mohammed, others with a deeper hunger
pursued a different path. While the ulama sought to define what it
meant to be a Muslim by creating laws delineating its practice, the
passionate Sufis were not satisfied with mere external observance.
They wanted to *feel*. Though deeply Muslim, they didn't crave
the imitation of Mohammed's practice, but the intimacy of his
connection. These were Islam's mystics. Had I been alive in the
Middle East during this time, I am quite certain I would have
found myself among them.

The earliest of these mystics were itinerant wanderers, floating
about in search of richer, deeper experiences—and other seekers.
Eventually, several consistent rendezvous points emerged as the Sufis

began to organize themselves. Sufism would ultimately develop into several different orders, such as the order founded by Rumi, famous for their whirling dervishes. After the period of military conquests ended, Sufism would grow and spread throughout the Muslim world, playing a key role in the spread of Islam.

Like the Byzantine and Sassanid empires before them, the Islamic Empire under the Umayyad dynasty began to crumble on the edges and implode from within. But Islam as a religion had found its footing. The first political empire fell. An anemic second empire arose in its place, with the perfunctory bloodletting. The political capitol moved eastward, from Damascus to Baghdad. But as the empire faded, the spirit of Islam burst forth as a supernova.

ISLAM SHINES – THE FIRST RENAISSANCE

The spiritual awakening associated with the teachings of Islam, combined with the cultural diversity of the peoples now absorbed by it, spilled over into the realms of science and reason. The Muslim conquerors were intolerant of internal power threats, but were lenient towards the people they conquered. This would prove beneficial in their hunger for knowledge. Long before Europe was even thinking about a Renaissance, the Muslim world was producing great thinkers, mathematicians, scientists, and artists, often rolled up into one person, the original "Renaissance men." Here are a few of my favorites:

Al-Razi was a renowned alchemist and philosopher, considered perhaps the best physician in the Muslim world.

Al-Farabi, possibly of Turkic origins from Central Asia, was known as "the second master" (second to Aristotle, himself) because of his high level of expertise in philosophy and logic. His other main contribution was a massive treatise on music, with less prominent contributions in the fields of mathematics, physics, and metaphysics.

Avicenna (Abu Ali Sina) produced a fascinating integrated treatise linking logic, physics, mathematics and metaphysics, showing an interaction between these categories, including multiple subcategories, to produce the individual effects.

Averroes (Ahmad ibn Rushd) was renowned for his extensive commentaries on the writings of Aristotle, breaking down complex meanings in a clear and understandable way.

Al-Biruni was a brilliant anthropologist and astronomer, producing some 146 titles in his lifetime. He assembled two extensive encyclopedic works including "Verifying All that the Indians Recount, the Reasonable and Unreasonable," which was a detailed description of the science, religion, literature and customs of India. He also amassed a detailed encyclopedia of virtually everything that was known in the field of astronomy.

Alhazan discovered that light travels in a straight line, contributing to the discovery of reflection and refraction, long before these concepts were fully developed by Isaac Newton.

Important contributions in the use of the sundial and the pendulum for timekeeping came from the minds of Muslim astronomers. Algebra was invented and combined with key advances in trigonometry to provide innovative calculations in the field of astronomy. Muslim chemists discovered alcohol, sulfuric and nitric acids, potassium, and more. They developed the techniques of sublimation, crystallization, and distillation, still in use today as methods of chemical analysis.

Muslim thinkers from this "Golden Age" of Islam endowed the world with scores of original contributions in the areas of mathematics, physics, chemistry, astronomy, medicine, social sciences, logic, and philosophy. Their discoveries are recognized as the stepping-stones for the discoveries of the European Renaissance centuries later. These men and their achievements deserve the same honor we bestow on men such as Leonardo da Vinci and Galileo.

Islamic Law Is Complete

Meanwhile, Islam's scholars went deeper into the definition of Islam as a religion and faced divergent ways of thinking. Rationalist thinkers were drawn to the fundamental principles of Islam and how to apply them relativistically in a culturally diverse world. Their thinking often involved philosophy, logic, and higher levels of reasoning—areas of the mind not yet even awakened in the Bedouins and sedentary tribes of seventh-century Arabia.

Traditionalists, on the other hand, favored literal interpretation of the Quran and rigorous imitation of the traditions of the Prophet and his companions. Much like Christian fundamentalists and the Bible, Islamic traditionalists believe that Mohammed represented divine perfection, both in the words of the Quran and in his living example. The only way to live a life that is pleasing to God is to live exactly as Mohammed and his companions had. This gave rise to the formal study of not just the Quran, but also the *Sunna*, or the traditions of the Prophet. But now a couple of hundred years removed, agreement on what those traditions were did not come easily.

> By the end of the tenth century, the general consensus was that the study of Islamic law was complete.

Several schools of thought emerged, each vying for exclusive validation from whoever happened to be the current monarch. Theological distinctions were often subtle, but nonetheless, taken very seriously. This is well illustrated by a question often asked of scholars in the presence of the monarch and his favored ulama council: "Is the Quran created by God, or is it uncreated and co-eternal with God?" It was a truly mind-bending question. The persecuted heretic's answer determined whether he was to be set free or returned to the dungeons. Christian inquisitors would obsess on an oddly similar question many centuries later: "Do the bread and the cup merely symbolize the body and blood of our Lord, or upon consumption do they *become* the body and blood?" The wrong answer could result in a very unpleasant stint in a medieval torture chamber for an unwary theologian.

By the end of the tenth century, the general consensus was that the study of Islamic law was complete. Although there were many differences between the schools, efforts to produce new discoveries were discouraged. This was right up the alley of the traditionalists, who created a new criminal charge—the crime of "innovation," which was viewed in the same light as the Christian crime of heresy.

The Crusades — Christian Jihad

For the first 400 years of Islam's existence, Christians enjoyed a protected status wherever they were within the empire. However, political developments toward the end of the second Muslim dynasty would upset this friendly balance and bring about a different sort of relationship, one not quite so chummy.

According to John Esposito, "Two myths pervade Western perceptions of the Crusades: first, that the Crusades were simply motivated by a religious desire to liberate Jerusalem, and second, that Christendom ultimately triumphed."[5]

The Crusades were the result of an unholy alliance between the Byzantine emperor, Alexius I, who sought divine legitimacy for his political and territorial ambitions, and Pope Urban II, who desired greater power and influence in the secular realm for the church. Ironically, together they created the pilgrimage, or crusade, to free Jerusalem from the Muslim infidels. Who the true infidels were may be judged by the words of Jesus himself, who taught, "by their fruit you shall know them," likening peoples' deeds to the fruit of a tree.

The invasion of Palestine was successful. The Crusaders established Christian sovereignty in the Holy Land when they overran Jerusalem in 1099. In the city of Acre, about 120 miles to the north, Richard the Lionhearted negotiated terms of surrender that included the safety of the city's inhabitants. He then proceeded to massacre the whole city, including women and children.

Almost ninety years later, the Muslims recaptured Jerusalem. I first learned of the fame of the victorious Muslim commander, Saladin, from my Algerian friend Sayid. Saladin never wavered in his commitment to the Islamic principles of warfare. He has been remembered throughout history for his compassion and fairness in dealing with his defeated Christian enemies. When treaties were negotiated, he was true to his word. Noncombatants were spared. He even left Christian churches and shrines untouched.

Sayid went on to tell me a curious story about another distinguished Muslim commander, this one from his home country. With excitement he told me of Elkader, a small town in America's heartland of Iowa, which was named after an Algerian Sufi named Abd el-Kader. El-Kader achieved hero status in Algeria for his long-standing and courageous resistance of French colonial invaders in the mid-1800s. He was widely known and admired for his unwavering stand on the observance of human rights toward his Christian adversaries. Eventually defeated and exiled to Syria, his final heroic act was to selflessly intervene on behalf of the Christian community in Syria, rescuing them from certain massacre by rioters. Sending his own sons into the streets to offer refuge, he sheltered large numbers of Christians, including several prominent leaders, in his own home. For his heroism he received international recognition, and the founders of the town in Iowa chose him as their town's namesake.

"By their fruit you shall know them."

It defies logic to ignore what happened during the Crusades, then scratch our heads and wonder where Muslim animosity toward Christians came from. This is not to say the Crusades play a key role in today's religio-political complexities, but the cornerstone remains embedded in the foundation. Where possible, wrongs should be acknowledged without excuse.

With increasing levels of irony, the end result of the Crusades for the Palestinian Christians was a loss in their status as protected ones. Many ultimately became Muslims. For Jews, in the kingdom representing Christendom, they were forcibly converted, exiled, or killed. Sadakat Kadri, author of *Heaven on Earth*, mentions a rabbi who recorded a travelogue of his journeys throughout the Middle East and North Africa during the Crusades. In Jerusalem, which had been occupied by the Crusaders since 1099, he had found only four Jews. In regions that were under Muslim rule, he estimated a count of 300,000.[6]

From Mighty Empire to Fractured Nations

In 1258 Mongol hordes commanded by the grandson of Genghis Khan overran the empire and captured Baghdad. The city was burned to the ground, the last caliph and his family were executed, and the Muslim inhabitants of Baghdad massacred. The days of Islam as a unified empire were forever over. According to Rory Stewart, author of *THE PLACES IN BETWEEN*, a book about his travel on foot across Afghanistan, the savagery of the Mongols dealt Islamic history a devastating blow: "he… obliterated the… great cities of the eastern Islamic world—massacring their scholars and artisans, turning the irrigated lands of central Asia into a waterless wilderness."

The Mongol empire lasted less than fifty years and the Islamic Empire reconstructed itself—this time as three rival sultanates. Islam became a kingdom divided against itself, establishing the footprint for the main divisions in today's world of Islam.

Sultanate Name	Years in Power	Territories	Dominant Sect
Ottoman Turks	1299-1923	Turkey, Eastern Europe, Middle East, North Africa	Sunni
Persian Safavid	1501-1722	Iran, North Caucasus (Russia)	Shia
Mogul	1520-1857	Indian subcontinent	Sufi/Sunni

But the winds of war in Europe would soon blow southward, forever changing the shape of the Muslim world. After thirteen centuries of war and empire building, World War I was about to catapult the Muslim world into a new universe. The era of empires and emperors was coming to a close, and the era of nation-states was about to begin.

After thirteen centuries of war and empire building, World War I was about to catapult the Muslim world into a new universe.

After being defeated in World War I, the Ottoman Empire was broken up into many pieces. Some regions took control of their own destiny and declared independence. Others had their fate assigned to them by various European post-war treaties and councils. As if the multiplying factions of Islam itself were not enough to keep the region immersed in conflict, now political boundaries were imposed by outside entities. Inevitably, these boundaries broke up contiguous ethnic and religious groups, and completely left others out, and would throw the entire region into a state of chaos.

No one even noticed the oncoming freight train. The Industrial Revolution was building steam in Europe, and colonialism was on board.

UNDER THE CRUEL HAND OF COLONIALISM

In the same manner that negative childhood experiences often define decades of adult life in the absence of effective psychotherapy, the Muslim world is still responding to abuses that took place during the era of European colonialism. At one point, the British Empire was so expansive that, as the old saying goes, the sun quite literally never set on it. At its largest point, it covered nearly one quarter of the Earth's total land area and encompassed almost the same fraction of its population.

The British Empire was the largest in history, occupying lands in most of the continents including, famously, Africa from "Cape to Cairo." Rooted in economic exploitation, the empire was heavily dependent on the steady flow of slaves from Africa. When required, the Europeans didn't hesitate to use military force to retain their advantage.

Once proud and powerful members of the Empire of Islam now found themselves British subjects. Of particular relevance for the future of Islam are the events that took place on the Indian subcontinent and in Egypt.

In India, it was the abundance of black tea that caught the eye of British magnates. Colonial businessman had learned that the potentates of Asia and Africa were often easily enticed by offers of cash to support their luxurious lifestyles. They would simply dangle money in front of the sultan or the khan who gladly accepted it in exchange for control of various commodities within the kingdom. The downside of the deal was that the subjects of the monarch were then forced to work as virtual slaves to make good on the deal. The inevitable result was rebellion on the part of the masses.

In India, after several decades of economic oppression by the British East India Company, civil unrest was on the rise. Complicated by several crop failures and a cholera pandemic, India's masses rebelled and the British government stepped in with their military, declaring the entire region a British colony in the mid-1800s.

In the ensuing rebellion by both Muslim and Hindu civilians and armed forces, Britain spared no one. Their brutal savagery conjures images of the Mongol hordes of Genghis Khan. According to a 2007 article in The *Guardian*, millions of civilians were slaughtered.[7] The soldiers of the crown hung resistors in trees, massacred a battalion of POWs, and plundered, pillaged, and razed the cities and villages of India. Britain ruled the entire subcontinent until 1947.

With all of India reeling from their crushing defeat beneath the fist of British power, they would be further subjugated by British arrogance. As Reza Aslan aptly put it, "In return for the pillaging of their lands, the suppression of their independence, and the destruction of their local economies, the colonized peoples were to be given the gift of 'civilization.'"[8]

Substitute the word "democracy" for "civilization" and this has a very familiar ring to it.

The British wore tight, uncomfortable clothing and sat in chairs at a table, daintily drinking tea out of an exquisite porcelain cup with a graceful loop as a handle, which they held in just a certain way. The Muslims wore flowing robes with graceful head pieces, sat on the floor on comfortable pads at a table only as high as a coffee table, reclining on thick pillows and drinking tea from cups that looked like small bowls—without the little handle—held in the palm of their hand, and slurped loudly. It's hard to imagine the British and the Indians doing almost anything similarly. Relations between men and women, how women dressed, how children were disciplined— the British way was the "civilized" way.

In the shadow of colonization, brutal and oppressive though it was, and its mission of civilization, the solemn duty of Christianization follows close behind. Plenty of good was done on the subcontinent by Christian missionaries, primarily in the areas of education and healthcare. Mission boards founded thousands of schools and hospitals throughout the region, leaving behind a legacy of educational opportunities and better health for millions. But however distinct these efforts may have been from those of the British government and the East India Company, it was impossible to keep them separate in the minds of the proud Muslims who saw only Western powers bringing Western military might, Western customs, and the now Western religion.

Bewildered and humiliated, Islamic leaders turned inward. What sin had they committed? They had ruled the subcontinent for centuries. How did they now find themselves subjugated to this Western power? Traditionalist ulama blamed the Sufi masses whose practices had become more and more syncretistic in their pursuit of spiritual ecstasy. The Sufi mystics blamed the traditionalists for their blind devotion to ancient practices.

A more modern version of Islam was struggling to be born.

For centuries Muslims had basked in the glory of a faith and practice that was at the same time a mighty empire. Now beneath the crushing humiliation of colonialists, what would Islam become?

The response of both the traditionalists and the Sufis was self-examination. Each underwent a revival, seeking to re-create their former greatness, but without addressing present realities. Their attempts to recapture the seventh-century magic did not produce a vibrant version of Islam for the nineteenth century.

Not all were looking backward.

Bold, modernist thinkers were emerging, moving past the "us versus them" mentality and digging deep to consider adapting to the West. Powerful ulama leaders were issuing fatwas declaring India to be a place of war inhabited by the enemies of Islam and requiring

Muslims to emigrate or to engage in jihad. In contrast, the new modernists rose above the fixation on retribution that has plagued Islam and opened their minds to intellectual and spiritual expansion.

The first of these forward-thinking modernists was Sayyid Ahmed Khan (1817–1898). Ahmed Khan was a purist and freethinker, a man I would have loved to meet. He was utterly devoted to the Quran but insisted on reading and understanding it for himself, rather than relying on the ulama to interpret it. Vehemently opposed to the approach of striving for a completely literal application of seventh-century scriptures in nineteenth-century India, his goal was to understand and apply the *principles* taught by Mohammed. I share the same way of thinking when it comes to the Bible and the teachings of Jesus. Ahmed Khan produced a multi-volume commentary from his studies of the Quran and openly criticized the ulama for creating a religion of their own, which was not in accordance with the teachings of the Prophet.

He promoted his teachings in books and journals, and at the educational institution he founded. Even though the majority of Muslims in India at that time continued to subscribe to the teachings and rulings of the ulama, Ahmed Khan's modernist approach received vast exposure and was considered a viable alternative by a significant minority. His influence was limited by the fact that he was a fairly high-ranking employee of the East India Company and was even knighted by the British crown, a fact that the ulama constantly used to discredit him.

While Ahmed Khan's days were waning, another great Muslim thinker was obtaining advanced degrees in Cambridge and Munich. Like Ahmed Khan, Mohammed Iqbal (1875–1938) was not one to let the ulama do his thinking for him. Although he had more traditionalist leanings than Ahmed Khan, he had a knack for applying traditionalist ideology to the modern world. The key to bridging the chasm involved making a distinction between essential truth and what might be considered optional or subject to the cultural norms of the time and place.

Iqbal's Western education gave him a unique perspective for articulating the Islamic mindset. He stood against such Western ideals as the separation of church and state, at the same time rejecting the meaningless traditions of the ulama. Even though he sought Sharia law as essential to the Islamic community, he saw a modern version that combined the spiritual principles taught by Mohammed with the issues faced by nineteenth-century Indians.

In the end, he would conclude that this ideal was impossible to achieve as a minority religion surrounded by Hindus. He became a major proponent for the establishment of the first Islamic state in the era of nation-states, Pakistan. Accompanied by the largest mass migration in history and mutual genocide numbering in the millions between Muslims and Hindus/Sikhs, Pakistan would emerge as a modernist Islamic state. They eventually held democratic elections and utilized a modern form of Sharia law.

Pakistan has had ups and downs since its creation but it remains a crown jewel representing the labors of these two great Muslim minds.

At the same time British troops were massacring millions of Indians, another crew of Brits was hard at work oppressing the Egyptians. The fine quality of Egyptian cotton was exactly what the doctor ordered for England's dwindling textile supplies. In addition, the Egyptian government utilized British industry in ambitious infrastructure projects, but soon found themselves on the bad side of inadequate financial management skills. Britain stepped in and effectively bought out the entire country, even Egypt's shares in the strategic Suez Canal.

Egypt was flooded with European workers and British businessmen. The financial burden of the government's ineptitude was passed down to rank-and-file Egyptians in the form of oppressive taxation. As surely as Britain had taken control of the Indian subcontinent with military might, they took over Egypt using economic power. Civil unrest among the Muslim populace simmered as they found themselves working harder and harder for less and less. And they were surrounded by arrogant foreigners profiting from their national assets and disrespecting cultural and religious norms. According to Aslan, "Cairo had become a virtual apartheid state where small pockets of tremendously wealthy Europeans and westernized Egyptians ruled over millions of impoverished peasants who labored on their lands and cared for their estates."[9]

Egypt produced their own modernist thinker—the father of the Middle Eastern Islamic awakening, Jamal al-Din al-Afghani (1838–1897). While still a teenager, al-Afghani had been sent to India to be educated in the sciences. One year later he witnessed the butchery of the British Army and it affected him deeply. Constantly hearing about the lofty Western ideals of freedom and democracy, he was disgusted by the unadulterated hypocrisy he witnessed in the repression of India's own bid for freedom.

An avid world traveler, al-Afghani was a brilliant thinker cut from the same cloth as the thinkers of the Islamic Renaissance. They thought of the universe as an integrated whole and developed unified models for describing it. Educated in Western democratic principles, of which Europe claimed to be the originators, al-Afghani had no trouble seeing the true source as the egalitarian community led by Mohammed in Medina twelve centuries earlier.

Each facet of the emerging modernist Islamic thinking had a unifying constant: the rejection of the ulama as of the divine keepers of the definition and practice of Islam. Furthermore, according to Aslan, al-Afghani felt that, the ulama bore the responsibility for the decline of Islamic civilization. In their self-appointed role as the guardians of Islam, the ulama had so stifled independent thought and scientific progress that even as Europe awakened to the Enlightenment, the Muslim world was still floundering in the Middle Ages. By forbidding a rational dialogue about the limits of law and the meaning of Scripture, the ulama... had become the true enemies of Islam.[10]

Al-Afghani was educated in the sciences, so he had a particular disdain for the ulama whose education was limited to historical studies of Islam's origins and traditions. He thought of Islam as not only congruous with the world of science but as the driving force behind it. He was a strong proponent for broad scientific study in the Muslim world, seeing it as the only way to compete with colonial Europe. Esposito quotes from a collection of al-Afghani's writings assembled by Nikki Keddie in her book, *An Islamic Response to Imperialism*:

The Europeans have now everywhere put their hands on every part of the world. The English have reached Afghanistan; the French have seized Tunisia. In reality this usurpation, aggression, and conquests have not come from the French or the English. Rather it is science that everywhere manifests its greatness and power.... Science is continually changing capitals. Sometimes it has moved from the East to the West, and other times from the West to the East... All wealth and riches are the result of science. In sum, the whole world of humanity is an industrial world, meaning that the world is a world of science.... The first Muslims had no science, but, thanks to the Islamic religion, a philosophical spirit arose among them... This was why they acquired in a short time all the sciences... Those who forbid science and knowledge in the belief that they are safeguarding the Islamic religion are really the enemies of that religion. The Islamic religion is the closest of religions to science and knowledge, and there is no incompatibility between science and knowledge in the foundation of the Islamic faith.[11,12]

Al-Afghani ultimately took his concepts to the most prominent center of Islamic education, al-Azhar University, which happened to be located in Cairo, where he would continue to see firsthand the impotence of Islam against the power of British colonialism. As the center for Islamic thought even today, al-Azhar was the ideal place for al-Afghani to proliferate his lofty modernist ideals, both in written publications and in the classroom. His torch would be passed on to two gifted disciples, but ultimately be extinguished by Islam's overpowering reactions to European colonialism— reactions that would draw Islam back into a descending orbit of traditionalism.

Al-Afghani's flame flickered back to life a few decades later in the form of Physics Nobel Laureate, Dr. Abdus Salam (1926–1996). I first heard about him from his grandson, a good friend of mine who serves as the imam of a small mosque in San Diego. Salam was a brilliant scientist and passionate social activist. He was the first Muslim and first Pakistani to win a Nobel prize in the sciences, awarded for his contribution to theoretical physics. Similar to the breakthrough that proved that electricity and magnetism are interconnected and part of a unified theory of electromagnetism, Dr. Salam postulated, and successfully proved mathematically, that what are known as "weak nuclear forces" are actually not different than electromagnetic forces. This pivotal contribution, unifying two of the four known fundamental interactions of nature, was subsequently validated experimentally by other scientists.

Throughout his distinguished career as a scientist, Dr. Salam worked tirelessly to promote opportunities for education in the sciences for students in the developing world. Salam was convinced that the key factor in imprisoning the majority of the world in misery and suffering was the lack of scientific development. At the age of 34, Dr. Salam proposed the founding of an international theoretical physics institute at a conference of the International Atomic Energy Agency, which reports to the United Nations. Although he was originally ridiculed for this suggestion, The Abdus Salam International Centre for Theoretical Physics became a reality in 1963, and Dr.

Salam became its first director. Earning a reputation as a scientific diplomat, Dr. Salam lobbied to bring about educational and research opportunities to other aspiring students in the developing world.

But, except for the rare shining star like Dr. Salam, the world of Islam has taken a step backwards in the decades following the departure of the colonialists. To understand this, we must recognize that it was the grandparents of today's working age Muslims who experienced the nightmare of European colonialism. Entire races and ethnic groups suffered deep, collective trauma. In the same way a boy who has been beaten by an abusive father might live out his entire life angrily proving to himself and to the world that he is worthy of respect, so the Muslim world is still living out their reaction to the violence and disrespect they experienced under colonialism. The expression of Islam that emerged does not reflect the essence of Islam in paradise, but rather a response to Western Christian oppression.

The reaction that would set the stage for the next century would be the angry rejection of all things Western.

Modern-day prophets and gifted thinkers such as Sayyid Ahmed Khan of India and Jamal al-Din al-Afghani of the Middle East were invalidated by Islam as a whole on the sole basis of their Western educational exposure. The ancient instinct for retribution was too powerful. Even though the modernists were unwavering in their deep commitments to the teachings and traditions of The Prophet, the traditionalist ulama prevailed. The wound to the soul of Islam was too deep. The reaction that would set the stage for the next century would be the angry rejection of all things Western.

The torches of these great modernist minds attempting to create a definition for Islam in a modern world would be reduced to flickering candles. The colonial era came to an end and the next several decades would see the births of multiple new nations and mad scrambles for power. The dream of a unified faith throughout the Muslim world would give way to Islamic nationalism and a kind of "every faction for itself" tribal mentality, which continues to this day.

THE BIRTH OF RADICAL TERRORISM - THE TERRIFYING STORY OF MOHAMMED AL-WAHHAB

It's not an overstatement to say that the influence of Mohammed ibn Abd al-Wahhab (1703–1792) was demonic. No person has done more to bring the dark blight of terror to the Middle East.

He was a villager of modest means from a small oasis in the heart of the deserts of Arabia, at that time under the authority of the Ottoman Empire. Receiving his religious education in nearby Arab cities including Medina, he developed a special affinity for the teachings of a fringe Islamic scholar by the name of Ahmad ibn Taymiyya (1263–1328). Taymiyya's doctrines were so out of sync with Muslim orthodoxy and practice that he had multiple stints in prison for heresy, eventually dying there.

Taymiyya conceived of God as distant and unknowable, with an unrelenting compulsion to punish. Though gifted in the areas of reason and debate, he was considered a heretic for applying modifications to the time-honored legal standard of the ulama— the four sources of knowledge: the Quran, the traditions (hadith), analogy, and consensus. Taymiyya's legal theory placed primary emphasis on one element of the science of evaluating the traditions: *Salafism*, or imitating the practices of the first three generations of Muslims. Of course, now five to six hundred years after all of these were dead and gone, this method was open to subjective interpretation. Taymiyya was famous for declaring his own harsh interpretation, vigorously arguing for it legally, then proclaiming anyone who disagreed with him an infidel and unilaterally carrying out the judgment of execution. His views were not taken seriously as they were considered outrageously punitive.

Four hundred years later, his views were taken seriously by al-Wahhab.

Al-Wahhab returned to his village as a hyper-radical and violent zealot. He had adopted Taymiyya's hard-core monotheistic view that denounced any form of ancestor veneration and mediation between man and God by a religious leader such as an imam. Both were quite common among Muslims. According to al-Wahhab, Muslims were called not only to practice Islam in this way but were divinely called to wage war against any who strayed from these principles. He also espoused Taymiyya's strict form of Sharia law that included harsh punishment for infractions.

Apparently seeing himself as a second coming of The Prophet, al-Wahhab gathered a small following. He was promptly chased out of town by horrified villagers after he and his crew took their extreme concepts from theory to practice and publicly stoned a young woman who had confessed to sexual immorality. Al-Wahhab was just a violent fanatic living in obscurity, but at the next oasis he would meet a small-time sheikh by the name of Mohammed ibn Saud (1726–1765). From this union, the seed of almost everything that is feared today in Islam would germinate.

Saud was a frustrated sheikh wanting to expand the sheikhdom but with limited financial resources. Possibly by promising Saud to enforce payment of the zakat tax for the poor, al-Wahhab persuaded him to provide refuge for him and his violent band. Al-Wahhab insisted on assuming the role of religious leader and requested an oath of allegiance from Saud to perform jihad against locals he considered unbelievers.

This seemingly insignificant meeting of the minds between Saud and al-Wahhab in the obscure deserts of Arabia, initially affecting only seventy households, would upset the delicate balance of power among tribes and become a tipping point with effects still being felt today. Jihad would indeed be waged, oasis by oasis, against fellow Muslims, as al-Wahhab's strict and violent version of Sharia law was imposed. Acceptance of the belief system of this fanatical sect took place out of fear of slaughter, and with each oasis settlement taken, the conscripted *mujahedeen* army grew in numbers and strength. Wahhabi-ism would eventually cover almost the entire Arabian desert, including the major cities, within fifty years of the sealing of the pact between Saud and al-Wahhab.

With Arabia in their control, the army of fanatics would push northward, setting their sights on Arab Sufis and Shiites. In 1802, in the Shiite holy city of Karbala, they massacred four thousand Shiite Muslims as they celebrated a holy day. A modern-day equivalent might look like a rogue fanatical Christian group sneaking into Joel Osteen's mega-church in Houston during their Christmas Eve service and annihilating the congregation with automatic weapons. The Ottoman Empire finally took notice.

The military strength of the Saud-Wahhab coalition proved ill equipped against the armies of the Ottoman Empire. The fanatics were crushed and sent back to the deserts of Arabia and the cities of Medina and Mecca returned to Ottoman control. The evil genie was back in the lamp, where he would remain for over a century. The Saud family would continue to fight, both against the Ottomans and internally amongst themselves, for control of the Arabian Peninsula for the next hundred years.

Fast-forward to the colonial era, the early 1900s. Reminding ourselves of the al-Afghani quote about the British having their hands in every part of the Muslim world, the British saw it as advantageous to weaken the Ottomans and control the Arabian Peninsula. To accomplish this, they provided military and financial support to the Saud family. It was World War I that brought down the Ottoman Empire, but, in the subsequent power vacuum, the Saud family wasted no time using their newfound military might to retake Medina and Mecca, publicly executing forty thousand men in the process. They declared their family monarchy over the "Kingdom of Saudi Arabia" in 1932.

The genie's lamp was uncorked, and the Saudi monarch summoned him forth. This violent expression of Islam was now legitimized and enforced throughout the entire Kingdom of Saudi Arabia. Executions by beheading, amputations, and repression of women are ongoing issues even today. To make matters worse, not long after the Saud family seized power, oil was discovered there. Saudi Arabia became a powerful force in the Middle East and a magnet for Muslim laborers from all over, all of whom were indoctrinated in Wahhabi-ism. And the Kaaba remains the centerpiece of the pilgrimage to Mecca, drawing three million Muslims annually.

With evangelistic fervor funded by millions of oil dollars, Wahhabi teaching spread throughout the Muslim world. Reza Aslan describes the pervasiveness of the Saudis' efforts:

> In 1962, their missionary efforts gained momentum with the creation of the Muslim World League, whose primary goal was the spread of Wahhabi ideology to the rest of the world... Since the creation of the Muslim World League the simplicity, certainty, and unconditional morality of Wahhabi-ism have infiltrated every corner of the Muslim world. Thanks to Saudi evangelism, Wahhabi doctrine has dramatically affected the religio-political ideologies of the Muslim Brothers, Mawdudi's Islamic Association, the Palestinian Hamas, and Islamic Jihad, to name only a few groups.[13]

With many Muslims still bearing scars from the chains of colonialism, for some, the command to wage "jihad" against foreign infidels would strike a chord. And the Brits were far from finished inflicting wounds in the Middle East and Persia. The United States would get in on the act also, as we will discover in chapter four. It was these very wounds that produced the angry radicals who filled the ranks of both Al Qaeda and the Islamic State. With the Saudis' help, they trace their origins in fatwas all the way back to Taymiyya, whose teaching would become the convenient theology of nearly all of today's Islamic terror groups.

The Wahhabi version of Sharia law is equally deviant, focusing almost exclusively on punishment, and taking special joy in imposing inhumane physical penalties. It was difficult to find any small area of everyday life that was not under the oppressive purview of Wahhabi-ism. In Hamid Algar's powerful essay on Wahhabism, he states that "... Smoking was ... prohibited, men were punished for not wearing beards of sufficient length, music was outlawed, and flowerpots deemed to offend public decency with their bright colors were smashed."[14] The rights of women were drastically curtailed.

Although secular power and religious dogma make excellent bedfellows initially, as soon as a measure of dominion is secured, idealistic principles become an impediment. With the now untold wealth of the king and thousands of princes who constitute the Saudi monarchy, Western alliances are needed in order to keep their wealth secure. US military presence in Saudi Arabia has resulted in a rift between Wahhabi religious leaders and the government. The United States, as the originator of the "war on terror," finds itself in the incongruous position of being staunch military allies with the nation that is the source of the ideology behind both Al Qaeda and the Islamic State groups.

Wahhabi-ism is hated and soundly rejected by Shiites, Sufis, and most Sunnis as an invalid expression of the Islamic faith. As such, it is excluded from any further discussion related to Islam in this book.

After being brutalized by colonialism, the Muslim world was broken into pieces. The evil *jinn* of the seventh century awakened.

Tyrants and warlords would emerge. Genocides and ethnic cleansing would take place, the rest of the world hardly knowing.

The empire was shattered, but what of the people? One-fourth of the world population still claims Islam as their faith. In spite of cruel colonialism and Saudi evangelism, the vast majority reject violence as a solution.

But have we heard *their* voices?

CHAPTER 2 NOTES

1. David Nicolle, *The Great Islamic Conquests AD 632–750: Essential Histories* (Oxford: Osprey, 2009), 49.

2. Nicolle, 7.

3. Nicolle, 84.

4. Jalal al-Din Rumi, *Love's Ripening: Rumi on the Heart's Journey*, Translated by Kabir Helminski and Ahamad Reswani (Boston: Shambhala Publications, Inc., 2008).

5. Esposito, 59.

6. Kadri, 43.

7. Randeep Ramesh, "India's Secret History: 'A Holocaust, One Where Millions Disappeared…,'" *The Guardian* (August 24, 2007), https://www.theguardian.com/world/2007/aug/24/india.randeepramesh.

8. Aslan, 228.

9. Aslan, 240.

10. Aslan, 235.

11. Esposito, 127.

12. Nikki R. Keddie, *An Islamic Response to Imperialism* (Berkeley: University of California Press, 1983), 17–19.

13. Aslan, 250.

14. Hamid Algar, *Wahhabiism: A Critical Essay* (Oneonta, NY: Islamic Publications International, 2002), 44.

WHO IS YOUR MUSLIM NEIGHBOR?

Present-Day Teaching and Practice of Islam

In the unrelenting cascade of counterterrorism thrillers and cable news coverage of terror incidents, the humble voice of Islam's mainstream has been silenced. This, combined with the fact that only 25 percent of Americans have ever met a Muslim, makes it easy to see why so many are misled and fearful. Who are today's Muslims? What do they believe and what are their hopes and dreams?

According to the Pew Research Center, as of 2009, the population of the Muslim world stood at 1.6 billion souls or about 23.4 percent of the world's population.[1] Estimates are as high as 1.8 billion in 2017. Approximately one in every four persons alive today is a Muslim. Let that sink in. Map 5 shows the distribution by percent throughout Africa and Asia of the 95 percent of Muslims who live in these continents.

A quick survey of the map reveals that the Arabic speaking Middle East is almost the smallest grouping, containing only 8 percent of all Muslims in the world. Almost one-third of all Muslims live in

India, Pakistan, and Bangladesh. Many are surprised to learn that the nation with the highest number of Muslims is Indonesia, with more than 200,000,000. That's a long way from Arabia. Between the Indian subcontinent and Indonesia, almost half the Muslims of the world are represented.

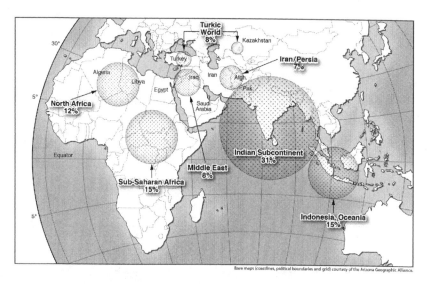

Map 5 — Distribution of Muslim Population by Region

For those curious about the absolute numbers, they are shown in Figure 1 on the next page.

The Muslim world is wonderfully diverse. As with Christianity, the practice of Islam is very much affected by local culture, not to mention the brand of Islam itself. In a recent visit to a small mosque in San Diego, a group of young Pakistani professionals eagerly told me that there are seventy-eight different sects of Islam. This is a very small number when compared to the estimated 40,000-plus Christian denominations and independent groups. But when overlaid upon the uncounted ethnicities, languages, and cultures represented by Islam, it is clear that Islam is not a monolith but a mosaic of diversity.

The disintegration of the political empire that had been merged with the teachings of Islam for thirteen centuries was a substantial first step in the liberation of Islam as a world religion. Forever free from the influence of emperors crazed by their thirst for power and wealth, Islam could pursue its spiritual identity. Smaller scale Islamic empires and monarchies emerged and continue to this day, but Islam as a whole exists distinctly from political power.

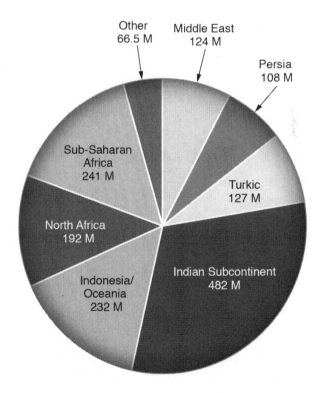

Figure 1 — Number of Muslims by Region

THE FOUR MAJOR DIVISIONS IN ISLAM

There are four major divisions in Islam: Sunni, Shia, Sufi, and Ahmadi.

Sunni

The Sunnis represent 90 percent of all Muslims. Except where noted, all of the descriptions of Islam I write about in this book refer to Sunni Islam. The term Sunni comes from the Arabic word *Sunnah* and refers to the traditions of the prophet Mohammed. Sunni Muslims don't think the successors of Mohammad had a direct connection to God. For this reason, they place heavy emphasis on the Sunnah as the means of finding direction in day-to-day life.

Shia

The Shiites make up the bulk of the remaining 10 percent of non-Sunnis. We have tracked their origins to followers of Mohammed's cousin Ali, who was rejected as the Prophet's successor. Shia Muslims believe in a divinely appointed leader who follows in the footsteps of Mohammed as both spiritual guide and secular ruler. Most of the world's Shiites reside in Iran, which would explain the rise to power of Shia cleric Ayatollah Khomeini during the Islamic revolution there. Three other nations have Shiite majorities: Iraq, Bahrain, and Azerbaijan, but there are also significant numbers of Shia Muslims in Pakistan, India, Turkey, Yemen, Afghanistan, Syria, Saudi Arabia, and Nigeria. Without powerful government oversight to hold the factions in place, the 1,400-year-old feud between the Shiites and the Sunnis is the first to boil over. We see this happening in 2018 in Iraq, Syria, and Yemen.

Shiites believe in the infallibility of their leaders—like the Pope to the Catholics. This explains why Shiites celebrate birthdays and deaths of leaders and make pilgrimages to their shrines. This practice is considered idolatrous by strict Sunnis. Shia Muslims also hold to the future appearance of a messianic figure known as the Mahdi, who will one day appear and rule the world with the justice of Mohammed. Over the centuries, various succession crises took place resulting in multiple offshoots. They are called "fivers," "seveners," and "twelvers," depending on how many of the previous imams they recognize.

Sufi

Flowing like life-giving blood through the veins of the Muslim body are Islam's mystics, the Sufis. They are not a distinct sect—they are Sunnis or Shiites who practice a deeper spirituality. Mysterious and uncounted, Sufis earnestly seek to experience the divine presence of Allah. Mystics embark on a journey of self-discipline in order to achieve purification of the soul. Dozens of Sufi masters have risen to prominence and followers have founded orders in their names. Each order has a unique pathway to a higher consciousness, and seekers are guided through a progression of steps and practices to achieve it. Disciples are only allowed to progress to the next level upon the approval of their master. Key elements of the Sufi orders are love for all mankind, transformation of the soul—from an inclination to desire evil to a state of contentment, an aversion to materialism, and participation in various practices to elevate consciousness.

The well-known "whirling dervishes" come from the Mevlevi Sufi order, founded by Rumi. The dervishes are dressed in white and orbit around their master, who spins on his own axis. I heard a Turkish master describe this practice as a means of aligning with the orbits of the solar system to draw closer to God. Spinning for sometimes hours, dervishes fall into a trance-like state and find intimacy with God.

Ahmadi

The Shia concept of the messianic Mahdi was taken to the next level by Mirza Ghulam Ahmad (1835–1908). Ahmad claimed to actually *be* the promised Messiah and Mahdi in fulfillment of several end-time prophecies made in the hadith. Ahmad, which is a variation on the name Mohammad, gathered a following of believers who came to be known as Ahmadi Muslims, or *Ahmadiyya*. Ahmad didn't bring any new teaching with him. He only claimed to be the fulfillment of Mohammad's original teaching, sent to bring peaceful revival to all the peoples of Islam.

Ahmadi Muslims practice Islam indistinguishably from the Sunnis. Along with the claim of a succession of Mahdis who followed Ahmad, they bring two major points of emphasis. Missionary activity is a high priority, and peace is promoted as a core teaching. They have branded themselves with the term "True Islam," nabbing up the domain name TrueIslam.com with Facebook and Twitter handles to match. They are freely critical of the power struggles and tribal infighting that occurred throughout the history of the Islamic Empire and today. As a result they have drawn the ire of Sunni leaders and—ironically, given their tagline—are not accepted as being true Muslims. In Pakistan, where their numbers are the greatest, they are legally forbidden to claim to be Muslims, and persecution is rampant. The Ahmadiyya have grown in numbers to more than ten million and are in most of the countries of the world.

Nobel Laureate Dr. Abdus Salam and his grandson, my friend Maaz, happen to be Ahmadi Muslims. I met Maaz at a social event put on by the Ahmadiyya Community of San Diego called Coffee, Cake & True Islam. Maaz is an industrial engineer and the father of a young daughter. In his spare time, he faithfully leads the small Muslim community that meets in an office on the back edge of a large industrial complex. Most, if not all, of the small group are from Pakistan. Maaz speaks perfect English, and we hit it off right away. When he realized that my concept of Islam and of Muslims was not based on the image presented in the US media, but on actual history, he lit up, and we connected on a different level. In addition to having many enlightening conversations about the spiritual significance of many of the Muslim rituals and beliefs, we have talked for hours about the many spiritual truths we hold in common. I find these times of rich spiritual fellowship extremely refreshing, and I often leave with tears in my eyes, thinking of the harsh results of the ongoing lack of understanding between Christians and Muslims. I truly consider Maaz to be my brother and I expect that he will follow in the influential footsteps of his grandfather.

The Sunnis, Shiites, Sufis, and Ahmadis are held together by the Quran. In addition to the Quran, they agree on other core elements of the practice of Islam, which have been distilled down to what we know as the five pillars. These two components are what form the common essence of all of Islam.

THE QURAN

The Quran holds a higher place in Islam than does the Bible to Christianity, or the Old Testament to Judaism. In pre-Islamic times, there was no concept of one all-powerful and loving God who cared for his creation and involved himself in their lives on an individual basis. On dark nights in the deserts of Arabia, terrified and confused souls sought solace and direction from the *kahin*, a kind of soothsayer or fortuneteller, who in turn would consult the *jinn*—spirits with some degree of power that occupy the atmosphere, and sometimes magic lamps. When consulted about the meaning of a dream, the location of a lost flock, or whether to take a certain bride, the kahins invariably provided their direction in the form of Arabic prose. And the answer to the question of the agonized seeker required no small amount of interpretation.

The words of the Quran were delivered in similar style, as contemplative prophetic musings in the form of beautiful Arabic prose. When pressed for an exhibition of miraculous powers as validation of his status as the Messenger of God, Mohammed's consistent response was that his only miracles were the prophetic recitations. Islamic tradition captures the essence of the miraculous powers of the Quran in the story of the conversion of Umar, one of Mohammed's first followers and his second successor. At first, Umar was a staunch opponent of Mohammed and angered that his own sister had become a follower. His anger boiled over on one occasion when he learned that Mohammed was teaching in his sister's home. With murderous intent, he set out for his sister's house with sword in hand. Upon entering and hearing the sound of Mohammed's voice, he was so affected by the beauty and profundity of the recitations that he immediately dropped his sword and became a follower. As Reza Aslan points out in *No god but God*, like Saul of Tarsus who ceased his persecutions of the followers of Christ when he was transformed by a vision of the Savior, "Umar was transformed by divine intervention: not because he saw God, but because he *heard* God."[2]

The power of the Quran is not limited to its meaning. *Baraka*, or blessing, is derived from the *sound* of the words itself. For those who don't speak Arabic, it is virtually impossible to experience and appreciate this element of the Quran. In most mosques around the world, Quranic readings are conducted exclusively in Arabic, regardless of the language of the listeners. The veneration of the words of the Quran reached such great heights that a vigorous doctrinal controversy arose as to whether the Quran was eternal and coexisted with God or was created. The dispute became so intense that the scholars of the time were tortured, exiled, and executed depending on their position, as you will recall from our discussion of the Umayyad dynasty in Chapter Two.

The Holy Quran contains 114 chapters and over 6,000 verses. Each chapter, known as a *surah* in Arabic, corresponds to a specific prophetic episode and has a one-word title. Surahs are sequenced according to length rather than chronology, from longest to shortest, with the exception that the first chapter is a short preamble. Each surah begins with the words, "In the name of God, the Merciful-to-all, the Mercy Giver."

Many people in the West are exposed to the Old Testament and the book of Leviticus for example, which contains hundreds of directly stated laws, ranging from what type of meats are forbidden to eat, to how long a woman must abstain from sex after her menstrual cycle. Not so with the Quran. Of the 6,000 verses, only about six hundred contain some form of law or directive, and the vast majority of these pertain to a religious ritual or prayer. According to Esposito, "Approximately 80 verses treat legal topics in the strict sense of the term: crime and punishment, contracts, family laws."[3]

Clearly, the Quran is not a book of law.

Much of the Quran consists of beautiful prose describing the nature of God—as one, as all-powerful, yet gracious and merciful, providing mankind and animals with everything they need. In return, man is expected to worship God, not simply by acknowledging his greatness, but by living a life that is worthy of his greatness. In the Quran, there is no separation between the worship of God and a person's works. One's deeds are a reflection of one's attitude towards God. The deeds that are required proceed from a heart of integrity and compassion—honesty in all spheres of life, generosity toward those in need, and respect for one's elders and family.

The Quran was insufficient as the sole basis for a comprehensive religious and secular legal code. Where the Quran was silent, a second source was equally authoritative—the holy grail of the original Muslim community's practices. The customs and traditions of this venerated group are known as the *Sunna*, from which the term *Sunni* is derived.

This would give rise to the study of what are known as the hadith, the collection of recorded sayings and practices of Mohammed and his key companions. This study was complicated because the scholars who dug into it were more than 150 years removed from the life of Mohammed. With four competitive schools of thought, the temptation to doctor or even invent hadith that were supportive of one's doctrines proved to be too great. There was a proliferation of conflicting hadith, giving rise to yet another area of study: determining the pedigree of the hadith. Each of the four centers of study had their own differing, authenticated versions.

Confusion as to the authenticity of all but the most principal hadith, along with the necessity for direction in matters not contained in the Quran or the hadith, would give rise to two other sources for direction: drawing analogies from comparable situations or events and consensus among the scholars.

The Four Sources of Sharia
The Quran
The traditions or Sunna, as defined by the hadith
Analogy
Scholarly consensus

I recommend reading the entire Quran but here is a representative example. I suggest the following English translation by my good friend and fellow peacemaker Safi Kaskas and his co-author the late David Hungerford: *A Contemporary Understanding: The Qur'an, with References to the Bible.* As with all translations, there is a tension between literal accuracy and literary style. As with the Bible, it is virtually impossible to capture the meaning of the original text with the original literary style.

> The Quran, Surah 11, The Prophet Hud, verses 1–11
> In the name of God, the Merciful to all, the Mercy Giver:
> Alif Lam Ra, (this is) a Book whose verses are perfectly constructed, then detailed directly from the grace of the

Wise, the Most Expert, so that you may worship no one but God. I am sent to you from Him to warn you and to give you good news. Ask your Lord to forgive your sins and turn towards Him in repentance. He will let you enjoy a good life until a specified time, and He will give His grace to everyone who was graceful. But, if you turn away, I dread the suffering (which is bound to befall you) on that Mighty Day. You must all return to God, as He has power over everything. See how they turn away, trying to hide from Him. Even when they cover themselves with their clothes, He knows all that they hide and what they reveal. He has full knowledge of what is in men's hearts.

Every living creature on earth depends on God for sustenance and He knows where it lives and where it dies. It is all in a clear record. He created the heavens and the earth in six days and the throne of His Majesty of His mightiness extends over the water. (He created this) in order to test which of you is best in deeds. And if you (Prophet) say, "You will be resurrected after death," the unbelievers will answer, "This is clearly nothing but sorcery." If We defer their suffering for a specified time, they are sure to say, "What is preventing it (from coming now)?" On the Day when it befalls them there will be nothing to divert it from them and they will be overwhelmed by the very thing they mocked. If We let man taste some of Our mercy and then take it away from him, he will abandon all hope, forgetting all gratitude. If We let him taste ease and plenty after hardship has touched him, he is sure to say, "Misfortune has gone away from me." He becomes overjoyed and boastful. Except those who are patient in hard times and do righteous deeds: forgiveness of sins awaits them and a great reward.

THE FIVE PILLARS

The five pillars of Islam address devotion to God and are practiced by the Sunnis, the Shia, the Sufis, and the Ahmadis. They are:

1. The Profession of Faith (*Shahada*)
2. Ritual Prayers Five Times per Day (*Salat*)
3. Alms Giving (*Zakat*)
4. The Fast of Ramadan (*Sawm*)
5. The Pilgrimage to Mecca (*Hajj*)

1. The Profession of Faith—Shahada. The profession of faith is the single entrance requirement into the Islamic faith. "There is no god, but God, and Mohammed is the messenger of God." Plain and simple, this is an acknowledgment of the oneness of the all-powerful Creator. There is no other god. Mohammed absolutely considered his God, *Allah* in Arabic, to be the same God as that of the Hebrews and the Christians. The second phrase is an acknowledgment that the words of Mohammed as received from the angel Gabriel, and thereby the words of the Quran, are the direct words of God. Making this proclamation makes you a Muslim.

2. Ritual Prayers—Salat. The required ritual prayers take place at five specific times each day: dawn, noon, afternoon, sunset, and before bed. In Muslim-majority countries, the faithful are summoned by the haunting cries of the muezzin from minarets piercing the heavens. Preferably performed in community, the prayers are recited by the imam or prayer leader using the identical words used by their ancestors for centuries. Any male may lead the prayers. Emphasis is placed on voice quality, since the sound of the words is as important as the words themselves. The leader sings the prayers out in deep, rich tones.

Devotees stand in compact and perfectly aligned rows on prayer rugs or inside rectangular markings on the carpet. Accompanying the prayers are postures of standing, bowing, and kneeling—both upright and with forehead to the floor, always facing toward Mecca. The leader usually pauses in the prostrated position, allowing all a few moments of personal prayer and worship. The prayers close with a ceremonial turning of the head to the right and to the left, repeating the words, *assalamu alaikum wa rahmatullah* ("peace be upon you and God's blessings") to neighbors on both sides.

I have visited several mosques in San Diego for Friday prayers. I'll never forget my first visit.

Leaving my shoes in one of the hundreds of cubbies stacked from floor to ceiling in the walls that form the entry area, with trepidation, I walk into a room filled with men sitting cross-legged and facing the front of the large, open room. I see the ebony skin color of Africans, the rich mocha colors of the Indian subcontinent, the tans of the Middle East, and a few with skin tone lighter than my own. Most are dressed normally, but a few are wearing white robes and some are dressed in their traditional national clothing. Along the back wall are several rows of women of all ages, mostly sitting in chairs or on the floor leaning against the wall. Some are wearing the hijab, others are not. Children are scattered around the room, some running around and playing, others sitting with their mothers, and a few boys are with their fathers in the front section. Several older men are seated in chairs along the sides or on the floor leaning against the walls. I take my place inside one of the rectangle outlines on the carpeted floor.

As men continue to trickle in, a heavyset man with the dark complexion of a Bangladeshi or Pakistani sitting towards the front stands up and walks to the microphone. With rich intonations, he begins hypnotically chanting in Arabic. His voice is continuous as when singing, not stopping between words and holding some syllables for several seconds while his voice rises and falls musically. It is the call to prayer. The room falls silent.

Allaaaah hu akbar, Allaaah hu akbar

Ash-hadu anla ilaha illah Allah

Ash-hadu anna muhammadar-rasulullah

Hayya as-salah

Hayya al-falah

Allahu akbar allahu akbar

La ilaha illa Allah

(All but the last two lines are repeated twice).

God is great, God is great
I bear witness that there is no God but Allah.
I bear witness that Mohammed is the messenger of
Allah.
Make haste to prayer.
Make haste to salvation.
God is great.
There is no god except Allah.

The call to prayer continues for several minutes, after which the speaker introduces himself as the chairman of the board of the mosque, makes some announcements, and then introduces the visiting imam. It is time for the *khutbah*—the sermon. I find myself listening to a sermon about the story of Moses from the Old Testament of the Bible.

In the moments after the khutbah, I notice men slipping forward to occupy each available rectangle on the carpet so that there were no empty spaces. The symbolism of a cohesive community is compelling. Everyone rises and the prayers begin. Since I don't understand Arabic, I focus on imitating those that I can see in front of me. We begin in a standing position with hands overlapped across the front about belt high. Some raise their hands to their ears as if listening. As the imam prays, we begin a sequence of bows, placing our hands on our knees as we bow. At a poignant moment in the prayer, the imam pauses and speaks the words *Allah-hu akbar.* In perfect unison, each person drops to their knees and bows with forehead to the floor, many repeating the words, *Allah-hu akbar.* I find myself swept up in the power of this sacred moment—shoulder to shoulder with several hundred fellow worshipers honoring God by bowing before him together. As we linger in this posture, I hear prayers whispered out on all sides of me. With the prompt of *Allah-hu akbar*, we rise to a vertical position, remaining on our knees. We repeat the cycle of prostration, pause for prayer, and rising several times, each change of position prompted by another *Allah-hu akbar*. As we are in the upright position on our knees, I notice a hand signal being passed down the rows. Each person sequentially points with their index finger. I take my turn and later learn that with this gesture, each is signifying that God is one.

We end up comfortably on our knees listening to a final prayer and the ceremonial *assalamu alaikum wa rahmatullah* ("peace be upon you and God's blessings") to the right and to the left, which closes out the prayers. Since this takes place on a Friday afternoon, most men of working age quickly rise, retrieve their shoes, and make their way back to work.

Those with time on their hands stay around for some chit-chat. I see families mingling and carrying on happy conversations, parents trying to gather up their small children, and baked goods for sale on a table in front. As I mingled about attempting to make conversation, most were friendly and welcoming. At this point it has every bit the same feel as being in church on Sunday morning.

I have heard many other khutbahs since then and find them to be quite similar to the many sermons I've heard in church. Recurring themes are trusting in God in difficult times, treating others with respect, honoring one's mother, husbands and wives having respectful interactions in the home, and, always something about helping those less fortunate.

3. Alms Giving—Zakat. All Muslims who are able are required to pay an annual tax of 2.5 percent on all of their income and assets. The tax is to be used to help orphans, widows, the poor, and for the propagation of Islam. In general, the zakat tax is considered an individual matter, but in a handful of nations, the tax is collected by the government.

Muslims take this much more seriously than Christians do their tithes. This became clear to me when I attended a fundraising event in

San Diego for the people of Afghanistan. The emcee was the leading imam of the largest mosque in San Diego. After a wonderful dinner and entertainment featuring traditional Afghan music, the imam took the stage. In my experience within the Christian community, the approach for solicitation of funds for benevolent causes has always been somewhat subdued. But, with the first words of the imam, I was ready to hide under the table.

Talk about pressure. He started at the high end—$5,000. Without batting an eye, he stated that until we had three donors, we wouldn't be moving to the next level. After about ten minutes of cajoling, the goal was met. From $5,000 we gradually transitioned all the way down to $10–$20, with arm-twisting directly proportional to the amount of the donation. And there were no private jets involved. Donations were going towards building schools in Afghanistan. I don't know what the final take was, but I can say that my dress shirt needed dry-cleaning.

I have a friend from Turkey named Aysun who is a wonderful example of practicing the third pillar. I met her at an international social event in San Diego. Her younger sister had won the US immigration visa lottery several years earlier and was living in the United States, so Aysun came for a visit. She loved it so much that she decided to apply for a student visa and enroll as a student at a small school in San Diego. She left a management position in Turkey, where she had supervised a large number of factory workers. I loved hearing her tell stories of her grandfather, a devout Muslim, who taught her of the importance of giving to those in need. Aysun was living on a shoestring budget as a student, but she often dug into her purse and pulled out a few dollars whenever she passed a homeless person on the street.

I have been to many Friday mosque visits and other special events, but I can't recall one of them without a solicitation of funds for the underprivileged.

4. The Fast of Ramadan—Sawm. A fast is declared for Muslims during the ninth month of the Islamic lunar year, the month of Ramadan. It was during the month of Ramadan that Mohammed received his first revelations from God. From sunrise to sunset for the entire month, Muslims are to abstain from food, drink (even water), and sex, and instead focus on devotion to God. Many read the entire Quran during Ramadan and spend extended amounts of time in prayer. During this season, abstention from anger is especially emphasized. The fast is intended to be a time of personal reflection, and daily meetings at the mosque facilitate this.

Since the Muslim calendar is based on the lunar year (354 days), Ramadan begins eleven days earlier each year. When Ramadan falls in the summer months it can be especially difficult. However, as my friend living in Jordan explained,

> The government shortens the work day by several hours. The short days and fasting means very little is accomplished business-wise during the month (important for people traveling to Muslim coutries during Ramadan). In Jordan, during Ramadan, it is illegal to eat, drink, smoke or chew gum in public between sunrise and sunset—even for non-Muslims. Some restaurants stay open for expats and tourists, but if they have windows facing the street, they must be blacked out. Also all liquor stores in Jordan close down for the entire month.

After the sun sets, families gather for *iftar*—the daily breaking of the fast. My friend in Jordan went on to tell me that most non-Muslim expats stay off the roads during the hour before sunset. Hungry drivers are on edge and in a rush to make it to their iftar destination on time. Some mosques offer daily iftar dinners especially geared to the needy and to the devout. Protocol is carefully observed. The iftar meal is complicated by the fact that evening prayers are also required at sunset. Typically dates are served before the prayers to take the edge off the hunger, the prayers are observed, and finally dinner. Restaurants usually change up their menus to serve a buffet or a set iftar meal. Families and friends often gather in homes to celebrate iftar, where the burden falls on the hungry homemaker to prepare the meal while fasting.

After dinner the night prayer is observed and most waste no time getting home to bed. Everyone is up early to eat breakfast before sunrise.

As the month wears on, fatigue sets in. It's a tough schedule. For the devout, spiritual momentum builds. The last ten days of Ramadan hold special meaning. It was during this window that the angel Gabriel appeared to Mohammed. Some linger in the mosque all night, hoping for a similar visitation and the promise of forgiveness.

The fast finally ends on the first day of the tenth month, which is a holiday known as *Eid al-Fitr*, or "feast of the breaking of the fast." Eid al-Fitr is a national holiday in most Muslim countries, and celebrated with a gusto matching that of Christmas in the West.

I was deep into my research for this book during the month of Ramadan 2017, so I got a lot of visibility into the observance of the fast. I even made a misguided attempt to keep the fast myself. However, the first day of Ramadan took place on Memorial Day, and I had a family barbecue planned that afternoon. Thinking I could start on the following day, I realized I had a business lunch scheduled. After a couple more days just like that, I realized what a challenge it would be for Muslims living in countries that don't observe the fast nationally, and I gave up my feeble attempt.

I found that Ramadan is a wonderful time for non-Muslims to get a clearer picture of the practice of Islam. In addition to a heightened observance of all things Islam, mosques all over the United States host iftar gatherings, and often open these up to the public. I attended several. I took a small group to one such gathering. My wide-eyed friends seemed a little frightened when I told them we would not be sitting together, but dispersing ourselves individually to maximize our experience. For the first hour, we sat with the congregation and watched a presentation given by a computer science professional about the physical and spiritual benefits of observing the Ramadan fast. Next we met Aigul, a member of the mosque Board of Directors, who graciously escorted the members of our group to their tables and introduced each to the others at the table. I later found out that she is an influential physician at a top medical center in San Diego. On the drive home I listened with joy to my friends' excited conversations about whom they had met and what they had learned. Each expressed surprise that they had not encountered any of the stereotypes they had expected – just ordinary people having pleasant conversations.

At the end of the month of Ramadan, I took another group to a large formal dinner event for the celebration of Eid al-Fitr. The month-long fast now complete, the atmosphere transitioned from somber introspection to celebration. The women were dressed in a vast array of colors and traditional fashion. There were Pakistani women wearing knee-length dresses with colorful pants. I saw Somalian ladies wearing full-length, long-sleeved dresses with a white hood over the head draping down past the shoulders and a round opening for the face. And others wearing flowing pastel-colored silks with scarves draped around their faces. Even the men broke out brightly colored robes and scarves.

Two large buffet tables were filled with copious amounts of herb-roasted chicken, sliced beef, bright yellow basmati rice, a variety of side dishes, and plenty of fresh pita bread and hummus. Most of the people in the room made multiple trips to the buffet table, returning to their places with heaping plates of food. Children, parents, grandparents, aunts, and uncles all sat together at the large tables. Happy conversations filled the eating space. I overheard a heated conversation among some men, including the imam, who was a single guy. I moved nearer to see what the conversation was about.

I chuckled when I learned they were roused by a recent NBA game. A comedian provided entertainment after dinner.

Not all celebrated. I sat at a table with a woman named, Aisha, who was present at the celebration without a husband, and with four grown children. Her eyes had the shape of sadness and exhaustion. I didn't bring up the subject of her husband, and in the course of our conversation she told me, with watering eyes, that she had almost no relatives left in Afghanistan; all had been killed.

The festivities were interrupted at the proper time so everyone could make their way back into the meeting area for the evening prayers.

5. The Pilgrimage to Mecca—Hajj. Every Muslim who is financially and physically able is required to make the pilgrimage to Mecca at least once in their lifetime. Pilgrims, known as *hajis*, may arrive during a prescribed five-day window scheduled about two months after the end of Ramadan. In Mecca they take part in the annual festival involving circling the black cube, known as the Kaaba, a ritual that has been taking place since before the life of Mohammed. The men dress in seamless white garments to symbolize unity and equality before God. The Kaaba is thought to have been built originally by the prophet Abraham and his son Ishmael. During the festival the hajis participate in several days of meaningful rituals and ceremonies to offer worship to God and commemorate the prophets.

At the close of the festival, Muslims celebrate their second major holiday, known as *Eid al-Adha*, or the "Feast of the Sacrifice." Eid al-Adha commemorates the willingness of Abraham to sacrifice his son according to the command of God, who then provided a ram for the sacrifice instead. In the Muslim version of the story, the son involved was Ishmael, while according to the biblical account in Genesis 22, the son was Isaac. For the feast, each family sacrifices an animal and divides the meat into thirds. One-third is given to the poor, another third to friends and relatives, and one-third is kept.

Some years ago I was with my family on holiday in Istanbul. It turned out to be the day before the Eid al-Adha feast. It seemed that the entire city had been turned into a stable. Everywhere I turned, whether in a parking lot behind a store, a vacant lot, or a post on a street corner, sheep were tied near a bundle of hay. They were awaiting sacrifice on the following day.

The five pillars are what bind all Muslims together. Just as with Christians, the level of commitment to the practice of the key tenets of their faith varies. Among the many Muslims I have met, most are very serious about their commitment to God and the practice of all five pillars. Even the secular-leaning Muslims I have met remain committed to caring for those less fortunate and maintaining a daily relationship with God through prayer.

ISLAM, JUDAISM, AND CHRISTIANITY

According to the Quran, Islam, Judaism, and Christianity are actually the same faith: *"He has ordained for you the same faith He commanded Noah (Nuh), and what we have revealed to you, and what We commanded Abraham (Ibrahim) and Moses (Musa) and Jesus (Esa): 'you shall uphold the faith and do not break up into factions.'"* (The Quran 42:13) More than twenty Old Testament prophets are validated by the Quran, including Jesus of Nazareth. The story told in the Gospels of Matthew, Mark, and Luke is virtually retold in the Quran and is known as the *Injil*. Mohammed considered Islam to be a clarification of both Judaism and Christianity for the Arab peoples. Mohammed rejected the controversial teaching that Jesus was the "Son of God," which he understood literally. He also repudiated the teaching that Jesus himself was God, a member of the so-called "Holy Trinity." This doctrine had emerged and was vigorously debated among Christians in the centuries just prior to Mohammed's lifetime. Islam is unwavering in its commitment to the unity of God, known as *tawhid*. There is no place in Islamic theology for a "Son of God," who is also God, or for a God made up of three distinct personalities.

Even so, mainstream Muslims have a great degree of respect for Christians and are well aware of the commonalities with Islam. In fact, Muslims believe that Islam is the fulfillment of Christianity, and that Mohammed merely pointed out areas in which Christians had corrupted the original teachings of Jesus. The Quran 5:46 says, "We sent Jesus (Esa), the son of Mary, to follow in the footsteps of those earlier prophets, confirming what was available of the Torah. We gave him the Gospel. It has guidance and enlightenment..."

Mainstream Muslims have a great degree of respect for Christians and are well aware of the commonalities with Islam.

For the most part, minority Christian groups peacefully coexist in Muslim-majority countries, as they have for many centuries. Palestinian Christians and Muslims stand hand-in-hand in resistance to the Zionist colonization of their ancestral homelands. Since the 9/11 attacks in 2001, the so-called war on terror and its conflation with a war on Islam have created political pressure between Muslims and Christians in many places. When this pressure breaks out into violence, it must be recognized that what drives this violence is not the ideology of either Christianity or Islam, but political injustices.

In the United States I have found that Muslims are willing participants in interfaith groups and activities. My good friend, Imam Taha Hassane, imam and director of the Islamic Center of San Diego, tirelessly attends and gives talks at interfaith gatherings all over San Diego. Imam Taha was named the 2018 Community Hero by the National Conflict Resolution Center and KPBS. In 2010 the UN unanimously adopted the observance of *World Interfaith Harmony Week*, which was proposed by King Abdullah II of Jordan, a Muslim.

REFUGEES

The Syrian refugee crisis played a significant role in the 2016 US presidential campaign—Donald Trump made this statement, "We cannot let them into this country, period." From the perspective of human suffering, the Syrian conflict can only be described as a nightmare from hell. In a September 2017 report by the Syrian Observatory for Human Rights, experts estimated that over 60 percent of Syria's entire population (a staggering fourteen million people) have been wounded or displaced.[4]

There are several factors leading to the choice to flee homes and risk perilous journeys to faraway places on such a massive scale. With five separate groups engaged in the fighting, and dozens of splinter factions, the entire country is a battleground. Government forces are indiscriminately utilizing high-tech Russian thermobaric bombs as well as low-tech "barrel bombs." These explosives often fall on densely populated neighborhoods resulting in a huge number of civilian casualties. Both types of munitions are hellish in their method of human destruction. According to Popular Science,[5] thermobaric bombs produce an incendiary blast, which literally burns the flesh off of those encompassed by it, and barrel bombs rip people to pieces leaving scattered body parts in the wake.

Another key factor leading to the desperate choice of becoming a refugee is that, with dozens of marauding factions seeking to boost their ranks, any non-fighting male is under constant threat of conscription, or of being accused of fighting for the enemy. If detained by the government forces of Assad, the likelihood of being tortured and murdered is high. Human Rights Watch has obtained smuggled photographs validating claims of systematic torture and murder of detainees on a scale numbering in the thousands.[6]

Talgat's decision to get his family out of Syria came in terrifying fashion. I learned of his story from an American friend living in

Amman, Jordan. When Talgat's teenage wife, Zauresh, went into labor for their third child in late 2013, the civil war had already engulfed them. Their home was in the border town of Daraa, which is known as the "cradle of the revolution." According to Public Radio International, the street graffiti protesting the Assad government that was the spark that set off the Syrian uprising was spray-painted in Daraa early in 2011.[7] When Talgat ran from his house to find emergency transport to the hospital for his wife, he found himself dodging artillery explosions and eventually detained at a military checkpoint. He finally secured transportation and made it home to find himself the father of his third child. Zauresh had given birth alone at home.

As horrifying as this experience must have been for his young family, the journey to a new life outside of war-torn Syria would prove even more difficult. Talgat, Zauresh, and their four children, one a newborn, were able to escape on foot across the nearby border into Jordan with barely more than their own lives. Life in Jordan was better than living in a war zone, but the struggle for survival continued. As an undocumented immigrant, Talgat was not allowed to work, and the government of Jordan provided no financial assistance to refugees. Unable to survive on meager handouts from nongovernment aid groups, after a few months Talgat decided to take his family to the capital, Amman, in hopes of finding under-the-table work. Over the next three years Talgat was able to provide for his family in this fashion, but was caught and reprimanded several times by labor officials. Eventually, his family was forcibly sent to a refugee camp with a stern warning that if they caught him working again they would all be taken back to Syria. With a family to feed, and no path to citizenship or opportunity to work legally, again, it was time for desperate measures.

After six months in the camp, Talgat and his younger brother set out on a desperate adventure to find a third brother who had made his way to Sweden, in hopes of paving the way for his family to live in Sweden. Of course, Talgat would have no choice but to leave his young wife and their four children behind. The child who had been born at home in Syria, a boy, abruptly stopped speaking after his father left.

The details of their journey are sketchy. Somehow they made the treacherous overland trek through Syria into Turkey, where they found a smuggler of human cargo who could transport them to Hungary. There they were forced to live in hiding for months, scratching for survival in the wild. The Hungarian police eventually caught up to them and they spent three months in jail. When they were released they were able to somehow make it to the Baltic coast and secure passage to Sweden. There they were able to find their brother and file the proper paperwork to become legal permanent residents.

Only one step remained. Filing the necessary documents to allow their wives and children to join them in Sweden and also become residents. This process takes about two years. Miraculously, five years after leaving their home in Syria, Talgat, Zauresh, and their four children were reunited in Sweden in January 2018.

As a footnote, my friend living in Amman who helped facilitate the reuniting of the family told me this: "One of Zauresh's brothers is named Jihad. He is one of the gentlest, kindest, most generous people I know. When I finally met him in Sweden, he had tears in his eyes when he thanked me for supporting his sister and wife when he couldn't."

A *New York Times* story reports that on August 31, 2016, during the Obama presidency, the United States reached its goal of admitting ten thousand Syrian refugees in a resettlement program.[8] This is only about two out of every one thousand refugees. Twenty-three other nations are ranked ahead of the US in receiving Syrian refugees including Germany, Sweden, and Canada.

WHO SPEAKS FOR ISLAM? ISLAM'S MODERATE MAINSTREAM

Beyond the Quran and the five pillars, what are Muslims all over the world really about? What are their hopes and fears, their dreams, and concerns?

Many Christians rely on statements from evangelical leaders such as Franklin Graham, who said, "It wasn't Methodists flying into these buildings, it wasn't Lutherans, it was an attack on this country by people of the Islamic faith,"[9] or televangelist Pat Robertson, who reveled in a hypothetical conflict between Muslims and gays[10] in the aftermath of the Orlando shooting in summer of 2016. Other Americans fall into the category of "I don't know."

Thanks to groundbreaking data collected by Gallup between 2001 and 2007, representing 90 percent of all Muslims worldwide, we are not limited to the irrational ranting of televangelists or non-factual news programs for an accurate understanding of the viewpoints of Muslims. John Esposito and Dalia Mogahed provide informative exposition of the data in their insightful book, *Who Speaks for Islam?*

When asked what the United States could do to improve their lives, the most common responses of Muslims from around the world were to reduce unemployment and improve the economic infrastructure.[11] When asked about their dreams for the future of their own countries, the majority cited improved economic conditions, greater security, and an end to civil tensions. Next in line were improvements in education, democratic ideals, and freedom of speech.[12]

Sound familiar?

Jobs, education, economic improvement, safety, freedom of speech... How can this be? The primary concerns of 90 percent of all Muslims on the planet are unemployment and education? What about all those reports telling us that the core beliefs of Islam involve extreme violence against all infidels? As we have shown, it is *not* a core belief, and as the survey results show, the primary concerns of the vast majority of Muslims do not include anything even remotely related to the violent subjugation of all to Islam.

When queried about the meaning of jihad, only the island nation of Indonesia thought the meaning of jihad was to sacrifice one's life for the sake of Islam. More common responses were, "a commitment to hard work," "achieving one's goals in life," "struggling to achieve a noble cause," "promoting peace, harmony, or cooperation and assisting others," and "living the principles of Islam."[13]

Focusing specifically on the 9/11 attacks, 93 percent of those surveyed did not agree with the statement that the attacks were "completely justified."[14] When questioned about their devotion to Islam, both the 93 percent who were against the attacks and the 7 percent who were for them considered themselves devoted Muslims. Those who condemned the 9/11 attacks often cited verses from the Quran as their justification.

Sharia law in its most authentic form emphasizes family law and social egalitarianism. It is seen as a form of legal protection against autocratic rulers.

Only a handful of countries surveyed returned majorities saying that Sharia law should have no place in government. But in the many countries where Sharia law was favored, only a minority favored it as the sole source of legislation. Most favor a balance between a secular legal system and Sharia law. I have spoken with many Muslims about Sharia law. They think of it as a means of living under the principles of social justice taught by Mohammed. Non-Muslims tend to be incredulous that Muslims favor Sharia law. Of course, most non-Muslims equate the term Sharia law to the oft-publicized Taliban version involving harsh punishments and enforcement of restrictions as ridiculous as displaying flowers that are too colorful. But Sharia law in its most authentic form emphasizes family law and social egalitarianism. It is seen as a form of legal protection against autocratic rulers. Muslims simply want to be governed with the fairness exemplified and taught by Mohammed in the Quran.

I find it curious that so many Americans find fault with Muslims for wanting their faith to have a place in legislation. Another Gallup poll, taken in 2006, produced results that show a clear majority of Americans want the Bible to be used as the source for laws in America. Nine percent of Americans would like the Bible to be the only source for legislation and 42 percent would like religious leaders to play a direct role in creating a constitution. American Christians had nearly identical responses to the people of Iran.[15]

Mohammed's teaching on women was revolutionary for seventh century Arabia– and for the rest of the world. He granted women equal status with men, rights to family inheritances, and fair treatment in the case of divorce.

In addition to misperceptions about what mainstream Muslims believe about jihad and Sharia law, most Americans seem completely in the dark when it comes to understanding the role of women in Islamic society. Most are aware of the voting and driving restrictions on women in Saudi Arabia that were in place until very recently. They know about religious police enforcing the proper dress of women in Iran. They have seen the images of women wearing full-body garments with only a mesh opening for vision in the oppressive heat of Afghanistan. But most seem ignorant of the fact that over the last few years, as Aslan states, the Islamic world has produced more female presidents and prime ministers than both Europe and North America combined.[16]

We have already seen that Mohammed himself was quite secure in the presence of strong women. We've learned that his first wife was fifteen years his senior and a prominent member of Mecca's elite merchant community. His youngest wife, Aisha, apparently had no problem standing up to Mohammed. Far from having a submissive role in a male-dominated society, in the famous "Battle of the Camel," the camel was Aisha's as she passionately led the army into the fray. Mohammed's teaching on women was revolutionary for seventh century Arabia—and for the rest of the world. He granted women equal status with men, rights to family inheritances, and fair treatment in the case of divorce.

Over time, the teaching of the various legal scholars throughout the world of Islam would follow regional cultural norms more than the example of Mohammed. For this reason, even today there is huge variety in the role and rights of women in Muslim-majority countries. While in Wahhabi-ist Saudi Arabia, women have been forbidden to drive until very recently, in neighboring United Arab Emirates, women are allowed to be commercial and military pilots. An October 2014 CNN story told about Major Mariam al-Mansouri, a "highly trained, combat ready pilot," who even led a strike mission against ISIS positions in Syria.[17]

In Afghanistan, Iran, and Saudi Arabia many women wear full-body burqas in public. In Turkey, it's a different story. My friend Dilara is the general manager for a Turkish high-tech company in partnership with a company located in the Middle East. When not running the business on-site, she travels the world engaging with executives of other companies. She has a daughter living in the US, so visits the states a couple times per year. An ultramodern woman with short cropped hair, she does Pilates daily, avoids red meat, has a housekeeper, and enjoys the finer things of life. Also from Turkey, Aysun and her sister, whom I mentioned in the discussion about the Five Pillars, love going to the nightclubs in San Diego. Aysun is naturally blonde and, when dressed to the nines, she and her sister look just like all the California girls at the clubs. They love a night on the town with good food, music, and dancing.

Nine Muslim women have been heads of state, with the women leaders of Mauritius, Bangladesh, and Kosovo in power as of early 2018. Megawati Sukarnoputri was president of the largest Muslim country in the world, Indonesia, leading over two hundred million Muslims. Bangladesh has had two female prime ministers.

In a wonderful TED talk entitled, "How Women Wage Conflict without Violence," filmmaker Julia Bacha cites a study conducted by Maria Stephan and Erica Chenoweth, documented in their book, *Why Civil Resistance Works*. In their study of the major nonviolent and violent conflicts that took place between 1900 and 2006, they found that nonviolent campaigns were more than twice as effective in producing the desired changes.[18] Bacha cites the research of Victor Asal, who indicates a major factor in the choice to use nonviolent resistance as a means of producing political change is whether women are allowed to play key roles in the public life of the society.[19] When will the war on terror end? Perhaps when the nations of the West have as many women heads of state as the Muslim world does.

The portrayal of Muslim women in the US media is almost exclusively an image of oppression and victimization. Esposito and Mogahed reference a recent survey of all photographs of Muslims in the American press. The survey revealed that three out of every four photographs of Muslim women showed them in a passive role. Compared to photographs of Muslim men, there were six times as many images of women who were portrayed as victims.[20]

Victim images of Muslim women were reinforced by Laura Bush, not long after her husband invaded Afghanistan. In a November 17,

2001 radio address on PBS, the First Lady declared that "because of our recent military gains in much of Afghanistan, women are no longer imprisoned in their homes. They can listen to music and teach their daughters without fear of punishment. The fight against terrorism is also a fight for the rights and dignity of women."[21]

In late 2015, I tuned into a prime-time CNN interview with Reza Aslan. Aslan was invited to the program as a subject matter expert for questions relating to Islam. "Does Islam Promote Violence?" was written in large block letters at the bottom of the screen as the segment began. They first played a clip from the Bill Maher show in which Maher, pausing for dramatic effect, states, "Not only does the Muslim world have something in common with ISIS, it has too much in common with ISIS," virtually equating the Muslim world with the Islamic State terror group. The lead interviewer next stated that Maher had gone on for five minutes talking about circumcision for women and not respecting the rights of women and then asked Aslan for his response. The dual CNN anchors then took turns interrupting Aslan while he was explaining that female genital mutilation (FGM) is not part of Islam, and that there have been seven female heads of state in Muslim countries. They kept trying to bring the conversation back to FGM in Somalia and voting restrictions in Saudi Arabia as if this represented the norm. Even in the presence of a religious scholar telling them otherwise, the prime-time news anchors were already convinced that Muslim women are victims of repression and violence. And if CNN is telling this story, what story are Fox News and Breitbart telling?

Fortunately, there are data to counterbalance the non-factual rhetoric that floods the airwaves. On the subject of higher education, while the countries of Brazil and the Czech Republic show 4 percent and 11 percent respectively for the number of women pursuing education after high school, in Iran more than half of college students are women. In Egypt, Jordan, and even restrictive Saudi Arabia, the numbers are in the 30 percent range.[22]

Since the colonial era, the Western world has been obsessed with the dress of the women of Islam. From the hijab to the burqa to the burqini, Westerners have long seen the modest dress of Muslim women as a symbol of oppression. But what do Muslim women think? When asked to compare themselves to women of the West, a common response was that it was the women of the Western world who lacked self-respect and submitted to the will of men in their style of dress. Esposito and Mogahed point out, "In both cases, the assumption is that women are either covering or uncovering to please or obey men."[23]

> Rather than being sources of repression, Muslim women see Sharia law and the teachings of Islam as means of protection from male-dominated government and culture.

What about Sharia law? When a woman from Islam's mainstream thinks of Sharia law, contrary to what we might first think, she actually thinks of it in a positive light. In a family law context, Sharia provides a layer of financial protection for women. In one example of Islamic jurisprudence, Esposito and Mogahed point out that a woman is never legally responsible for supporting herself or anyone else, even if she is wealthy. This being the case, brothers receive double the inheritance of the daughters upon the passing of their parents. A woman is free to have a job, but never obligated to work. Her closest male relative is obligated to provide for her. Under this framework, the man is legally responsible for providing not only for his immediate family, but also for any women in his extended family who lose their source of support through death or divorce.[24]

Examples such as this help us to understand why 81 percent of Iraqi women answered that religious authority should play a direct role in the creation of family law.[25] In fact, when queried about what is the most important thing to advance the progress of Muslim women, the answer most frequently given was "attachment to their spiritual and moral values is critical to their progress."[26] In African nations where female genital mutilation is practiced, Muslims agree that this is irreconcilable with the teaching of Islam.

Rather than being sources of repression, Muslim women see Sharia law and the teachings of Islam as means of protection from male-dominated government and culture.

What about Muslim men? Do they feel that women's rights should be restricted in comparison to their own? With regard to voting rights, 87 percent of men in Iran are in favor of women being allowed to vote. Even in Saudi Arabia, where women were restricted from voting at the time of the survey, 58 percent of the men were in favor of women being allowed to vote. In virtually every country surveyed, clear majorities of the men answered that women should be able to work in any field for which they are qualified.[27] In further data analysis, Gallup found that there was no correlation between the religious commitments of Muslim men on either side of this issue. Such data reveals that restriction of women's rights in Muslim countries is not due to the teachings of Islam.[28]

When it came to those who committed honor killings, in the country of Jordan, 69 percent did not perform their daily prayers and 56 percent did not perform the fast of Ramadan. In fact, many had histories of violent behavior. Thirty-five percent had already served sentences for previous crimes, 32 percent were illiterate, only 4 percent had attended college and 24 percent were brought up in broken homes.[29] Clearly, something other than the teaching of Mohammed had driven these men to murder their own female relatives.

The Gallup survey results presented by Esposito and Mogahed paint a substantially different picture of today's Muslims than Bill Maher and CNN. And every Muslim I meet seems only to confirm their conclusions. There is Mohammed, a young, intelligent PhD software engineer from the resort city of Agadir in Morocco. We met at an international social event in San Diego a couple of years ago. He was excited about my book project from the beginning. When I told him the title of the book, his eyes got big and he told me about his American workmates. They had confronted him about why Muslims had an inherent and violent anger towards the USA. Mohammed was very proud to tell me that, on the contrary, Morocco was the first country to recognize the United States as a nation when we declared independence. He is equally frustrated with the US media as he is toward the radical imams who violate the Quran and recruit terrorists, and with their ignorant followers who are "too lazy to study the Quran for themselves."

Mohammed got impatient with me when I asked him about women wearing the hijab. "Morocco is a free country. If they want to wear it they wear it, and if not, they don't," he quipped. Always quick to respond to my questions with substantive answers, Mohammed knows the Quran, and prefers not to focus on rules, but on the heart of Islam and the principles behind the rules.

Or what about Rashid, whom I met in Grand Junction, Colorado when I was there for my father's hip replacement surgery a couple of summers ago? I ran across the street from the cheap hotel where I was staying to have dinner at a local restaurant. I sat down at the bar next to a Middle Eastern looking young man, always looking for opportunities to interact with Muslims. Rashid was an engineering student from the United Arab Emirates (UAE), a small country on the southeastern edge of the Arabian Peninsula. Rashid stayed permanently at the cheap hotel right next door to mine, and all his schooling expenses were paid by his father. I was a bit curious about his choice for housing. Surely there must be less expensive and more convenient options near the university where he studied. I don't remember much about the conversation except him telling me when he was traveling in the Middle Eastern countries lacking oil revenues such as Jordan or Lebanon, the locals could always spot travelers from the Gulf States and tried to charge them extra for taxi rides and other services.

What I do remember is after we had dinner, exchanged phone numbers, and then left for our hotel rooms, before I reached my room, I received a somewhat shocking text message from Rashid, propositioning me for sex.

The vast majority of Muslims are concerned with the same things we are concerned with … Like us, they have hopes for a bright future for their children.

Or my good friend Fayaz Nawabi, who came to the United States from Afghanistan as a refugee. As he was growing up in the US, he had difficulty adjusting to the various moves and life changes. He became angry and rebellious, and even started a gang in his middle school. He is a born leader. Amazingly, by the age of thirteen he had memorized the entire Quran. At the same time, he loved sports and often listened to sports radio and was a frequent call-in participant known as "the kid." After stints as an ESPN radio producer and at an investment banking firm, Fayaz became discontent with the corporate world and went back to school. He studied public administration and city planning at San Diego State University, with an associate's degree in Japanese thrown in for good measure. He has developed a keen interest in politics, and you will find him all over the place in the San Diego local political scene. He continues to serve as a part-time imam for several of the mosques around town. Watch for Fayaz to emerge on the larger political scene—he recently ran for a seat on San Diego's City Council.

The vast majority of Muslims are concerned with the same things we are concerned with. They are city council candidates, accountants, software engineers, and struggling students. They are at varying places on the sexuality continuum. They are fleeing homes they have had in their families for generations, under waves of violence—desperate for a breath of peaceful air. Like us, they have hopes for a bright future for their children. And they have no interest in strapping on a vest full of explosives and detonating it in a crowd of Americans.

But what about 9/11? George W. Bush, Donald Trump, and much of America seem to be mystified about why Islamic extremists are compelled to commit acts of terror against American citizens.

We're about to go behind the curtain and shine a light on the ominous dark power of Islamic terror.

CHAPTER 3 NOTES

1. Pew Research Center, *Mapping the Global Muslim Population* (October 7, 2009), http://www.pewforum.org/2009/10/07/mapping-the-global-muslim-population/.

2. Aslan, 158.

3. Esposito, 76.

4. "About 465 Thousand Persons Were Killed and 6 Years of the Syrian Revolution and More than 14 Million Were Wounded and Displaced" *Syrian Observatory for Human Rights* (March 13, 2017), http://www.syriahr.com/en/?p=62760.

5. Kelsey D. Atherton, "Thermobaric Bombs and Other Nightmare Weapons of the Syrian Civil War," *Popular Science* (October 5, 2016): 4, https://www.popsci.com/thermobaric-bombs-and-other-nightmare-weapons-syrian-civil-war.

6. "Syria: Stories behind Photos of Killed Detainees," *Human Rights Watch* (December 16, 2015), https://www.hrw.org/news/2015/12/16/syria-stories-behind-photos-killed-detainees#.

7. Hugh McLeod and a reporter in Syria, "Syria: How It All Began" *PRI* (April 23, 2011), https://www.pri.org/stories/2011-04-23/syria-how-it-all-began.

8. Haeyoun Park and Rudy Omri, "US Reaches Goal of Admitting 10,000 Syrian Refugees. Here's Where They Went," *New York Times* (August 31, 2016), https://www.nytimes.com/interactive/2016/08/30/us/syrian-refu-

gees-in-the-united-states.html.

9. Christopher Mathias, "A Pastor Who Said Islam Is 'Evil' Is Speaking at Trump's Inauguration," *Huffpost* (January 18, 2017), https://www.huffingtonpost.com/entry/franklin-graham-islamophobia-trump-inauguration_us_587e3ea5e4b0aaa369429373.

10. Dan Evon, "Pat Robertson Comments on Orlando Shooting," Snopes (June 15, 2016), https://www.snopes.com/news/2016/06/15/pat-robertson-orlando-shooting-comments/.

11. John L. Esposito and Dalia Mogahed, *Who Speaks for Islam?* (New York: Gallup Press, 2007), 62.

12. Esposito and Mogahed, 94.

13. Esposito and Mogahed, 21.

14. Esposito and Mogahed, 69.

15. Esposito and Mogahed, 49.

16. Aslan, 72.

17. Dana Ford, "UAE's First Female Fighter Pilot Led Airstrike against ISIS," *CNN* (October 9, 2014): 13, https://www.cnn.com/2014/09/25/world/meast/uae-female-fighter-pilot/index.html.

18. Julia Bacha, "How Women Wage Conflict without Violence," *TED: Ideas Worth Spreading* (June 1, 2016), https://www.ted.com/talks/julia_bacha_how_women_wage_conflict_without_violence/transcript?language=en.

19. Bacha.

20. Esposito and Mogahed, 100.

21. Esposito and Mogahed, 101.

22. Esposito and Mogahed, 103.

23. Esposito and Mogahed, 110.

24. Esposito and Mogahed, 119.

25. Esposito and Mogahed, 113.

26. Esposito and Mogahed, 113.

27. Esposito and Mogahed, 121.

28. Esposito and Mogahed, 123.

29. Esposito and Mogahed, ___. [need page number]

Why Do They Hate Us?

THEY HATE OUR FREEDOM?

I CRY,

THEY DIE

IS THIS THE FATE TO BE?

SHE SINGS BLOODSHED

AND THE PEOPLE HOLD THE FLAG;

DANCING A JIG LIKE THEY WERE FREE,

MISUNDERSTANDINGS LED BY EARTHLY GREED,

'TIS SUICIDE!

WE ARE ONE!

THIS DEATH LURKS IN THE CENTER OF OUR BEING.

MY BROTHER HOLDS THE TRIGGER ON THIS GUN

THE BULLET SPLITS MY HEART

MY SOUL RISES ABOVE

AND CRIES FOR THOSE WHO STILL

THINK THEY ARE ALIVE

IN A CESSPOOL OF BLOOD

NO MY BROTHER!

YOU KILL THE HEART OF THE BODY,

AND THERE IS NOTHING LEFT,

PLEASE DON'T FORGET TO LOVE!

Kimba Buske

On December 2, 2015 twenty-eight-year-old Syed Farook and his wife Tashfeen Malik dropped their six-month-old daughter off at his mother's house and left for work. Farook worked for the San Bernardino County Department of Public Health, which was holding a semi-annual training event and holiday luncheon at an off-site location. He left the event at about 10:30 a.m., leaving a backpack on the conference table. Half an hour later, Farook returned with his wife. They were both armed with semi-automatic weapons and wearing black ski masks and tactical vests. They shot their way into the building and quickly entered the conference room, where there were about eighty people enjoying a break in the proceedings. For the next two or three minutes, the two unloaded magazines containing more than one hundred rounds of ammunition on Farook's helpless coworkers. The couple escaped and fled, but it only took the police a few hours to find them, and the two went down in a horrific shootout not far from their San Bernardino home. In total, fourteen were killed, and twenty-four injured, including two police officers. Malik had pledged allegiance to ISIS on her Facebook page only a short time before the attack. It was the worst Islamic terrorist incident in the US since 9/11.

As the front running candidate for the Republican presidential primary, Donald Trump wasted no time making a statement to the press. In addition to calling for "a total and complete shutdown of Muslims entering the United States," candidate Trump echoed the question asked by President Bush after 9/11, more than fourteen years earlier. Trump said, "It is obvious to anybody the hatred is beyond comprehension. Where this hatred comes from and why, we will have to determine."[1]

We have already learned that the vast majority of Muslims do not hate Americans, and that the original teachings of Mohammed forbid killing except in self-defense. But what about the radicals? What about Al Qaeda and Osama bin Laden? What about ISIS and the Taliban? Why are these Islamic extremists targeting Americans? Why did nineteen Middle Eastern Arabs hijack crowded airliners and fly them into buildings? Was George W. Bush right when he said, "They hate our freedoms?"

"They hate our freedoms" is an explanation we all seem comfortable with. And tragically, we seem agreeable to the so-called war on terror, which has cost the lives of hundreds of thousands of Muslims. But as someone who has lived five years in the Muslim world, I found Bush's explanation unsatisfying. With respect to direct causality, surely there must be a more definitive answer. Why would well-educated men from stable family backgrounds forfeit their lives in order to kill hundreds of American civilians? How could the culture that I had experienced as so hospitable and gracious produce men who would fly airliners into skyscrapers? "They hate our freedoms" wasn't doing it for me. Suicide attacks are the acts of desperate men and women. I had to know why. With trepidation, I set out to explore the subterranean caves of Islamic terror. I was shocked by what I found lurking within the deep labyrinth.

I considered myself well-informed on world affairs, especially those involving the Muslim world. That self-evaluation would change. But I had to ask myself: If I was misinformed, what about the other three hundred million Americans, many of whom have never been to Canada or Mexico, let alone Turkey or Morocco?

Since the early 1950s, the US has been involved in military or covert intervention in twelve out of the sixteen Middle Eastern and Persian-speaking nations.

The first clues to finding an answer to our question, "Why do they hate us?" go back to the days of European colonialism. The abuses perpetrated in the Muslim world by colonial powers came to an end barely a generation-and-a-half ago. The inhabitants of the Indian subcontinent will never forget the cruel subjugation of the British. After World War I, it was Britain and France that carved up the Middle East and North Africa. They didn't relinquish control of Palestine and Algeria until after World War II.

After World War II, with Muslim anger still smoldering, the United States inherited the leading role in the Middle East tragedy. Since the early 1950s, the US has been involved in military or covert intervention in twelve out of the sixteen Middle Eastern and Persian-speaking nations. Only the tiny Gulf States—Oman, UAE, Qatar, and Bahrain—have been spared. Added to these twelve are the African nations of Libya, Egypt, Sudan, Ethiopia, and Somalia, as well as Pakistan and Indonesia, for a grand total of nineteen Islamic nations in which the United States has had military and/or covert involvement in recent decades. With many of these, our involvement is ongoing. On top of that, the United States has played a key role in supporting Israel's ongoing colonization of Palestine, resulting in a massive humanitarian crisis and over five million Palestinians currently in refugee camps.

So what makes a radical? As we take our first steps into the labyrinth of terrorism, the first demon we encounter is the Islamic

Revolution of Iran. For many of us, this was our first taste of anti-American sentiment in the Muslim world. In November 1979, an angry mob of students stormed the US Embassy in Tehran and took fifty-two embassy workers hostage. In the ensuing days, we saw masses of angry Muslims burning American flags and effigies of Jimmy Carter on the nightly news. Even though technically not an act of terror—all hostages were released after 444 days—this event served as a high-profile spark that would ignite a flame of Islamic fundamentalism.

In the absence of an explanation, Americans were left to draw their own conclusions about Muslims and ask, "Why do they hate us?" It would not be until several decades later that we would learn about the covert CIA activity that triggered this event.

WE HATE THEIR FREEDOM? — THE BRITISH, THE CIA, AND IRANIAN OIL

Iran is one of the few ancient civilizations still in existence today, and had always been ruled by various monarchs. By the end of the colonial era Iran was in a bitter struggle for democracy and was attempting to free itself from the tyranny of the Qajar dynasty. In his book, *All the Shah's Men: An American Coup and the Roots of Middle East Terror*, Stephen Kinzer writes about the little-known story of Iran's unsuccessful attempt at becoming a democracy.

In the waning years of the Qajar dynasty, the last two shahs had developed an insatiable thirst for extravagance. After depleting the wealth of the populace, they became so desperate they began selling off the rights to Iran's most valuable natural resources, including petroleum. The shah inked a sixty-year deal with the British that, in 1920, netted him only £47,000 for an entire year of oil production.[2] Iran had become, quite literally, an extravaganza for the British.

While the Anglo-Iranian Oil Company (AIOC) was enjoying its

status as the most profitable British business in the world, conditions for the Iranian workers were appalling. They were paid fifty cents a day and denied basic benefits such as vacation pay, sick leave, and disability compensation. Oil workers lived in a squalid shanty town near the oil fields lacking running the water and electricity. Not far away in the British sector, according to Kinzer, "there were lawns, rose beds, tennis courts, swimming pools and clubs,"[3] and no Iranians allowed.

As virtual slaves to the British, Iranian workers, farmers, and merchants coalesced into a democratic reform movement. After several decades of bloody struggle against the British-backed monarchy, in April 1951, Iran emerged with its first democratically elected prime minister, a passionate champion of workers' rights named Muhammad Mossadegh. The Iranian dream of democracy had seemingly been fulfilled.

Mossadegh was so well known for his efforts to bring democracy to Iran that he was named Time Magazine's Man of the Year in 1951—over Harry Truman, Dwight Eisenhower, and Winston Churchill. But Mossadegh was *persona non grata* among the Muslim clerics. He was educated in the West and a proponent of secular democracy—he was a Muslim moderate.

Mossadegh's first order of business was to reconfigure Iran's oil policy to put more of the black gold's wealth where it belonged—in the hands of the Iranian people. At peak annual production during World War II, Britain was extracting more than sixteen million tons of oil, for which Iran was guaranteed a minimum sum of £975,000 per the latest renegotiated agreement.[4] This amounted to pennies per barrel when the price of crude was ten tô twenty dollars per barrel. A US State Department financial analysis showed that the AIOC was cashing in to the tune of a 3,000-percent profit margin.

At a time when the United States via Aramco (the Arabian-American Oil Company) had negotiated a 50/50 profit share with Saudi Arabia, Britain refused to negotiate with Mossadegh on any level. In their own words, they sought only to "cow these insolent natives,"[5] who did not appreciate "the immense service to mankind of the British people in recent times."[6] To the bitter end Mossadegh held firm on his demand for an evenly split profit share of a nationalized Iranian oil industry. Britain too held firm on their demand for a flat fee structure while refusing to divulge how much oil they were producing.

The Brits tried all manner of legal maneuvering, taking their case to the United Nations and to the World Court. This only served to put Mossadegh on the world stage as a champion of democratic reform and as a defender of Iran against imperialist injustices. British hawks at the highest government levels pushed Britain to the brink of invading Iraq. In the end, the British used their naval might to put a chokehold on Iran's economy by blockading their ports. They virtually shut down Iran's oil production by prohibiting any access by European oil tankers. This pushed Iran to the point of insolvency and created deep economic hardship for Iran's people. Mossadegh eventually caught the Brits in a plot to overthrow the Iranian government, at which point Mossadegh threw them out of Iran and closed their embassy. Mossadegh and his National Front followers were willing to pay any price to free themselves from tyranny—from both ancient dynasties and corporate empires.

The British were now without a base of operations in Iran and seething at the fact that this "insolent native" was standing up to their empire. In order to execute their plans to overthrow Mossadegh, England turned to their newfound ally, the United States. Under Harry Truman, the United States was openly supportive of Iran's democratic government and pressured AIOC to begin sharing its wealth more equitably with Iran.[7] For the last two years of his presidency (1952–1953), Truman stood up to Great Britain, insisting that nothing should be done that "would appear to be in opposition to the legitimate aspirations of the Iranian people."[8] He firmly opposed military and covert operations to overthrow Mossadegh and worked to broker a compromise.

For this reason, the US was held in high esteem by the Iranian people unlike Britain and the USSR. Both Truman and his predecessor, Woodrow Wilson, had publicly supported Iran in their quest for a democratic government and in their standoff with the British. America was seen as a country that sought to improve the quality of life of impoverished Iranians without imposing America's lifestyle and beliefs.[9]

Global events produced a crossroads for the US government in this profound moment in history. In a decision known only to a handful of men, US policy towards Iran took a sharp right turn. Triggered by fear of communism, the US government directly produced an outcome in Iran that lit the fuse of an incendiary device so powerful that more than 65 years later, East and West are still being consumed.

According to Kinzer, the tipping point came when North Korea invaded South Korea in June 1950 with support from the communist governments of both the USSR and the People's Republic of China. The United States was the principal player in the UN force supporting the South, with strong participation on the part of the British. British support for the US in the Korean War would play a key role in the Iran crisis. Prior to that Latvia, Lithuania, Estonia, Bulgaria, Romania, Hungary, Poland, Czechoslovakia, Albania, and Yugoslavia had all already fallen like dominoes to communist control. And in 1949, the forces of communist leader Mao Zedong had defeated their pro-Western opponents in China and the Soviet Union had conducted their first nuclear weapon test in Kazakhstan.[10]

A few years earlier, Truman had commissioned the Central Intelligence Agency in response to the attack on Pearl Harbor and the growing threat of communism. The CIA had the vague and dubious charter of conducting covert, subversive activities directed against communism. So, while Truman was standing with Iran's democratic government, an eager CIA operative was setting up shop in the US Embassy and taking over Britain's vast network of anti-Mossadegh operatives. According to Kinzer, "This network had been assembled at great cost and had shown its ability to spread inflammatory rumors, place provocative articles in newspapers, manipulate politicians, influence mullahs, and produce hired crowds on short notice."[11]

Truman's successor, Dwight Eisenhower, would follow suit with Truman in supporting Iran initially. In the end, it was Eisenhower's secretary of state and head of the CIA, brothers John and Allen Dulles, who made the fateful decision for all of America. Mossadegh was not associated with Iran's communist party, but he was a proponent for worker's rights, and his government was considered weak. And Iran shared its northern border with the Soviet republics of Armenia, Azerbaijan, and Turkmenistan. For the Dulles brothers, the risk of Iran becoming another communist domino overrode its quest to become a democratic state. Not to mention the enticement of Iran's immense oil reserves.

Operation Ajax was sanctioned reluctantly by Eisenhower and vigorously by Winston Churchill, and only publicly admitted to some fifty years later by both the United States and Britain. The operation was executed by CIA operative Kermit Roosevelt, grandson of former president Theodore Roosevelt. Roosevelt's strategy was to hire criminal gangs to stir up the minority anti-Mossadegh insurgents in street riots and bribe military leaders to assault the Prime Minister's residence with tanks. The CIA had Iran's most recent shah waiting in the wings to resume his monarchy once the democratic government was toppled.

The first coup attempt failed. Roosevelt had underestimated Mossadegh's popularity and the hired insurgents were outnumbered in the streets by pro-Mossadegh demonstrators. Roosevelt needed to find a way to keep the Mossadegh supporters off the streets in order for his plan to succeed. The CIA operative, feeling desperate now, hatched a deceptive plan to use Mossadegh's own sense of honor to take him down. But he would need the help of the US ambassador, Loy Henderson.

Roosevelt was well-versed in the character traits of his target, so he knew that Mossadegh trusted people with a childlike innocence and was deeply compassionate. Mossadegh had no idea the CIA was in Tehran. Roosevelt instructed Ambassador Henderson to meet privately with Mossadegh and tell him that Americans were being harassed by his supporters—a complete fabrication. He told him to say that children were being greeted with obscenities and "Yankee go home" was being shouted in anonymous phone calls. And, with vicious duplicity, Henderson added that he would reassure Mossadegh the United States had "no intention of interfering in the internal affairs of a friendly country."[12]

Ambassador Henderson played his role to perfection, embellishing his claims of harassment with stories of vehicles belonging to Americans being vandalized in the streets. Mossadegh responded exactly as predicted. Shocked and dismayed that his supporters were mistreating the guests of Iran, he called his police chief and instructed him to put an end to the trouble in the streets. This proved to be a fatal mistake.

Up until that point, Mossadegh had remained true to his commitment to democracy and freedom of speech, and allowed the street protests to continue unimpeded. This had previously worked in his favor: His own supporters were able to keep the growing number of paid protesters in check. But now the balance of power in the streets would shift. Kinzer writes:

> Mossadegh sent the police out to attack a mob that included many of his own most fervent supporters. Then, to assure that his partisans would not return to the streets the next

day, he issued a decree banning all public demonstrations. He even telephoned leaders of pro-government parties and ordered them to keep their people at home. He disarmed himself.[13]

The growing number of bribed military officers and gang leaders now faced no opposition as they converged on Mossadegh's residence with their ranks of insurgents. Mossadegh was eventually forced to flee after a close range battle that lasted several hours and resulted in the loss of three hundred lives. The insurgent forces claimed victory.

In the aftermath of the staged coup d'état, Iran's champion for democracy was eventually forced to turn himself in to the new government. He was then ironically convicted of the false charge of treason, spent three years in prison, and died while under house arrest. In his trial, he is captured on camera proclaiming his innocence and defiantly shouting that his only crime was to stand against the oppression of foreign governments.

The coup would completely extinguish any hope for a democratic government in Iran. With the military now in charge, the US puppet, Mohammad Reza Pahlavi, the now famous "Shah of Iran" was installed as an autocratic monarch.

And the flow of oil resumed.

An international consortium was put in place to determine how shares in Iran's oil industry should be distributed. The Brits retained only a 40-percent share, 40 percent would now go to five American companies, and the remaining 20 percent was split between the Dutch and the French. Iran was paid a handsome billion dollars for the 60-percent share that went to the non-British companies, and they would enjoy a 50/50 profit sharing agreement with all companies. In the ultimate irony, the British and Anglo-Iranian Oil walked away with only a 40-percent share and a 50/50 profit share. Had they simply negotiated with Mossadegh in good faith, they would have retained their 100 percent share at the 50/50 profit-sharing level. The whole thing was nothing but a pissing contest. Britain and the people of Iran were the huge losers, and United States oil companies, along with a couple of military contractors, were the big winners. To the people of Iran, the CIA's role was only too obvious.

In place of their democratically elected prime minister, the people of Iran now had the military and an obvious puppet of the United States calling the shots. Whether they would see any of the now lavishly abundant oil revenues was completely up to the shah. The seeds of revolution had been deeply sown. They had nothing to do with Islam, and everything to do with the oppression of a corrupt monarch and the overthrow of their democracy by foreign powers.

While the shah would do much to modernize Iran, his own extravagance would far outshine any economic improvements for millions of Iranians. The *New York Times* reported that, in 1971, the shah spent one hundred million dollars on the 2,500-year anniversary of the Iranian monarchy, complete with chefs from Paris and luxurious designer porcelain and crystal.[14] Student protests were brewing months before the festivities even began.

At the same time, any resistance was dealt with harshly. Viable opposition political parties were banned, and an internal surveillance organ known as SAVAK was created, which had strong ties to the CIA. By the late '70s, there were as many as 2,200 political prisoners in Iran, with reports of torture emerging. The shah also purchased eighty F-14 Tomcats, along with more than 280 Phoenix missiles from Grumman Aerospace and Hughes Aircraft, making Iran the only nation besides the United States to operate this powerful interceptor jet.

Even though Americans were oblivious to the CIA operation to overthrow the government of Iran, the citizens of Iran were not. With the number of Iranians recruited and paid at every level, it would have been impossible to keep this operation a secret. The shah's cozy relationship with the United States would take care of any doubters. Unrest would eventually boil over, and the shah fled Iran in January 1979. While the US media portrayed a violent scene of Islamic fundamentalist revolutionaries, the real picture was pointed out by Reza Aslan.

> [Iran's] clergy, its intellectuals, the merchant class, and nearly every sociopolitical organization in Iran—from the Communists to the feminists—put aside their ideological differences and joined together in an anti-imperialist, nationalist revolt against a corrupt monarchy. Despite the post-revolution propaganda, this was by no means a monolithic revolutionary movement initiated at the behest of the Ayatollah Khomeini with the aim of establishing an Islamic theocracy. On the contrary, there were dozens of diverse and sometimes conflicting voices raised against the Shah. Khomeini's, for better or worse, is merely the loudest.[15]

Meanwhile, members of the disintegrating government and many Iranians fully expected another CIA-directed military coup to reinstate the shah or install someone else. It was for this reason that students stormed the US Embassy in Tehran, the base of operations for the CIA, and held fifty-two members of the diplomatic corps and operatives hostage for 444 days.

We can only imagine what the world might look like today if the US government had chosen to support Mossadegh and Iran's fledgling democracy rather than backing the British. Perhaps the fear of communism was legitimate, but from an ethical perspective, the end never justifies the means. The subterfuge and treachery used to take down Mossadegh is unforgivable in the court of human decency.

There can be no doubt that United States intervention rallied the Iranian people under the banner of Islam. The US and Britain had set the table for the Shia cleric, Ayatollah Ruhollah Khomeini. He would have little trouble pulling the people of Iran together, not as much *for* Islam but *against* imperialist oppression. This was only the first cord of the powerful bonds that would lash anti-Americanism to radical Islam.

Since Iran's Islamic revolution in 1979, the United States has maintained a diplomatic policy of direct confrontation with Iran. In contrast, after a cooling-off period of more than a decade, the Iranian government has made multiple overtures to the United States for a normalizing of diplomatic relations. Professors John Mearsheimer and Stephen Walt, in their book *The Israel Lobby and US Foreign Policy*, describe pre-9/11 attempts by Iran's president to smooth things over with the US government:

> On May 23, 1997, Mohammed Khatami was elected president of Iran. He was even more enthusiastic than his predecessor about improving relations with the West, and the United States in particular. He made conciliatory remarks in his inaugural speech on August 4 and in his first press conference on December 14. Most important, he went out of his way in a lengthy CNN interview on January 7, 1998, to express his respect for "the great American people" and "their great civilization." He also made it clear that Iran did not "aim…to destroy or undermine the American government" and that he regretted the infamous takeover of the US Embassy in 1979. Recognizing the existing hostility between Tehran and Washington, he called for a "crack in this wall of mistrust to prepare for a change and create an opportunity to study a new situation."[16]

Again, during the US invasion of Afghanistan in the aftermath of 9/11:

> Iran helped the United States topple the Taliban in the fall of 2001 by providing advice on targets to strike in Afghanistan, facilitating US cooperation with the Northern alliance and helping with search and rescue missions. After the war Tehran helped Washington put a friendly government in place in Kabul. At the same time, Iran's president Khatami made it clear once again that he wanted to improve relations with the United States and saw events in Afghanistan as a major step in that direction.[17]

In spite of these overtures and Iran's direct collaboration in the "war on terror," George W. Bush named Iran as a member of his self-styled "axis of evil" in his State of the Union address on January 29, 2002. In so doing, he effectively ended any hope of normalizing relations with Iran.

Admittedly, the political situation with Iran is complex, primarily centered around their nuclear ambitions and statements made regarding the legitimacy of Israel. Even so, I find it ironic that Iran gets the "evil" label, given this history.

As a footnote, less than three weeks after the storming of the US Embassy in Tehran, a student protest at the US Embassy in Pakistan erupted into an all-out assault in which a US Marine would die of a bullet to the head. Pakistan's president, Muhammad Zia-ul-Haq, virtually abandoned the one hundred-member embassy staff to the mercy of the rioters. The US Embassy was burned to the ground, but the embassy staff miraculously survived in a steel-lined vault. The riot was triggered by false radio announcements from Khomeini that the Americans were responsible for an attack on the Great Mosque in Mecca the day before.

This incident is virtually unknown in the United States and was somehow smoothed over. Were it not for the miraculous preservation of the embassy staff, it could have triggered a US military intervention by President Carter in Pakistan, and in Iran, where the hostages would be held for another four hundred-plus days.

THE CIA GOES JIHADIST IN AFGHANISTAN – FROM SINGLE SHOT RIFLES TO STINGER MISSILES

Just as the US had feared a Soviet takeover of Iran, the Soviets feared a US invasion of Afghanistan. In addition to sharing almost six hundred miles of border with Iran to the west, Afghanistan's northern boundary was shared with the Tajik, Uzbek, and Turkmen Soviet republics. As home to over a dozen major ethnic groups and uncounted tribes, Afghanistan's rural territories had always enjoyed a great deal of autonomy from the central government. The pro-

Soviet Marxist People's Democratic Party of Afghanistan had seized power in April 1978, with the help of the Afghan army, and was in the process of implementing a Soviet-style program of modernizing reforms across Afghanistan. The communist regime had very little popular support, and strong tribal factions resisted these reforms as un-Islamic. An active rebellion against the communist government ensued. The Soviets feared their foothold in Afghanistan would be lost to a pro-American government and feared a US military presence on their doorstep.

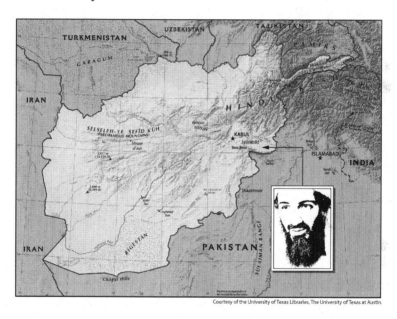

Courtesy of the University of Texas Libraries, The University of Texas at Austin.

Map 6 — Afghanistan

Pulitzer prize-winning author, Steve Coll, in his book, *Ghost Wars: The Secret History of the CIA, Afghanistan, and bin Laden, from the Soviet Invasion to September 10, 2001* tells the virtually unknown story. He explains, "With a base secured in Afghanistan, the KGB chief feared... that the United States could point Pershing nuclear missiles at the Soviet Union's southern underbelly, where its defenses were weak."[18] And so, three weeks after American hostages were taken in Iran, "the Politburo's inner circle made the first tentative decision to invade [Afghanistan]."[19] It was a nuclear chess match being played out on the game board of ancient Persia. By the end of 1979, one hundred thousand Soviet troops were making their way into Afghanistan in order to prop up the pro-Soviet government and quell the rebellion. Now it was the USA's turn to make a move.

The United States' only interest with Afghanistan was keeping it from becoming another Soviet satellite. The CIA would stop at nothing to accomplish this. Only weeks after reaping the consequences of overthrowing a democratic government in Iran, the CIA would once again meddle. But, this time they would create a Pandora's box of terror. The evil entities released in Afghanistan roam the world to this day, infecting it with a black plague of death.

Within days of the Soviet invasion, National Security Advisor to then president Jimmy Carter, Zbigniew Brzesinski, penned a classified secret memo to President Carter. He warned him of the likely Soviet takeover but proposed a strategy of resistance that involved providing arms to tribal resistance fighters via Pakistan and soliciting additional support from other Islamic nations. He noted that, since Pakistan was in the midst of serious negotiations with the United States regarding their nuclear capability, US nuclear nonproliferation policy towards Pakistan could be affected. He also strategized that the United States should work in concert with other Islamic countries such as Saudi Arabia, both in a propaganda campaign and in a covert action campaign to help the rebels—a strategy that would prove to be hugely, and horrifically, successful. Brzesinski hoped that Afghanistan would prove to be a Vietnam for the Soviet Union. This strategy was to remain in effect virtually untouched for the next ten years.

Absent from this strategy were three essential considerations: (1) What was best for the people of Afghanistan and how would they be affected? (2) In the event that this strategy proved successful and the communist government was removed, what clear objectives and procedures were in place for the formation of a new government in Afghanistan? (3) What would be the long-term impact of funneling militant jihadists into Afghanistan, arming them, and then training them in terror tactics? The single-minded focus on ridding Afghanistan of communism to the exclusion of these considerations would have disastrous consequences.

Afghanistan's "rebels" consisted of local villagers turned fighters, led by tribal leaders. Each tribe functioned autonomously from other tribes, as they always had, defending only their own families and villages. Larger ethnic groups and tribes were more organized on a regional level. Although Kabul University had a "Faculty of Islamic Law" with professors dedicated to Islamic revivalism, the vast array of rural tribal groups practiced a moderate and syncretized version of Islam, in which local customs were combined with Islamic teachings. They were more concerned with day-to-day survival than with religious nuance. At some point along the way, perhaps part of Brzesinksi's propaganda campaign, these humble villagers became known as *the mujahedeen*, or "those who wage jihad." In the United States, the mujahedeen achieved legendary status as defenders of Afghanistan against Soviet tyranny.

Help for Afghanistan's resistance fighters came from multiple sources:

- The CIA and the US State Department ultimately contributed over three billion dollars in weapons, cash, and training. Nearly all of it was administered by neighboring Pakistan intelligence to the tribal groups of their choice, with little accountability.

- Saudi intelligence had a formal agreement with the US to match funds dollar for dollar. They sent the cash directly to the Saudi Embassy in Washington, to be passed on to the CIA.

- Independently from the Saudi government, Wahhabi religious groups, including mosques, charities, clubs, and schools, sent huge cash donations directly into Afghanistan. They also sent their most fanatical members to become mujahedeen.

- Pakistan, which shares a 1,500-mile border with Afghanistan, also had a large contingent of independent "irregulars" join the ranks of the mujahedeen, providing sizable independent and untraceable cash donations.

- Independent jihadists from as far away as Indonesia and Algeria made their way to Afghanistan, along with fighters from virtually every country in the Middle East.

- Even Iran eventually got involved in support of Afghanistan's Shiite minority.

Rivers of cash began to flow into Afghanistan. On the ground, there was no plan for its distribution or a unified force to receive it. It turned into a free-for-all of tribal leaders, each vying for his own piece of the action. All three of the major benefactors (the United States, Saudi Arabia, and Pakistan) had their favorites. The favored tribal leaders would emerge as powerful warlords. The factions of the civil war that would take place after the Soviet pullout were being formed in the early days of the invasion.

It started with hundreds of thousands of 1950s vintage single-shot rifles, tens of millions of bullets, and a few thousand RPG-7 grenade launchers. From there, according to Coll, the CIA's only strategy was to sit back and watch.[20] As the Soviets upped the ante, the mujahedeen would graduate to Chinese-made AK-47s, 60 mm mortars, and 12.7 mm heavy machine guns, as well as fleets of large trucks and SUVs. In the end, to match the influx of lethal Soviet MI-24 helicopter gunships, the now ethnically diverse mujahedeen were supplied with General Dynamics fire-and-forget, shoulder-launched anti-aircraft missiles. The Stinger missile system was a game changer. Effective to 25,000 feet, it struck fear into the hearts of the Soviet helicopter pilots.

While the United States and the Saudi governments were flooding Afghanistan with cash and weapons, Saudi religious groups seized the opportunity for Wahhabi indoctrination. "Middle-class, pious Saudis flush with oil wealth embraced the Afghan cause as American churchgoers might respond to an African famine or a Turkish earthquake," wrote Coll.[21] Thousands of Islamic religious schools, known as *madrasas*, were constructed along the Pakistan/Afghanistan border. The madrasas operated with direct financing from Wahhabi mosques and charities, and were used for indoctrinating not just the mujahedeen, but also the thousands of Afghan refugees flooding into Pakistan.

In the mix of missiles and madrasas, a wealthy Saudi businessman was starting to appear in high profile diplomatic encounters between the Saudi and Pakistani governments. His name was Osama bin Laden. Bin Laden was using his wealth to establish himself as a powerful independent player in the network of Wahhabi madrasas, full of radical jihadists from all over the Muslim world. In this cash-rich, hidden sanctuary far from any semblance of government visibility, bin Laden found the conditions perfect for recruitment of radicals.

In January 1981, ownership of the resistance transferred from Jimmy Carter to the more hawkish Ronald Reagan. With a fresh cabinet stacked with staunch anti-Communists, the CIA's role in the Soviet-Afghan conflict was expanded. In addition to a surge in funds allocated for Afghanistan and approval for the use of high-technology weapon systems, a major change in tactics was implemented. The time had come for "intensified training of Islamist guerrillas in explosive and sabotage techniques, and targeted attacks on Soviet military officers," according to Coll.[22] The CIA's next move was to train an army of terrorists in the technologies of explosives and detonation.

Though obliviously self-destructive, the CIA terror tactics proved effective against the Soviets. By 1986, Mikhail Gorbachev was looking for a way out of Afghanistan. By the time Colonel-General Boris Gromov walked over the Afghan-Uzbek Bridge, crossing back into Soviet territory in February 1989, Afghanistan had become the largest refugee-producing country in the world. Total war casualties stood at one million Afghan civilians, innumerable wounded, and some six million refugees, hosted by both Pakistan and Iran.

The children of Afghanistan have suffered indescribable horrors as a consequence of the millions of landmines left scattered across the countryside. The Soviets and the communist army of Afghanistan placed the vast majority of these mines, some looking nightmarishly like a child's toy. But all parties in the struggle used landmines and many were supplied by the United States. The annual casualty count stood at almost 1,300 as late as 2014, according to a 2015 report by The-Monitor.org. Eighty percent of the victims are civilians, and 50 percent are children—killed, or maimed for life.[23]

The Soviets left behind their best effort at a communist government and attempted to prop it up from afar. But now without a common enemy, the mujahedeen turned their armaments on one another. And taking out the pro-Soviet government was a foregone conclusion.

The Afghan civil war was complicated by the fact that all four major players supporting the mujahedeen had diverging motives and conflicting strategies:

1. For the United States, the Soviet exit from Afghanistan was only a blip on the radar screen—until it was too late. Having become aware of the growing problem of radical militants finding sanctuary for training and organizing in the ungoverned reaches of Afghanistan, the CIA would use their limited leverage to channel funds and weapons to a cagey Tajik warlord named Ahmed Shah Massoud, who was considered the most moderate. Massoud would eventually emerge as the leader of what became known as the Northern Alliance. He aligned himself with Pashtun royalists from the line of previous Afghan monarchs. A major part of the Northern Alliance operation was financed by Afghanistan's opium poppy production, which accounts for more than 90 percent of the world's heroin supply according to a June 7, 2016 article by NPR.[24]

   Meanwhile, the United States—and the rest of the world—had their eyes fixed on other astonishing developments such as the breakup of the Soviet Union, the tearing down of the Berlin wall, and Saddam's invasion of Kuwait. At the same time, the CIA contingent assigned to Afghanistan reported "the rising presence of radical Arab, Indonesian, Malaysian, Uzbek, and other volunteer fighters... and jihadist training camps," according to Coll.[25]

2. The government of Pakistan had a powerful interest in creating a next-door neighbor that was both stable and compatible. Then president Zia—a devout Muslim—had his own ideas about how to make this happen. Having lived through the birth of

Pakistan, he was connected to its founding Islamist principle. While radicals such as bin Laden dreamed of returning to a stateless Islamic empire, Islamism recognizes state boundaries and seeks to create a functioning government around Islam. Zia was ideologically aligned with the more intellectual Muslim Brotherhood, founded in Egypt in the early '50s. He shied away from the Arab jihadists who were infiltrating Afghanistan. As the one who was making the calls on the distribution of the six billion dollars of aid that came through formal channels, Zia made sure that the lion's share was directed toward tribal leaders who saw the Muslim Brotherhood as their inspiration. Of these leaders, Gulbuddin Hekmatyar would emerge as the principal player and chief rival to the Northern Alliance. Hekmatyar wasted no time using his funds to go after any potential mujahedeen rivals.

3. The Saudi government plugged into a former professor of Islamic law at Kabul University, Abdurrab Rasul Sayyaf, who was more than happy to promote Wahhabi doctrine in return. Through Sayyaf, Saudi Arabia was able to bypass Pakistan and have direct access to the mujahedeen. With his newfound Saudi wealth, Sayyaf was able to form his own Afghan rebel party.

4. Independent Saudis continued funneling dollars to their madrasas on the border. Now a gathering place for Islamic radicals from around the world, international networks of Islamist fighters began to take shape. Even before the departure of Soviet troops,

this group began to find itself drawn to a broader cause: the overthrow of corrupt and secular governments in the Middle East. This Pandora's box of terror created by the CIA's strategy in Afghanistan thrived almost undetected in the greenhouse conditions at the Afghanistan-Pakistan border.

The communist government would fall to Massoud in 1992, three years after the Soviet pullout. But neither he nor any of the other factions was able to establish a stable government. The fighting continued. The warlords had long ago been corrupted by their immersion in a world of Soviet atrocities and suitcases full of cash. They had amassed personal fortunes. The bloody civil war raged on with no end in sight.

ON REAPING AND SOWING AND THE CREATION OF MONSTERS – THE TALIBAN

Meanwhile, a significant number of mujahedeen who were members of a pious Islamic religious order known as the Taliban, or "students of Islam," began returning home to the Kandahar area in the south of Afghanistan. Similar to the Franciscan monks, the Taliban subsisted on contributions for services such as teaching the Quran, leading prayers, and mediating disputes. They began to organize themselves under the leadership of Mullah Mohammed Omar, a soft-spoken and humble man who rarely left Kandahar. He had been content to lead prayers in a poor village until he was chosen to be the leader of the Taliban.

The Taliban distinguished themselves from the warlords because they seemed unaffected by the attractions of money and power. They publicly condemned the warlords for their ill-gotten wealth, for their practice of kidnapping and raping Afghan girls, for their engagement in the world of heroin, and for their indiscriminate killing of civilians. These humble defenders of a people ravaged by war achieved an almost mythological status. No one seemed to mind that they adhered to a very strict and austere interpretation of Islam, very much in line with the Wahhabi sect of Saudi Arabia.

The Taliban got their start as a competing faction in the civil war by executing vigilante attacks against small time warlords around Kandahar. With a few successes under their belt, local merchants banded together and hired them to keep the region secure. By 1994, one alliance at a time, the Taliban started to gain strength. Tribal groups that had belonged to one of the major factions began defecting to the Taliban. Before long, the governments of both Pakistan and Saudi Arabia began channeling their support to the Taliban as the front-runner in the civil war, hoping for a quick resolution. The austere Taliban were about to get another financial boost from bin Laden's vast financial reserves.

OSAMA BIN LADEN FINDS SANCTUARY

After the Soviets pulled out of Afghanistan in 1989, bin Laden had returned with his family to his father's construction business in Saudi Arabia. It didn't take long before he was involved in another jihadist cause—arming a resistance against the Soviet-backed government of Yemen, Saudi's next-door neighbor on the Arabian Peninsula. But bin Laden's convictions—and his self-image as Allah's holy warrior—were about to collide with the harsh realities of royalty.

In August 1990, Saddam Hussein invaded Kuwait in a desperate attempt to multiply his oil revenues to pay off debts from the Iran-Iraq war. The Saudis were fearful that Saddam would not stop at Kuwait and called upon the United States for military protection. Within days, upwards of 100,000 US troops were on the ground in Saudi Arabia. Fresh from the mujahedeen victory over Soviet infidels in Afghanistan, bin Laden requested an audience with the royal family's senior princes. He denounced the presence of this non-Muslim army and passionately argued that he was able to lead a jihadist army and defeat the Iraqis himself. When confronted with the fact that Kuwait had no caves or mountains like Afghanistan, and that Hussein had four thousand tanks, along with chemical and biological weapons, bin Laden replied simply that he would fight him with faith.

The faith of the Saudi monarchs was lacking, and bin Laden's offer was rejected. From that point he labeled the US forces as foreign occupiers of Saudi Arabia. After being discredited by even his own family, bin Laden was eventually forced to leave Saudi Arabia. Saudi police told bin Laden that it was for his own protection, and that the Americans were trying to kill him. Bin Laden would never return to Saudi Arabia.

Only an hour-and-a-half flight from bin Laden's home in the coastal city of Jeddah, changes were underfoot in the African nation of Sudan. Hassan al-Turabi had emerged as a leading figure in the ruling National Islamic Front political party in Khartoum. A Paris-educated law graduate with a strong Islamist pedigree, al-Turabi was a self-proclaimed defender of oppressed Muslims everywhere. Al-Turabi welcomed a broad spectrum of Muslim resistance movements. He even granted asylum to secular terrorists such as Carlos the Jackal. He made it known to bin Laden that he was welcome.

Bin Laden wasted no time setting up his operation in Khartoum. He used his wealth to buy off government officials and set up a powerful business network. But not without observation. On the CIA's radar now, bin Laden became a major focus of their operation out of the US embassy in Sudan. Bin Laden operated a kind of jihadist foundation that received proposals for various projects and provided funding for those he considered meritorious. Bin Laden and the CIA played a cat-and-mouse game in Khartoum for almost ten years. Although the CIA knew he was funding terrorist activity, they were never able to connect the dots between bin Laden's bank accounts and the funds used for purchasing explosives and paying terrorists. And he was never directly involved in any terrorist incidents.

Bin Laden surrounded himself with fellow Arabs as bodyguards and moved about freely. He became so emboldened that, at one point, he attempted to assassinate the team of CIA agents who were shadowing him in Khartoum. In the end, the government of Sudan would give in to US diplomatic pressure, and bin Laden was asked to leave. By now he had also been permanently exiled from Saudi Arabia. Bin Laden was a wealthy financier of terrorism and the owner of a substantial business empire, but now he was out of options. There was only one place left for him to go. He would return to the ungoverned reaches of eastern Afghanistan, where he had gotten his start as a holy warrior. And now it was personal between bin Laden and the United States.

In early 1996 the government of Sudan leased an airliner from Afghanistan and helped bin Laden make his exit. Coll writes, "It required two flights back and forth to move bin Laden, his three wives, his children, his furniture, and his followers to Jalalabad."[26] Notably, he did not fly into Taliban-held territory. The Taliban had not yet broken onto the scene by the time bin Laden had departed Afghanistan for Jeddah in 1990. Neither side knew the other. But within months of bin Laden's arrival in Jalalabad, Taliban forces moved in and took control. The Taliban were now barely more than one hundred miles from Massoud's government center in Kabul. Bin Laden seized the opportunity to use his wealth to buy the favor of the Taliban. "The Saudi provided about three million dollars from his personal treasury to pay off the remaining commanders who stood between the Taliban and Kabul," according to Coll.[27]

In late September 1996, the Taliban took control of the government of Afghanistan. Now bin Laden was virtually untouchable. Still stinging from the role of the United States in his hardships, bin Laden issued a *fatwa* (an Islamic religious decree usually reserved for influential religious leaders) entitled "Declaration of War against the

Americans Occupying the Land of the Two Holy Places." Meanwhile the CIA's hands were tied since they only had access to the Northern Alliance, and that access was tenuous. In the end, the CIA recruited a few members of the Northern Alliance to try to capture bin Laden. They authorized the use of lethal force if necessary. But bin Laden had become skilled in the use of evasive tactics and he was surrounded by Arab commandos. In the five years bin Laden roamed Afghanistan before 9/11, the CIA recruits were not able to make even a single attempt to capture him.

The CIA attempted an alternate tactic with the advent of surveillance drones in the late '90s. They hoped to confirm a sighting and take bin Laden out with a cruise missile. The video cameras picked up views of bin Laden on multiple occasions, but the CIA's recruits on the ground were never able to confirm it so didn't fire the missile. Several times the US State Department attempted to negotiate with the Taliban to hand over bin Laden, even though they never formally recognized them as the legitimate governing power of Afghanistan. The Taliban kept the CIA at bay with excuses and claims that they wouldn't allow any terror attacks to be launched from Afghanistan. Meanwhile, bin Laden lavishly supported the Taliban and moved about freely.

From late 1999 through early 2001, 9/11 mastermind Khalid Sheikh Mohammed was assembling his team of nineteen in the US—fifteen Saudis, two Emiratis, one Egyptian, and one Lebanese. President Bill Clinton, the House of Representatives, and virtually the entire United States were fixated on the impeachment proceedings for the charges of perjury and obstruction of justice related to Clinton's testimony in the Monica Lewinsky affair. The CIA had no idea of the nature of the attack, or where and when it might be, but they were certain that a major attack was coming, and tried to sound the alarm. But the ones that mattered in the Clinton administration weren't listening.

In January 2001, all eyes were on the Florida recount in the infamous Bush vs. Gore election. The 5 to 4 Supreme Court decision would put a president in the White House whose only political experience was six years as the governor of Texas. And nine months before the hijacked airliners smashed into the twin towers, America's national security apparatus was dismantled and reconfigured. Newly appointed National Security Advisor, Condoleezza Rice, demoted counterterrorism expert Richard Clarke from the National Security Council. According to Coll, Clarke had been "publicly described as the government's best expert on terrorism policy and the bin Laden threat." In spite of US embassy bombings in Kenya and Tanzania in 1998 and an attack on the USS Cole only three months before the Bush inauguration, the threat of terrorism, and specifically that of bin Laden and al Qaeda, his terror network, dropped off the national radar screen. Clarke had requested a Cabinet-level meeting about the imminent threat of al Qaeda. He wanted to propose several strategies for the containment of bin Laden. That meeting never took place, and the US would continue its policy of nonparticipation in matters relating to the Taliban government—or the al Qaeda leadership safely embedded within it.

Coll's detailed account of the events leading up to 9/11 closes with the CIA's September 10 briefing to President Bush and his cabinet. In the ultimate irony, Coll writes that "they analyzed the consequences for America's covert war against al Qaeda."[28] Less than twenty-four hours later, the metastasizing cancer implanted by the United States in Afghanistan found its way back to its source.

WILL GODZILLA BE TAMED? THE US INVASION OF AFGHANISTAN

Now it was impossible for the United States to keep its head in the sand regarding the mess we had made in Afghanistan. In a mind-boggling turn of events, only nine years after turning off funding for Afghan fighters to resist the Soviet invasion, the United States was launching an invasion of its own, less than a month after 9/11. American and British pilots conducted air strikes targeting the Taliban government in Kabul and al Qaeda training camps, and US troops moved in. A few months later, in December 2001, a hand-picked group of twenty-five prominent Afghans selected royalist Hamid Karzai as the interim leader of Afghanistan and began the process of forming a new government.

But, as the Soviets found out, establishing central governance among the array of Afghan tribal factions, not to mention the Taliban, would prove to be impossible. The rugged Hindu Kush mountains offered endless hiding places and escape routes including deep, underground caves. Afghan fighters had been defending themselves for decades against Soviet gunships and enemy tribes—and they had been well armed and trained by the CIA. More than fifteen years later, the Karzai government was still intact but the resistance was alive and well. In April 2017, Taliban forces attacked the army headquarters in Mazar-i-Sharif, killing 160. One week earlier, the US military dropped the "Mother of All Bombs (MOAB)" on ISIS targets near the Pakistan border. The MOAB bomb contains the most powerful non-nuclear warhead in America's arsenal.

AFGHANISTAN—THE LONG VIEW

In the 1970s the American people feared the spread of communist totalitarianism and lived under the threat of nuclear attack. The United States had been humiliated in a failed attempt to prevent a communist takeover of South Vietnam, driven to intervene by our adherence to the domino theory of communist expansion. Less than five years after the fall of Saigon, the Soviets were sending troops into Afghanistan. It seemed both strategic and noble to help the people of Afghanistan defend themselves against communist invaders.

CIA tactics were successful against the Soviets, but something went horribly wrong in the execution. 9/11 was a direct side effect.

I make no claims to be an expert in political science or covert affairs. But as a voting citizen of the United States, I own a share of the responsibility for actions taken under the direction of our elected officials. Hindsight offers a few simple lessons for future reference:

1. The United States all but created al Qaeda: limitless cash and weapons, no accountability or oversight, training in explosives and detonation, a wide-open door for Muslim radicals, thousands of madrasas to train them in jihadist theology, even US-provided schoolbooks to make sure the next generation grew up as jihadists, according to The Washington Post.[29] The only thing left for bin Laden was to organize.

2. Neither the CIA nor the State Department had any plan for rebuilding Afghanistan and reestablishing a viable government if their tactics against the Soviets proved successful. This resulted in a horrific civil war and the ultimate emergence of the Taliban. After providing $3.2 billion in aid, the United States had no access to Afghanistan, while bin Laden had the perfect sanctuary.

3. The motivation for aiding Afghanistan was ultimately about American interests. There is no indication of any contemplation of what might be best for the people of Afghanistan.

And, we are all left to wonder: which was worse, the Cold War, or the War on Terror?

A WAR OF AGGRESSION – THE INVASION OF IRAQ

Terror-induced trauma has a desired effect. After 9/11, Americans felt vulnerable, and we were desperate to do something that would help us feel safe again. It somehow seemed right to invade Iraq and take out the monster that was Saddam Hussein. But the strategic logic behind this decision has yet to be uncovered. According to Mearsheimer and Walt in *The Israel Lobby*, Bush's director of policy planning in the State Department, Richard Haass, when asked why the United States invaded Iraq, said he would "go to his grave not knowing the answer."[30]

There was no evidence to indicate that Hussein played any role in the 9/11 attacks. In fact, Iraq was on bin Laden's list as a corrupt government to topple. In spite of intelligence briefings to the contrary, Mearsheimer and Walt point out, "Intrusive UN inspections had eliminated Iraq's nuclear program and eventually led Saddam to destroy his biological and chemical weapons stockpiles as well."[31]

And yet, the United States Congress voted 70 percent in favor of joint H.J. Res. 114, "Authorization for Use of Military Force Against Iraq Resolution of 2002." American news outlets looked on, waxing patriotic and cheering for our troops. Dozens of sympathetic nations were even convinced to participate in the invasion and occupation.

Operation Iraqi Freedom began on March 20, 2003. US news reports showed fantastic footage from "shock and awe" aerial bombardments and scenes of Iraqis toppling the statue of Saddam Hussein. No weapons of mass destruction were found after months of searching. A little more than a month after they began, George W. Bush declared that "major combat operations in Iraq have ended." Bush was standing beneath a banner that read "Mission Accomplished" on the USS *Abraham Lincoln*, where he had been flown for the photo op.

But the war dragged on for eight more brutal years. And none of the major news outlets reported on studies, such as the one conducted by faculty of the Johns Hopkins School of Public Health, indicating that more than 600,000 Iraqis had lost their lives by mid-2006.[32]

Barack Obama successfully campaigned on assurances of getting the United States extracted from Iraq, and he tried to make good on his promise. But in 2013 horrific stories of beheadings and other atrocities began to emerge from western Iraq. In the vacuum left by the destruction of Iraq's government, a group calling itself the Islamic State took over large swaths of northern and western Iraq and proclaimed an Islamic caliphate. And they were gaining momentum. A US-led coalition began making airstrikes on ISIS positions in August 2014. At the end of 2017, after over three years of fighting, the government of Iraq announced that its war with ISIS was over. As with the US airstrikes on Baghdad, there were heavy civilian casualties in the bombing raids on Raqqa in western Iraq. Civilian casualties are high but, as of yet, uncounted. The government of Iraq is doing its best to contain the seething unrest of various insurgent groups. Suicide attacks and car bomb explosions remain commonplace occurrences.

ON THE MORALITY OF AN UNPROVOKED INVASION

What I find most disturbing about the US invasion of Iraq is the absence of ethical analysis in its aftermath—by the US government, by the news media, or by the American people. A war of aggression is a crime, according to the Rome Statute of the International Criminal Court,[33] and violates the charter of the United Nations. Over a half a million innocent people are dead as the result of a preemptive invasion carried out under false pretenses. Yet the United States has moved on with hardly a passing glance, not to mention any regrets. With profound sorrow, I ask myself and all of us collectively: America, where is your conscience?

George W. Bush and Donald J. Trump want to know the reasons that Muslim radicals hate us. A careful look at the history of CIA intervention in Iran and Afghanistan shows us that, "they hate our freedom" isn't one of them. After the invasions of Afghanistan and Iraq, I can't help wondering if it's the Muslim community who should be asking the question, "Why do they hate us?" and if Bush got his answer backwards.

THE REAL SOURCE OF TERRORISM – RELIGION OR POLITICS?

So far we've only viewed the highlight reel of US covert and military activity in the Muslim world. Other involvement in recent decades includes:

- Indonesia: In 1965 the CIA played an active role in the overthrow of the parliamentary democracy in Indonesia, where more Muslims live than in any other country, and installed General Suharto in a military coup. A massive purge of communist sympathizers took place immediately afterward, with up to one million executions. The CIA has been implicated as complicit in this purge, according to an October 2017 story in The Guardian.[34]

- Egypt: The US State Department and the CIA supported a military coup in Egypt in 1952.

- Libya: After repeated skirmishes that included an airstrike against Colonel Qaddafi's residential compound, the United States military participated in a 2011 NATO coalition with airstrikes and a naval blockade that resulted in the overthrow and murder of Qaddafi. In the ensuing anarchy, which continues as of the writing of this book, ISIS has emerged as a major player, requiring further US airstrikes. As a result, Libya has been named as a failed state.

- Sudan: In 1998, the United States destroyed the al-Shifa pharmaceutical factory in Khartoum, mistakenly believing it to be producing chemical agents.

- Somalia: In October 1993, a joint special ops force was dispatched to Mogadishu to kidnap two key players in the ongoing civil strife there. During the operation, two Blackhawk helicopters were shot down, and in the ensuing urban battle, hundreds of Somalis, including civilians, were killed, and eighteen American soldiers died. The incident was portrayed in the 2001 feature film Black Hawk Down. "The Obama administration has intensified a clandestine war in Somalia over the past year [2016], using Special Operations troops, airstrikes, private contractors and African allies in an escalating campaign against Islamist militants," according to an October 2016 story in The New York Times.[35]

- Pakistan: Since 2004, the CIA has attacked thousands of targets in northwest Pakistan near the Afghanistan border with missile launches from drones. The Prime Minister of Pakistan, Nawaz Sharif, has made it known that he considers this a violation of the territorial integrity of Pakistan and actually detrimental to Pakistan's own efforts at eliminating terrorism, and has repeatedly demanded an end to the strikes.

- Syria: In 2011, Syria erupted in civil war, with multiple rebel factions seeking to overthrow President Assad, who is supported by Russia. The United States has had on-again off-again involvement, at first supporting rebel factions with arms and airstrikes, then attacking ISIS with airstrikes. With both the dead and refugees counted in the millions, this tragedy is ongoing with no end in sight.

- Jordan: A November 2016 story in The Washington Post reports three Army special forces soldiers were killed at a Jordanian military base, bringing to light a CIA operation in which approximately 2,000 US troops are working in Jordan to train "moderate" Syrian rebels.[36]

- Lebanon: The United States has been deeply involved in Lebanon since 1958. After the 1982 Israeli invasion of Lebanon, US involvement, and lack thereof, resulted in the Israeli-backed massacre of over 1,000 Palestinian refugees. In 1983, "American airstrikes and the utilization of big guns from the battleship New Jersey resulted in large-scale civilian casualties," according to an April 2006 article in Foreign Policy in Focus.[37] Anti-US sentiment climaxed with the October 1983 suicide bombing of the Marine barracks near the Beirut airport, killing 241 US servicemen.

- Yemen: The United States has been conducting cruise missile strikes, naval bombardments, air strikes and drone strikes against terrorist targets in Yemen. The US is also supporting the Saudi-led coalition against Houthi rebel forces, who have taken over a significant part of Yemen in a civil war that erupted in full force in 2015. The Saudi bombing raids have attracted the attention of human rights observers for indiscriminate targeting and the killing of thousands of civilians.

Add to this the United States supporting the corrupt and oppressive regime of Saudi Arabia and sending almost $4 billion per year of military aid to Israel in their ongoing colonization of Palestine.

In a key address to the Council on Foreign Relations in December 2002, a little over a year after the 9/11 attacks, Richard Haass openly admitted that United States interests have trumped regional democracy in numerous situations:

> At times, the United States has avoided scrutinizing the internal workings of countries in the interest of ensuring a steady flow of oil, containing Soviet, Iraqi and Iranian expansionism, addressing issues related to the Arab-Israeli conflict, resisting Communism in East Asia or securing basing rights for our military. Yet by failing to help foster gradual paths to democratization in many of our important relationships—by creating what might be called a "democratic exception..."[38]

It's clear that this policy has changed little since Haass described it in 2002.

So, in light of the political nightmares of Iran, Afghanistan, and Iraq, in light of the long list of nations the United States has subjected to drone attacks, military assault, or government meddling, are we to suppose that Islamic radicals are motivated by religious conviction? Were 9/11, the Boston Marathon bombing, and San Bernardino motivated by Muslim fanatics bent on murdering infidels and subjecting the world to Islam as we are led to believe by evangelicals and far right outlets?

Or could it be that they hate having their democratic governments overthrown or the presence of foreign troops in their homelands, or perhaps they resent being invaded?

With the ongoing "war on terror," saber rattling with Iran and the uptick in anti-Muslim sentiment with the Trump presidency, the soil is becoming increasingly fertile for producing radicals—both Muslim and anti-Muslim.

I recently had lunch at a popular Middle Eastern café in San Diego with my good friend, a software developer named Mohammed. As we enjoyed our kebabs and basmati rice, he told me that he had stopped watching television because he found it too depressing to keep seeing Islam portrayed as a religion of violence and Muslims as terrorists. But, more than the media, it was the radical imams using phrases from the Quran to recruit suicide bombers and fake jihadists that roused my Muslim friend's anger. And he quoted with passion the Quran 5:32, *We decreed to the Children of Israel that if anyone kills a human being, unless it is in punishment for murder or for spreading corruption on earth, it will be as though he had killed all of human beings.* His sentiments have been echoed many times in many conversations with gentle-spirited Muslims.

Militant leaders often use a thin veneer of Quranic justification to inflame religious fervor. But a basic understanding of the Quran and an examination of recent history make it obvious that Muslims are radicalized by unwanted foreign presence in their homelands, and not by Islamic ideology itself. One need only consider the well-known profiles of al Qaeda founders Osama bin Laden and Dr. Ayman al-Zawahiri, along with many of the 9/11 attackers themselves, to confirm the political rather than religious motivation of so-called "Islamic" terrorists. Esposito and Mogahed tell us that although analysts expected to find lack of education and poverty among the suicide jihadists, instead they found men who were "well-educated, middle to upper class, and from stable family backgrounds... [some] exhibited behaviors hardly practiced by a religious Muslim. A number of them drank heavily and frequented strip clubs and porn shops."[39]

In the years leading up to 9/11, Bin Laden consented to several interviews with Western journalists from his hideouts in Afghanistan. Excerpts from a March 1997 interview conducted by Peter Arnett of CNN are especially insightful:

Arnett: Mr. bin Laden, you've declared a jihad against the United States. Can you tell us why?

Bin Laden: We declared jihad against the US government because the US government is unjust, criminal and tyrannical. It has committed acts that are extremely unjust, hideous and criminal whether directly or through its support of the Israeli occupation of (Palestine). And we believe the US is directly responsible for those who were killed in Palestine, Lebanon and Iraq. The mention of the US reminds us before everything else of those innocent children who were [redacted due to extreme violence] in the recent explosion that took place in Qana (in Lebanon). This US government abandoned even humanitarian feelings by these hideous crimes. It transgressed all bounds and behaved in a way not witnessed before by any power or any imperialist power in the world.

Arnett: the United States government says that you are still funding military training camps here in Afganistan for militant, Islamic fighters and that you are a sponsor of international terrorism; but others describe you as the new hero of the Arab-Islamic world. Are these accusations true? How do you describe yourself?

Bin Laden: The US today as a result of the arrogant atmosphere has set a double standard, calling whoever goes against its injustice a terrorist. It wants to occupy our countries, steal our resources, impose on us agents to rule us based not on what God has revealed and wants us to agree on all these. If we refuse to do so, it will say you are terrorists. With a simple look at the US behaviors, we find that it judges the behavior of the poor Palestinian children whose country was occupied: if they throw stones against the Israeli occupation, it says they are terrorists whereas when the Israeli pilots bombed the United Nations building in Qana, Lebanon while it was full of children and women, the US stopped any plan to condemn Israel. At the time that they condemn any Muslim who calls for his right, they receive the highest top official of the Irish Republican Army (Gerry Adams) at the White House as a political leader, while woe, all woe is the Muslims if they cry out for their rights. Wherever we look, we find the US as the leader of terrorism and crime in the world. The US does not consider it a terrorist act to throw atomic bombs at nations thousands of miles away, when it would not be possible for those bombs to hit military troops only. These bombs were rather thrown at entire nations, including women, children and elderly people and up to this day the traces of those bombs remain in Japan. The US does not consider it terrorism when hundreds of thousands of our sons and brothers in Iraq died for lack of food or medicine.[40]

Bin Laden's reference to the bombing of Qana, Lebanon in both answers referred to the 1996 Israel Defense Forces (IDF) shelling of a UN compound in southern Lebanon. Eight hundred Lebanese civilians had taken refuge in the compound and over 100 were killed in the attack, along with four Fijian UN workers.

Clearly bin Laden saw himself and his Muslim comrades on the receiving end of lethal American aggression, and thus justified in fighting back with terrorism. He specifically mentioned two actions that he directly associates with the United States: (1) Support of the Israeli occupation of Palestine and the IDF attack on UN compound in Lebanon, (2) the casualties in Iraq as a result of UN sanctions (in place from August 1990 through May 2003). Elsewhere in the interview bin Laden mentions the presence of US troops in Saudi Arabia and US support of corrupt dictators in the Middle East.

In January 2017, just before leaving office, President Barack Obama received a letter from 9/11 mastermind Khalid Sheikh Mohammed, who is being held in Guantánamo while he awaits his death-penalty trial. The entire letter is eighteen pages long and is available on the website of the Miami Herald;[41] I encourage you to read it in its entirety. On pages six and seven, Sheikh Mohammed directly addresses the reasons for the 9/11 attacks, which I quote verbatim (warning: The letter contains highly offensive statements):

> When Shaikh Osama bin Laden, may Allah have mercy upon him, and the mujahadeen publicly declared war against you and your nation, they warned you, your nation, and your allies in the plain light of day. Before 9/11, the mujahadeen asked you to lift the unjust sanctions against Iraq, the sanctions that you in the West imposed in which caused the death of 1 million women and children. They asked you to stop supporting the Jewish occupiers, to stop supporting the corrupt Arab regimes, to withdraw your soldiers, and to close your military bases in the Arabian Peninsula, but to no avail. Uncle Sam always turned a deaf ear to the mujahadeen's admonishments. He will only wake up after the ax already has fallen.

> You have been killing Muslims in Palestine for 60 years: expelling more than 4 million Palestinians; destroying their homes, schools, mosques, and markets by supporting Israel militarily, economically, and politically; and by protecting all of their crimes through the UN Security Council. In return for those 60 years, Allah aided us in conducting 9/11, destroying the capitalist economy, catching you with your pants down, and exposing all the hypocrisy of your long-held claim to democracy and freedom.

> It was of the utmost necessity to find the best way to stop your brutal foreign policy in our land. We did not start the war against you through the events of 9/11.

> The two blessed attacks in Washington and New York adhered to all universal laws and were a natural reaction to your destructive policies towards the Islamic world; your

unlimited support to Israel, the Jewish Zionist state; and your continued support and protection for dictatorial rulers in the Islamic world aimed at protecting your own interests.

Therefore, on 9/11 you reaped some of what you sowed in Indonesia when the US government and the CIA backed and supported the Indonesian dictator Suharto when his army-led massacres slaughtered hundreds of thousands of landless farmers.

... On 9/11 you reaped some of what you sowed when you established military bases in the Arabian Peninsula in Tabuk, Dhahran, Bahrain, Kuwait, Oman, and U.A.E.—which is prohibited by Sharia laws—to secure a nonstop flood of oil to your country at the cheapest price; and to support the dictatorial rule of monarchial (sic) families, and oppressive, corrupt, dynastic regimes and looting the wealth of the Muslim Ummah population; and to accomplish your military objectives there.

On 9/11 you reaped some of what you sowed in the political arena when you blocked resolutions in the United Nations Security Council more than 45 times to protect repeated Israeli crimes.

On 9/11 you reaped some of what you sowed when the US government backed and supported Israel's "iron fist" and their army's invasion of Lebanon in 1982 that killed more than 17,000 civilians and when you backed and supported the Army of the Israeli government during their invasions of Lebanon in 1982–83, 1993, and 1996 and the Qana massacre.

On 9/11 you reaped some of what you sowed when your government was backing the Shah of Iran and Safak, the brutal Iranian intelligence agency, for 40 years.

Khalid Sheikh Mohammed refers specifically to several of the items addressed by Richard Haass in his address to the State Department on so-called "democratic exceptions." He repeatedly addresses United States covert and military interventions including those in Vietnam, the Philippines, and South and Central America. There is no mention of hating our freedom. There is no mention of subjugating the planet to Islam. He states that the 9/11 attacks were a reaction to our "destructive policies towards the Islamic world" and a means of stopping our "brutal foreign policy." To be clear, violence for violence is never a solution. I categorically condemn the 9/11 attacks and all other forms of terror.

I present bin Laden's interview and Khalid Sheikh Mohammed's letter for two reasons: (1) to illustrate the clear political motivation behind the 9/11 attacks and (2) as difficult as it is, to take a cold, hard look at the specific reasons given for the attacks.

We already know that 7 percent of Muslims who took the Gallup poll thought 9/11 was justified. Further analysis by Esposito and Mogahed of this 7 percent of potential radicals reveals several interesting facts. Compared with 52 percent of the moderates, 67 percent of this group has secondary or higher education. Sixty-five percent have average or above average income. No difference exists in the unemployment rates of either moderates or radicals. Almost half of those in the radical group hold positions of supervising others, compared to 34 percent among the moderates, and 64 percent of them felt that their standard of living was improving.[42] It wasn't the economically disenfranchised who supported the 9/11 attacks. It was educated, successful Muslims—those likely to be well informed about history and current events.

Over 90 percent of both groups consider themselves religious—devotion to Islam was not a distinguishing factor between a radical and a moderate. Even more interestingly, when specific answers were requested for a reason as to why the 9/11 attacks were or were not justified, in Indonesia for example, those who were against the 9/11 attacks often cited the Quran as justification. Those who felt the attacks were justified gave secular and worldly responses such as, "The US government is too controlling toward other countries, seems like colonizing."[43]

In their eye-opening chapter, "What Makes a Radical?" Esposito and Mogahed quote from an interview of Robert Pape, author of *Dying to Win: The Logic of Suicide Terrorism*, which exhaustively analyzes every suicide attack from 1980 to 2004:

> The central fact is that overwhelmingly suicide-terrorist attacks are not driven by religion as much as they are by a clear strategic objective: to compel modern democracies to withdraw military forces from the territory that the terrorists view as their homeland. From Lebanon to Sri Lanka to Chechnya to Kashmir to the West Bank, every major suicide-terrorist campaign—more than 95 percent of all the incidents—has had as its central objective to compel a democratic state to withdraw.[44]

Esposito and Mogahed go on to state that even though these attacks are politically motivated, "religious and secular groups alike often frame their terrorist acts within a powerful religious context."[45] Foreign occupation lights the flame, religion is used to fuel it.

DO MUSLIMS HATE US?

What about the 1.5 billion Muslims throughout the world who have no interest in attacking the United States? How do they feel about United States political involvement in the Middle East? Esposito and Mogahed provide several valuable insights from the survey data. In all but ten of the countries surveyed, the majority feel that the United States is not serious about advocating for democratic forms of government in the region.[46] In fact, America is seen as openly hypocritical. Our self-concept is rooted in what is known as "American exceptionalism"—that we are inherently different from other nations in our staunch commitment to democratic ideals and human rights. But Muslims see a decades-long history of putting aside any requirements for democracy in the name of keeping the oil flowing or establishing remote military bases—while autocratic dictators abuse the human rights of their citizens.

> Respondents were asked: "Suppose someone from the government of the United States were to ask you in private, what is the most important thing the United States could do to improve the quality of life of people like you in this country. What would your recommendation be?" The most common responses, after "reduce unemployment and

improve the economic infrastructure," are "stop interfering in the internal affairs of Arab/Islamic states," "stop imposing your beliefs and policies," "respect our political rights and stop controlling us," and "give us our own freedom."[47]

On a more personal level, Muslims feel generally disrespected by Americans. When asked, "What do you admire least about the West?" among the top responses was hatred or degradation of Islam and Muslims.[48] In terms of what the West can do to improve relations with the Muslim world, those surveyed were clear about their desire for respect and understanding. The most common answers were:

- demonstrate more respect; more consideration

- do not underestimate the status of Arab/Muslim countries

- demonstrate more understanding of Islam as a religion, and do not downgrade what Islam stands for[49]

Esposito and Mogahed cite another Gallup poll, this time of American households. In answer to the question about what we admire most about Muslim societies, the most frequent answer was "nothing" and the second most frequent answer was "I don't know." These two answers represented 57 percent of those surveyed[50] and would seem to validate the above responses from our Muslim counterparts.

THE HUMAN COST

The price of immoral political acts is paid one soul at a time. When suffering takes place far away, the temptation is to impersonalize it, and this somehow makes it easier for us to ignore its cause. But is a life lost at the World Trade Center any more valuable than one lost in the carpet bombing of Baghdad? May our hearts be stirred with compassion as we consider the human suffering of those affected by

United States foreign policy. And may we be moved to do our part to see an end to the "war on terror" and healing of our relationships with Muslims everywhere.

Statistics are impersonal, and pondering suffering on this scale can be overwhelming. But, if you can, try to get past the numbers. And do your best not to envision distant "others," who somehow don't matter as much. Every victim represents a shattered family, living with the darkness of loss.

- Richard W. Cottam, in his book, *Human Rights in Iran under the Shah*, reveals that under the US-installed puppet, the shah of Iran, as many as 125,000 sons and fathers were held as political prisoners, and many suffered brutal torture.[51]

- Cottam also points out that in the run-up to the expulsion of the shah in the revolution, as many as 70,000 unarmed civilians were killed by forces loyal to the shah.[52]

- The people of Afghanistan were ruthlessly brutalized during the Soviet invasion and occupation of the '80s. Exact numbers are impossible to determine; the following are estimates provided by M. Siddieq Norzoy in his April 2012 article for the *Middle East Institute*:

  o 1.8 million killed, many of whom were civilians

  o 1.5 million disabled, more than 300,000 children, most torn apart by landmines, which were placed by the tens of thousands all over the rural countryside

- 7.5 million became refugees to escape
    the hell[53]

- In the 9/11 attacks, almost 3,000 were killed
  and more than 6,000 wounded. The death toll
  continues to rise from those affected by breathing
  the toxic dust cloud.

Casualties since the subsequent "war on terror" have skyrocketed. Detailed studies entitled "Costs of War" have been conducted by the Watson Institute for International and Public Affairs at Brown University:

- In the invasion and occupation of Afghanistan by
  the United States, as of July 2016 casualties are
  estimated as:

    - 73,000 fighters supporting al Qaeda or
        the Taliban

    - 54,000 civilians

    - 39,000 national military and police, mostly in
        Afghanistan, who are part of the US installed
        government there

    - 6,000 US military and contractors[54]

- In the war on Iraq, based on unsubstantiated
  claims of the existence of weapons of mass
  destruction there, the bloodletting gets worse:

    - 36,000 opposition fighters (supporting
        Saddam Hussein, or resistance fighters
        opposing US-backed government forces after
        his death)

- 137,000-165,000 civilians, direct casualties of war

- 12,000 national military and police

- 8,000 US military and contractors[55]

Total direct casualties of the "war on terror" are almost 400,000 souls, while indirect civilian casualties of the Afghanistan and Iraq offenses are estimated to be 800,000, all but about 14,000 being local inhabitants, for a grand total of 1.2 million deaths and uncounted injuries. It is impossible to determine the emotional toll on nations of such numbers.

Meanwhile, 320 million Americans, including presidents and members of Congress, both Republican and Democrat, seem oblivious of our very recent history and actually believe that the reason for radical Islamic hostility towards the United States is the ridiculous notion that they hate our freedom. With respect to addressing any of the real issues of causality, on the contrary, the United States has doubled down on those very issues.

CONCLUSION

Why do they hate us? First and foremost, Gallup survey data shows that over 90 percent of the Muslim world does *not* hate us. They might disagree with our policies, but the concept of using terror tactics against the United States is not considered an option for them. Just like us, they want to live their lives in peace, provide for their families, bury their elderly after a long and peaceful life, and see their children grow to be contributing members of society.

As for the 7 percent who do consider terror to be an option, the reasons for their anger toward the United States have consistently been shown to be political in nature—a direct consequence of several decades of US intervention and military presence in the region.

Support for monarchic rulers with records of human rights abuses in return for oil and military bases adds fuel to the fire.

> The belief that the reason for Islamic terrorism is that "they hate our freedom," or that Muslims are religiously motivated to subjugate the world to Islam has resulted in wholesale irrational fear (Islamophobia), and the use of strategies and tactics that, rather than address legitimate political grievances, exacerbate those very grievances.

In response to the 9/11 attacks, the United States was confronted with an opportunity for self-examination in an effort to understand what could have provoked them. Instead, President Bush pointed the finger and said, "They hate our freedom," and doubled down on the same foreign policy that produced the issues in the first place. The United States initiated a catastrophic "war on terror" that has resulted in the deaths of over one million Muslims. The war on terror has also served to destabilize the region and has ultimately resulted in putting ISIS on the map in Iraq, Syria, Yemen, and North Africa.

The belief that the reason for Islamic terrorism is that "they hate our freedom," or that Muslims are religiously motivated to subjugate the world to Islam has resulted in wholesale irrational fear (Islamophobia), and the use of strategies and tactics that, rather than address legitimate political grievances, exacerbate those very grievances.

We can sit back and point the finger at politicians and the government, or we can accept our own responsibility as part of the system. We have more power than we give ourselves credit for. Let's find out how we can make a difference.

CHAPTER 4 NOTES

1. Jeremy Diamond, *Donald Trump: Ban All Muslim Travel to U.S.* (December 8, 2015), https://www.cnn.com/2015/12/07/politics/donald-trump-muslim-ban-immigration/index.html.

2. Stephen Kinzer, *All the Shah's Men: An American Coup and the Roots of Middle East Terror* (Hoboken, NJ: John Wiley & Sons, 2003), 50.

3. Kinzer, 67.

4. Kinzer, 52.

5. Kinzer, 95.

6. Kinzer, 78.

7. Kinzer, 87.

8. Kinzer, 110.

9. Kinzer, 86.

10. Kinzer, 84.

11. Kinzer, 168.

12. Kinzer, 174.

13. Kinzer, 176.

14. Charlotte Curtis, "Tent. City. Awaits Celebration: Shah's 'Greatest Show,'" *New York Times* (October 12, 1971), 39:2, https://www.nytimes.com/1971/10/12/archives/tent-city-awaits-celebration-shahs-greatest-show.html.

15. Aslan, 193.

16. John J. Mearsheimer and Stephen M. Walt, *The Israel Lobby and U.S. Foreign Policy* (New York: Ferrar, Straus, and Giroux, 2007), 290.

17. Mearsheimer and Walt, 302.

18. Steve Coll, *Ghost Wars: The Secret History of the CIA, Afghanistan and bin Laden from the Soviet Invasion to September 10, 2001* (New York: Penguin Press, 2004), 49.

19. Coll, 49.

20. Coll, 57.

21. Coll, 82.

22. Coll, 126.

23. Lauren Perci, "Landmine Monitor 2015: Casualties and Victim Assistance," *Landmine & Cluster Munition Monitor* (May 1, 2015), http://www.the-monitor.org/en-gb/reports/2015/landmine-monitor-2015/casualties-and-victim-assistance.aspx.

24. Tom Bowman, "Afghan Governor Wants Government to Control Poppy Crop," *NPR* (July 6, 2016), https://www.npr.org/2016/07/06/484894669/afghan-governor-wants-government-to-control-poppy-crop.

25. Coll, 227.

26. Coll, 325.

27. Coll, 332.

28. Coll, 576.

29. Joe Stevens and David B. Ottaway, "From U.S., the ABCs of Jihad," *Washington Post* (March 23, 2002), https://www.washingtonpost.com/archive/politics/2002/03/23/from-us-the-abcs-of-jihad/d079075a-3ed3-4030-9a96-0d48f6355e54/?utm_term=.425cf198cf88.

30. Mearsheimer and Walt, 229.

31. Mearsheimer and Walt, 229.

32. Gilbert Burnham, Shannon Doocy, Elizabeth Dzeng, Riyadh Lafta, and Les Roberts, *The Human Cost of the War in Iraq: A Mortality Study, 2002–2006* (Cambridge: Center for International Studies, Massachusetts Institute of Technology, 2006).

33. "Rome Statute of the International Criminal Court" (United Nations: Office of Legal Affairs, July 17, 1998), http://legal.un.org/icc/statute/99_corr/cstatute.htm.

34. "Files Reveal US Had Detailed Knowledge of Indonesia's Anti-Communist Purge," *The Guardian* (October 17, 2017), https://www.theguardian.com/world/2017/oct/17/indonesia-anti-communist-killings-us-declassified-files.

35. Mark Massetti, Jeffrey Gettleman, and Eric Schmitt, "In Somalia, U.S. Escalates a Shadow War," *New York Times* (October 16, 2016), https://www.nytimes.com/2016/10/16/world/africa/obama-somalia-secret-war.html.

36. Thomas Gibbons-Neff and Joby Warrick, "Army Special Forces Soldiers Killed in Jordan Were Working for the CIA," *Washington Post* (November 12, 2016), https://www.washingtonpost.com/world/national-security/army-special-forces-soldiers-killed-in-jordan-were-working-for-the-cia/2016/11/11/8c6b53de-7b66-40ed-9077-bf954070f2be_story.html?utm_term=.51f8748f1143.

37. Stephen Zunes and John Gershman, "The United States and Lebanon:

A Meddlesome History," *Foreign Policy in Focus* (April 26, 2006), http://fpif.org/the_united_states_and_lebanon_a_meddlesome_history.

38. Richard Haass, "Towards Greater Democracy in the Muslim World" *US Department of State Archive* (December 4, 2002), https://2001-2009.state.gov/s/p/rem/15686.htm.

39. Esposito and Mogahed, 69.

40. Peter Arnett, "Transcript of Osama bin Laden Interview by Peter Arnett," *Information Clearing House* (March 1997), http://www.informationclearinghouse.info/article7204.htm.

41. Khalid Shaikh Mohammad, "Letter from the Captive Mujahid Khalid Shaikh Mohammad to the Head of the Snake, Barack Obama," *Miami Herald* (January 8, 2015), https://www.miamiherald.com/latest-news/article131466809.ece/binary/ksmlettertoobama.pdf.

42. Esposito and Mogahed, 71.

43. Esposito and Mogahed, 73.

44. Robert Pape, "The Logic of Suicide Terrorism: An Interview with Robert Pape," by Scott McConnell, *The American Conservative* (July 18, 2005), https://www.theamericanconservative.com/articles/the-logic-of-suicide-terrorism/.

45. Esposito and Mogahed, 77.

46. Esposito and Mogahed, 53.

47. Esposito and Mogahed, 61.

48. Esposito and Mogahed, 61.

49. Esposito and Mogahed, 61.

50. Esposito and Mogahed, 1.

51. Richard W. Cottam, *Human Rights in Iran under the Shah*, Case W. Res. J. Int'l L. 121 (1980): Available at https://scholarlycommons.law.case.edu/jil/vol12/iss1/7, 1980.

52. Cottam.

53. M. Siddieq Noorzoy, "Afghanistan's Children: The Tragic Victims of Thirty Years of War," *Middle East Institute* (April 20, 2012), https://www.mei.edu/publications/afghanistans-children-tragic-victims-30-years-war.

54. Brown University, Watson Institute for International and Public Affairs, *Costs of War* (January 1, 2018), https://watson.brown.edu/costsofwar/.

55. Brown University.

PEACE *Is* POSSIBLE

THE PERCEPTION OF HOSTILITY

In the midst of an ever-escalating "war on terror," raging Islamophobia, immigration bans, and reciprocal terror incidents that are tragically mindless in whom they victimize, dare we consider a vision of peaceful coexistence? A vision in which a Muslim doctor and a Wall Street banker pass each other on the busy New York streets and exchange a friendly greeting, each seeing only another man working hard to provide for his family? One in which two ladies walk together, chattering excitedly about their social lives and not even noticing that one of them is wearing a long black scarf and the other a delicate summer dress? A community where Muslims and non-Muslims carry on normal lives, barely noticing their differences?

This is an idealistic vision to be sure, but not one that requires miraculous intervention to realize. We can all take simple steps to begin reversing the ominous momentum of mistrust, hatred, and violence. Rebecca Cataldi, a conflict resolution specialist at the International Center for Religion and Diplomacy in Washington DC, in her insightful paper, *Clash of Perceptions: Hostility Perception and the US–Muslim World Relationship*, points out the importance of the bilateral perception of hostility between Muslims and Americans in the exacerbation of ongoing conflict.

In her description of "hostility perception theory," Cataldi explains that if one person's perception of another is that he is hostile and harbors ill will, that person's interpretation of the words and actions of the other will automatically catapult off of this perception to some imagined evil intent. This almost inevitably results in creating "self-fulfilling prophecies where one expects the other to behave belligerently, takes defensive action and relates negatively to the other, and then ends up producing the very belligerent behavior in the other that one expected and sought to avoid.[1] Without a change of perception, there is little hope of reversing this dynamic.

We can all take simple steps to begin reversing the ominous momentum of mistrust, hatred, and violence.

With this in mind, let us re-examine President Bush's post-9/11 question and answer in his address to Congress. "Why do they hate us?'" The insidiousness of this question lies in the ambiguity of the pronoun "they." Tragically, the president never clarified that "they" referred to a small band of Wahhabi radicals headed by Osama bin Laden. I believe our lack of awareness of the teachings of Islam, helped along by a steady stream of negative media images, produced an unconscious substitution of the word "Muslims" for the pronoun "they." President Bush never said it, but what Americans heard was, "Why do Muslims hate us?"

With the awful images still replaying in our heads, Bush's answer imprinted a powerful perception in our minds. And with that perception branded upon our collective psyche, America had no problem getting behind the invasions of two nations. There can be no doubt this perception of hostility continues to be in operation en masse in the United States today.

The media were not unaffected and continue to play a key role in reinforcing this perception. In the run-up to the US invasion of Iraq, news anchors were almost universally outspoken in their support of the impending invasion. With Fox News leading the way and across the full political spectrum to MSNBC News, untold hours of news programming created a virtual high school pep rally atmosphere in their coverage of America's unjustified invasion and war of aggression. It seemed as if news producers, writers, and anchor people alike all believed what President Bush had implied—Muslims are attacking us because they hate our freedom.

Americans are still hard-pressed to find any news coverage about Muslims in a post-9/11 world that doesn't also involve an act of terror. In news stories about various violent acts in the United States, if a person with an Islamic background is involved, it's called an act of terror. This is never the case if the perpetrator is non-Muslim. The relentless association of Muslims with terror, along with the absence of any portrayal of Muslims in a context of normal life continues to reinforce the false perception of hostility.

And Donald Trump leaves no room for doubt about his perception in a 2015 CNN interview when he said: "I think…Islam hates us."[2]

Even before 9/11, a deep foundation for a negative image of Muslims was already in place. It was laid almost imperceptibly over many decades by a force so pervasive it was virtually unnoticed. In his comprehensive work, *Reel Bad Arabs*, the late Jack Shaheen reviewed the more than 900 films featuring Arabs, produced primarily in the United States, between 1896 and 2001. He found that all but fifteen of the 900 films portrayed Arabs in a negative light. Four dominant categories of Arab characters were portrayed in his exhaustive review: sheikhs, maidens, Egyptians, and Palestinians—and almost always as villains. "We see them assaulting just about every imaginable foe—Americans, Europeans, Israelis, legionnaires, Africans, fellow Arabs, even—for heaven's sake—Hercules and Samson."[3]

Examples in *Reel Bad Arabs* are prolific. In 1951, Columbia Pictures released the first Hollywood feature film that portrayed Arabs as terrorists—*Sirocco*, starring Humphrey Bogart. Set during the Syrian struggle for independence from France after World War I, the film opens with a bomb exploding in a restaurant frequented by French officers. Syrians are portrayed by American actors wearing a ridiculous combination of costumes from Arabia, Cairo, and Africa. The French are portrayed as men of honor, while Syrian freedom fighters are depicted as treacherous and ruthless. All speak English with American accents. When a French emissary is sent to the Syrian insurgents, his throat is cut, and Humphrey Bogart shrugs and replies, "What did you expect?" The film closes with a black African Muslim throwing a grenade into Humphrey Bogart's room, killing him.

In *Captured by Bedouins* (1912), a British officer rescues an American maiden who had been kidnapped in the desert by Bedouin thieves. US cavalry troops arrive on the scene, just in time to gun down the fair maiden's Arab abductors. And speaking of gunning down Arab attackers, dozens of movies, made as early as the colonial era, depict British, French, American, and Israeli soldiers obliterating woefully overmatched Arab fighters. Shaheen found dozens of cases of anti-Christian Arabs, in one case referred to as "dirty, filthy swine." Islamic women are portrayed as virtual slaves, either oppressively clothed in a full-body burqa and serving a cruel husband, or wearing see-through leggings as belly dancers, and doing service of another kind. Egyptians are portrayed as Nazi sympathizers, swindlers, or mummies, with plenty of begging children thrown in for good measure.

Perhaps hit hardest by stereotyping in the film industry are the Palestinians. In the forty-five action films reviewed, more than half filmed in Israel, not a single one shows Palestinian families struggling to survive in refugee camps or living under occupation. "No movie shows Israeli soldiers and settlers uprooting olive orchards, gunning down Palestinian civilians in Palestinian cities," Shaheen wrote. Seven films involve Palestinian terrorists using nerve agents or threatening to detonate a nuclear warhead. Desperate Palestinians are depicted threatening and injuring Western women and children in eleven movies.

Black Sunday was telecast for several years on Super Bowl Sunday after it was released in 1977. I caught myself with my mouth hanging open several times as I watched it recently. In the opening scene, Israeli Mossad agents sneak into a house in Lebanon and wipe out a dozen or so Palestinians, apparently in the throes of plotting an attack on Israel. The female villain is spared. For unknown reasons, she makes her way to the United States and hooks up with a disillusioned Vietnam veteran serving as a pilot of the Goodyear blimp. Together they plot to blow up the blimp at field level at the Orange Bowl in Miami, where the Super Bowl is being hosted. The hero, a Mossad agent whose entire family had been murdered by Palestinians, works behind the backs of inept FBI agents to save the day. As the movie approaches the climax, the woman terrorist enters the blimp cockpit and shoots the pilot in cold blood. As the blimp lifts off, she sprays the ground with machine gun fire taking out the entire ground crew. She tosses bodies out of the blimp and shoots down a pursuing helicopter, but not before the heroic Mossad agent is dropped onto the top of the blimp. He manages to shoot both the pilot and the Palestinian woman, but not before they light the bomb fuse. Still on top of the blimp, he somehow attaches a cable from another helicopter to the blimp and rides it as it is towed out over the ocean. Not surprisingly, just after he leaps off the blimp clinging to the cable, the bomb explodes and no one is harmed. At no point was there any mention of why the Palestinians were resorting to terror, but there was a dramatic scene in the hospital highlighting the heartbreak of the Mossad agent. As they queried him about next of kin and went down the line from father to mother to children, he continued to repeat that each had been killed. It was impossible to miss the message.

I see the effect of this perception on social media all the time. In January 2018, a friend of mine living in Palestine posted pictures of three Palestinian boys she had run into on her morning walk to the language school where she taught English. The bespectacled boy and his two brothers looked to be laughing and giggling, while giving the thumbs-up signal to my friend as she passed by. The boys' Bedouin grandmother invited her in for tea. The first comment under the post from an American friend was one of surprise, "They seem very friendly." To which my friend replied, "The Arab people are exceptionally warm and hospitable... It breaks my heart that there is such a false negative perception about these lovely brothers and sisters." The other friend then commented, "Because of extremists...I can't fault any wariness unless you get to know some of them." The perception of the person living among them was that they are "exceptionally warm and hospitable," and the perception of one who lived far away and was only exposed to Hollywood movies was one of wariness, because you never know when one might be an extremist. Knowing many Arabs myself, my heart breaks with my friend's heart.

It's to be expected that Hollywood would produce over-dramatized action films energized by real terrorist incidents. The problem comes when there is no balancing representation, either in real life through travel or friendship, or on the screen. There is no shortage of action films, dramas, or even musicals depicting other cultures in a positive light. From *Dr. Zhivago* to *Fiddler on the Roof*, from *Hawaii* to *The King and I*, I'm sure we can all string together a long list of delightful productions featuring positive depictions of cultures around the world. But where are the fair representations of sheikhs as elderly men of wisdom? Where are the docudramas featuring Arab women such as the intriguing Ivonne Abdel-Baki, who is a graduate of Harvard University's Kennedy school of Government, has served in multiple high-level diplomatic and political capacities in Ecuador, and is fluent in five languages? Where is the musical that features Arab life and culture in a positive light?

The stereotype of Arab as terrorist is one Hollywood just won't let go of. In 2018, Amazon ran a high-octane Super Bowl ad promoting their new *Jack Ryan* series. Complete with voice clips from three presidents, rapid-fire building explosions, and close-ups of Muslims, the ad left no doubt about Amazon's intent to cash in on the business of Islamophobia.

President Bush's post-9/11 speech and more than one hundred years of negative screen images have had a profound impact on our perception of Muslims. And this image has been reinforced by yet another powerful group that has taken aim at the Arabs.

Modern Zionism emerged in the late 1800s in Europe. Zionism is a Jewish nationalist movement that, for obvious reasons, set its sights on Palestine as a homeland. In both ideology and in actual practice, Zionism extends the right of full citizenship to Jews only. Zionist leaders developed wealthy and powerful networks in both Britain and the United States. These networks put their wealth and power to bear on creating a pro-Zionist narrative in the news media. In her book, *Against Our Better Judgment*, journalist Alison Weir provides extensive data showing an almost universal pro-Zionist bias among American media outlets. This was evident as early as 1917, in a study of four leading newspapers.[4]

During the following thirty years leading up to Israel's military takeover of Palestine in 1948–1949, Zionists became extremely proficient in their ability to control the narrative as portrayed in the US media. When Israeli forces took over Palestine, more than 700,000 indigenous Palestinians were expelled from their ancestral homelands and became refugees. But, as Weir points out, the pro-Zionist narrative in the United States was so pervasive that, in a State

Department study in March 1949, they found that the American public was not even aware of the Palestinian refugee problem.[5]

The media blackout in the United States on news pertaining to the Palestinians is in full force today. Two generations of Palestinians have been born in refugee camps and their numbers have swollen to five million according to the United Nations Relief and Works Agency (UNRWA). The remaining Palestinian territories, Gaza, and the West Bank, have been occupied or blockaded by the Israelis since 1967. But I have yet to meet a rank-and-file American who is not either shocked or outright disbelieving when I describe the plight of the Palestinians. One woman I recently spoke with simply said, "I don't believe they would do that," referring to the Israelis driving out the Palestinians from their homelands. The typical American doesn't know what "the occupied territories" means, and I doubt whether many could explain the meaning of the term "Israeli settlers."

Extensive studies of media coverage of the Israeli-Palestinian conflict have been published by several groups and reveal an unmistakable bias towards Israel.

Are Americans just hopelessly ignorant about the history and current events of the Middle East? Perhaps. But evidence shows that our ignorance is helped along by a well-orchestrated propaganda campaign by the Israel lobby. For some the ignorance is willful, as in the case of Christian Zionists, who believe that the Jewish takeover of Israel and Jerusalem is a divine inevitability and welcomed prophetic fulfillment signaling the second coming of Christ. For the rest of us, it would take a serious amount of digging to get to the truth. Extensive studies of media coverage of the Israeli-Palestinian conflict have been published by several groups and reveal an unmistakable bias towards Israel. Exhaustive statistics have been collected on countless facets of media coverage of this issue. For brevity I randomly selected a single statistic: the evening news coverage by ABC, CBS, and NBC on child fatalities in a one-year period (September, 29 2000–September 28, 2001) during one of the Palestinian rebellions. On average, the deaths of children on either side were over ten times more likely to be covered if the child killed was an Israeli.[6] For every Israeli child's death reported on the news, it took ten Palestinian children to die before they could get the same coverage as the one Israeli child. A wealth of data confirms this pattern of reporting in every aspect and in every medium, whether television, newspapers, or Internet. An excellent source of this extensive data is *IfAmericaKnew.org* under their "media analysis" tab.

The American public has swallowed the Israel lobby's version of the story hook line and sinker: Arabs have an inherent hatred for Jews, as taught by the Quran. Without any provocation, Palestinian terrorists launch a steady stream of deadly rockets and suicide attacks on peace-loving Israeli civilians. Palestinians are an ever-present existential threat to Israel and any violence on the part of the Israelis towards the Palestinians is wholly defensive in nature, and an important aspect of the "war on terror." This narrative has become another key element supporting the false perception of Muslim hostility.

I recently had a brief conversation with a close friend about the topic of Israel and Palestine and the fact that I would be addressing it in my book. She is a well-educated, progressive thinker, who often accesses nontraditional media sources. Her immediate response in the discussion was, "That must be difficult for a researcher; how can you tell which stories to believe?" Given that she is well-informed and someone that I respect very much, it was a powerful illustration of the pervasiveness of the Zionist narrative. It seems that almost everyone I talk to, even though they might have a willingness to evaluate the conflict with fairness, is unaware of its one-sided history. They are unaware that more than 700,000 Palestinians have been dispossessed from their homelands and don't know that there are now over five million Palestinian refugees living in fifty-eight UN-registered camps in the Middle East. They are ignorant of the fact that Israel has occupied or blockaded all remaining Palestinian land and continues to dispossess Palestinians to this day. They lack awareness that any slight attempt at resistance is met with crushing violence. And I can almost guarantee that the vast majority of the American populace is unaware that since September 2000, more than 2,000 Palestinian children have been killed by Israelis compared to 134 Israeli children who have lost their lives at the hands of the Palestinians.[7]

I point this out not to criticize my friend or anyone else for not knowing the facts, but to highlight the difficulty of simply getting our hands on them. A complete discussion of the influence of Zionist wealth and activism in the United States is beyond the scope of this book, but I refer the reader to the following sources: *The Israel Lobby and US Foreign Policy*, by John Mearsheimer and Stephen Walt (2007, Farrar, Straus and Giroux), the Washington report on Middle East affairs (www.wrmea.org), and *Against Our Better Judgment*, by Alison Weir.

The perception of Americans that Muslims are hostile toward us is only one side of the equation.

In her description of Hostility Perception Theory, Cataldi points out that very often in conflict, the perception of hostility is bidirectional. We've taken a hard look at our own side of the equation, but what about the other side? Do Muslims believe that Americans, in general, maintain an attitude of hostility towards them? Certainly, after the invasions of Afghanistan and Iraq, and considering the rhetoric coming from President Trump, and the rise of Islamophobic incidents in the

United States, it would be reasonable to assume that many Muslims believe that Americans harbor hostility towards them. More recent survey data summarized by Cataldi confirms this assumption. But Cataldi highlights additional data from the previously cited Gallup survey not long after 9/11 that can give us more insight:

- "Eager to have better relations with the West" was one of the most frequently chosen responses when asked to associate various statements with their society.

- In Saudi Arabia, Morocco, and Lebanon, twice as many people are concerned about better relations between the West and Muslim cultures than are not concerned.

- The percentage of Muslims who say they admire nothing about the West was 6.3 percent in Jordan and 1 percent in Egypt.

- Muslims responded that they admire much about the West including freedom, human rights, democracy, equality, justice, hard work, and open-mindedness.[8]

In precisely the same time period that George W. Bush was convincing America that Muslims hate our freedoms and justifying invasions of two Muslim countries, Muslims were responding to Gallup surveys with answers stating that what they admired most about the West was its freedom.

The Gallup surveys in which this data was collected took place between the years 2001 and 2006. George W. Bush made his infamous statement that "they hate our freedoms" on September 20, 2001. The invasion of Iraq commenced on March 19, 2003. In precisely the same time period that George W. Bush was convincing America that Muslims hate our freedoms and justifying invasions of two Muslim countries, Muslims were responding to Gallup surveys with answers stating that what they admired most about the West was its freedom. It is difficult to imagine a more profound illustration of the consequences of Bush's false perception.

CAN YOU RESPECT A MUSLIM?

But, what about us? How can we do our part to reverse the momentum? It's often said that the first step toward change is awareness. Knowledge can definitely prepare us to break down long-standing misperceptions. But what about the psychological effects, which affect us more subtly? Is it possible to modify our psyches, conditioned by a lifetime of programming? How can we address the thoughts and fears that creep into our minds?

In my own experience, psychological change requires firm intention motivated by an impossible-to-ignore hunger for things to be different. It requires action and the investment of energy. In order to diffuse our innate fears of Muslims, I know of no force more powerful than that of face-to-face interaction. When two good-hearted souls hold eye contact and hear one another's stories, hearts soften. When each sees with compassion the tears of pain in the eyes of the other, imaginary walls crumble. And when they continue spending time together, the day arrives when they forget they are different.

For those who haven't already, it's time to consider befriending a Muslim.

For some of us that's as easy as striking up a conversation with a coworker. For many others it can be as daunting as skydiving. One thing is certain, it isn't going to happen without deeply motivated intention. For myself, even though I had lived in the Muslim world for five years, I was not immune to the programming. In my head I knew, but my subconscious produced the very fears that I'm writing about.

Ironically, I started the book project a year before I did anything about those deep-seated fears. I got my first opportunity to visit a mosque with a group of progressive thinkers and leaders in San Diego who are part of a church known as Sojourn Grace Collective. We attended a weekly open house called "Coffee, Cake, and True Islam," hosted by our local Ahmadiyya Muslim community. We had a mutually supportive interchange of thoughts. I was caught off guard when someone from our group asked the imam, "How would you and your members feel about attending events with our gay community?" You could have heard a pin drop when the imam paused before answering. I think he surprised everyone with his answer: "Though we may not agree with homosexuality, we stand against discrimination against the LGBTQ community and understand that this is a personal decision between them and God." Even with this tense moment, it was a good first visit.

Having broken the ice, I asked my friend, the software engineer named Mohammed, if I could attend Friday prayers with him at the mosque. He said I was welcome. After the sermon and the prayers, I stayed around for a few minutes and found a few friendly faces to introduce myself to. The broken ice was thawing. I went back alone several times, got to know some of the members, and organized several group visits to the mosque. I have visited other mosques and have come to feel very comfortable mixing with the Muslim community.

I didn't know it yet, but I still had ground to cover. This would come to me in a moment of clarity while I was spending time with

Maaz, the imam of the Ahmadiyya community that hosted my first visit to the mosque. I returned many times to their Tuesday night event, and often it was just Maaz and me. We drank tea, chatted, and gradually got to know each other. Often, we talked about unpleasant news surrounding things like Trump's executive order banning citizens of certain Muslim countries from entering the United States. But we also talked about everyday things that friends talk about: family stuff, problems at work, or plans for the weekend. We met for a burger once after we hadn't seen each other for a while. As we were catching up, I had the sudden realization that I looked at Maaz only as my friend. Nothing else about him entered into my consciousness as we chatted like a couple of old buddies. And in this moment I knew.

My ultimate goal in writing this book is for the information I share to become the catalyst for hundreds of thousands of relationships like the one I have with Maaz.

Several groups that facilitate Muslim/non-Muslim interaction have recently come onto the scene. For those who are a little shy about initiating on their own, it's possible that an Ecosia search will turn up one of these groups in your area. If not, the month of Ramadan can be an excellent opportunity to meet Muslims. Many mosques host iftar gatherings in the evenings throughout the month and open these to the public. Generally, a nice meal is served, and an adventurous soul can find herself sitting at a table with a couple of Muslim families or a talkative group of ladies.

During the course of my networking activities with the Muslim community, I found myself consistently running into the same gentleman. He was a soft-spoken, elderly man named Mohammed, who goes by his middle name, Aziz. I asked him to meet me for coffee. As he started to tell me his story, I found myself captivated. He had been serving as a finance minister in the government in Kabul during the communist takeover in the early '70s. One night, during the Soviet-style purge of the former government, he got a call from a friend warning him, "They are coming for you tonight." He fled with his family, taking only what they could carry, and walked for twelve days before reaching safety in Pakistan. After some time, Aziz and his family were allowed into the United States as refugees and have become US citizens.

In 2016 Aziz started an organization called We Love Our Neighbors. He is quietly passionate about working for peace. He explained that Christians and Muslims make up over half of the population of the world, so he focuses on promoting love and unity between these two groups, one neighborhood at a time. Aziz humbly does this work on a volunteer basis while still providing for his family as a real estate agent.

We have become close friends and solid partners. He has been especially helpful in planning and facilitating events put on by the nonprofit I founded, *Salaam*. On one occasion I took a dozen or so non-Muslims to an iftar gathering at a local mosque during Ramadan. When we arrived it was packed with around 300 people. The easy solution would have been to put the new guests together at a new table, but I was hoping that my visitors could be dispersed at separate tables, full of Muslim guests. When I asked Mohammed about this, he immediately went into action, disappearing into the crowd and then coming back to escort each guest, one at a time, to the next open spot he had found (or created). My guests had a delightful evening and were among the last to leave.

The pinnacle of sweet friendship provides a new vantage point to enjoy the view. Having broken through the misconceptions, we see only fellow travelers on the journey. We learn to savor our common humanity and celebrate our differences. And from this vantage point it becomes impossible not to notice that our new friends are hurting. When we hear a group of our coworkers making disparaging remarks about the Muslim woman downstairs who comes to work in her hijab, it affects us differently. In the past we might not even have noticed this conversation. But now we do. When we hear our friend's country listed on an executive order banning anyone from this country from entering the United States, we feel a part of their pain. And we feel differently now about the "war on terror."

Under the leadership of Donald Trump, attitudes and policies toward Muslims have taken a turn for the worse. In Trump's nationally televised speech at the CPAC conference in late February 2018, on the subject of immigration, he revived the well used poem from his campaign trail called, *The Snake*. In the story told in the poem, a woman is attacked and killed by a snake she had cared for after it had been wounded. Trump's punch line—and the defining principle of his immigration policy—was, "You knew damn well I was a snake before you took me in."

In a time when government leaders are fanning the flames of Islamophobia, citizen diplomacy is called for. Rebecca Cataldi points out: The most powerful way to affect the national conscience is to change people's perceptions at the grassroots level.[9] Opportunities for activism and advocacy are abundant for those who want to go beyond changing their own perception. Equipped with a solid understanding of the teaching and practice of Islam, we can interject truth to that conversation about what the Quran teaches about women, for example. Or we can invite a mixed group of Muslims and non-Muslims over for dinner and facilitate a warm conversation.

The ultimate experience for exposure to Muslim culture, and the most life-changing, is traveling to a Muslim majority country and spending at least a few weeks there.

Muslim advocacy groups such as CAIR (Council on American-Islamic Relations) or the Muslim American Society's (MAS) public affairs and civic engagement arm would be delighted to have your volunteer support. Getting involved with organizations that support war refugees, both locally and internationally, is a wonderful way to affect the Muslim side of the hostility perception equation.

The organization I created, *Salaam*, gives seminars and workshops, and facilitates interaction between Muslims and non-Muslims through friendship dinners and joint service activities. Based in San Diego, we provide training materials and on-site support to enable individuals and families to do citizen diplomacy in their own city.

The ultimate experience for exposure to Muslim culture, and the most life-changing, is traveling to a Muslim majority country and spending at least a few weeks there. I can promise you this will affect you profoundly, on the very deepest levels, and you will never see the world—or yourself—the same way again.

The list of destinations is virtually endless: the beach cities of Morocco, exotic Cairo, Istanbul or the Aegean coast of Turkey, the former Soviet republics of Turkmenistan, Uzbekistan, Tajikistan, Kirghizstan, and Kazakhstan. Beirut, Amman, and Jerusalem are excellent options for seeing the Middle East. Of course, a thorough review of state department updates throughout the planning process is essential.

For the especially adventurous, I offer the following suggestions to maximize your experience:

- Don't do the tourist package or stay in five-star hotels.

- Travel with only what you can carry on your back, or a small roller bag.

- Do not move about in a large group speaking English and laughing loudly. It's easy for locals to assume that you are laughing at them and it's a bit disrespectful.

- Do your best to dress like the locals. You will be accepted more quickly if you do not look like a giraffe among zebras.

- Use Airbnb if possible. Many Airbnb rentals are located in neighborhoods rather than tourist districts, and hosts can be fantastic tour guides.

- In choosing your destination, try to choose a spot where your Muslim friends in the United States have family or friends. This will ensure that you experience the iconic Muslim hospitality.

- For those wishing to get a firsthand look at the realities in Israel/Palestine, I recommend plugging in to a peacemaking group such as The Global Immersion Project. They will provide you with well-balanced exposure to peacemakers from all sides—Christians, Muslims, and Jews.

- Take a few months before your journey to familiarize yourself with the written and spoken language. Not only does this decrease your stress level by making you more aware of what is happening around you, it will help you to interact directly with the locals.

- The ultimate prize is to be invited by a local family to a meal in their home. This is where you find yourselves on the pages of National Geographic magazine, experiencing the core element of a culture—a family at home.

From acquiring accurate information, to spending time with Muslims, to travel to the Muslim world—the journey out of fear and false perceptions is difficult but rewarding. Whether you find yourself sitting at a table with a refugee family at a friendship dinner in your home city, or cross-legged on the floor as guests of a family in Morocco, your experience will be satisfying. It's my dream that as more and more choose friendship over fear, it will in time affect America's national conscience and lead to a foreign policy based on respect.

ON AN ETHICAL FOREIGN POLICY

I'm not a foreign policy expert, but I am a voter. As such, I speak to my current representatives, vote for candidates, and speak my voice into coalition platforms supporting the following principles:

a. **Formal apologies for wrongs committed, and reparations for those wrongs**

The United States should absolutely make an international public apology for the role that we played in taking down the democratically elected government of Iran headed by Prime Minister Mohammed Mossadegh. We should also acknowledge that the invasion of Iraq was unjustified. We should provide funding for the rebuilding of infrastructure, schools, hospitals, etc. We should make reparations to individual families who have been negatively affected by the war.

b. **Not just about American interests**

A policy that only pursues "American interests" and uses bullying tactics to achieve them should be brought to an end. All foreign policies should be evaluated relative to how they affect the populace of the countries involved.

c. **The role of the CIA**

The charter and oversight process of the CIA must be overhauled. Their role must be limited to intelligence gathering related to credible threats. Missions involving the overthrow of foreign governments put in place by democratic processes must be immediately curtailed.

Those involving any kind of government overthrow must be subjected to critical evaluation by an oversight body comprised of elected officials. The use of covert operations must be considered a last resort after all forms of diplomacy have failed.

d. **Ending wars**

Efforts should be stepped up to end US military involvement in both Afghanistan and Iraq. The people of Afghanistan and Iraq should be allowed the right of self-determination. If internal factions are unable to find a mutually satisfying solution through democratic means, the United States should only play a support role and convene an international body including representatives from internal factions, regional stakeholders, and neutral observers. Experts in conflict resolution should be employed to facilitate talks pertaining to forming a government wherein all stakeholders are represented.

e. **Diplomacy as a weapon against terror**

Funding for wars should be redirected to diplomatic efforts including relief, resettling and repatriating of refugees, education, rebuilding of infrastructure, etc.

f. **Supporting democracy**

When unrest flares up in nations without democratic representative forms of government, the US should step up diplomatic efforts in support of populaces seeking democratic representation. An example of missing an opportunity to support a movement to democracy took place in Tunisia in January 2011.

The day before Tunisia's entrenched dictator had fled to Saudi Arabia with tens of thousands of Tunisians demonstrating in the streets, then Secretary of State Clinton made a speech in Doha, Qatar. She directly addressed the corrupt, despotic leaders of the Middle East and prodded them to stop dragging their feet on democratic reforms. Yet when asked directly about the US position on the street protests taking place in Tunisia, her answer was, "We can't take sides." As Mark LeVine incisively pointed out in his January 2011 opinion column in Al Jazeera.com, had Secretary Clinton and the US State Department under President Barack Obama chosen to actively support democratic reforms, "it could have done more to defeat the forces of extremism than a million soldiers in AfPak (the Afghanistan/Pakistan military theater) and even more drone strikes could ever hope to accomplish." Without any direct intervention, the United States government could have stepped up diplomatic pressure to urge internationally-monitored elections and refused to recognize any government that is not democratically elected.

g. **A fair and equitable peace process for Palestine that acknowledges past wrongs**

High on the list of issues that must be kept before our politicians is that of an equitable peace in Palestine. My expectations for a peace process would be as follows:

- Acknowledgment of and reparations for the ethnic cleansing of the 700,000 Palestinians from their ancestral homes.

- The right of Palestinians to return to their homelands.

- An end to the apartheid policy of Israel's government. Palestinians living in Israel should have the same rights as Jews.

- The right of Palestinians for self-determination of their government—either as full citizens in a one-state solution, or as citizens in an independent Palestine in a two-state solution.

- The US allotment to Israel of $4 billion per year should be withheld until Israel demonstrates their commitment to a peace process that conforms with these expectations.

Final Words

As we have seen, the world of Islam is an elaborate mosaic of geographical regions, exotic cultures, languages, ideas, and practices. This book presents only a sketch of that mosaic. Two overarching ideas stand out as foundational to an accurate understanding of the 1.7 billion Muslims of today's world.

The first is that mainstream Muslims are our allies against terror. They attend millions of mosques all over the world that teach tolerance and respect for human life and are often themselves the targets of extremists. Secondly, it is undeniable that acts of terror are incited by political acts and not by the teachings of Islam.

The combined misunderstanding of both of these concepts results in policies that double down on previous political acts that have provoked extremist terror. In contrast, actions that reflect an accurate understanding will go directly towards eliminating the political triggers of terror.

The road before us to higher places is steep and our destination is yet distant at the mountaintop. Without an unwavering commitment to the pursuit of understanding, reconciliation, and change, we won't reach our goal. I hope this book will help us stay the course. It is my humble offering.

CHAPTER 5 NOTES

1. Rebecca Cataldi, "Clash of Perceptions: Hostility Perception and the US–Muslim World Relationship," *Journal of Peace, Conflict & Development,* 18 (2011): 27–46.

2. Anderson Cooper. "Donald Trump: 'I Think Islam Hates Us.'" CNN: Anderson Cooper 360 (March 2016), https://www.cnn.com/videos/politics/2016/03/10/donald-trump-islam-intv-ac-cooper-sot.cnn.

3. Jack G. Shaheen, *Reel Bad Arabs: How Hollywood Vilifies a People* (Brooklyn, NY: Olive Branch Press, 2001), 14.

4. Alison Weir, *Against Our Better Judgment: The Hidden History of How the U.S. Was Used to Create Israel* (Scotts Valley, CA: CreateSpace, 2014), 85.

5. Weir, 86.

6. "Off the Charts: Accuracy in Reporting of Israel/Palestine," *If Americans Knew* (December 2004), https://ifamericaknew.org/media/net-report.html#rt.

7. https://ifamericaknew.org/ (home page).

8. Cataldi.

9. Cataldi.

Appendix: People and Places of the Muslim World

The Muslim world can be divided into seven distinct groupings by region and language.

    a. The Middle East

    b. Persia/Iran

    c. The Turkic World

    d. The Indian subcontinent

    e. Oceania/Indonesia

    f. North Africa

    g. Sub-Saharan Africa

Iran, also known as Persia, has been broken out from the Middle East because (1) a different language is spoken there, Farsi, (2) it has existed as a civilization from ancient times compared to the recent creation of the modern nation-states of Arabic speaking Middle East, (3) the Shia version of Islam is practiced there, compared to mostly the Sunni version in the Arabic-speaking nations. Afghanistan and Tajikistan have been combined with Iran/Persia because, as once part of the ancient civilization of Persia, both speak a dialect of Farsi.

The Turkic world is also grouped by language. In addition to Turkey, the former Soviet republics of Kazakhstan, Uzbekistan, Kyrgyzstan, Turkmenistan, Azerbaijan, and the Uighurs of Northwest China all speak languages from the Turkic family.

From the Muslims in the surf towns and fishing villages of Indonesia and Malaysia who have distinctly Asian features, to the masses of colorful humanity inhabiting the Indian subcontinent, to the Uighurs of Northwest China and peoples of the Central Asian steppe who are of Mongol and Turkic descent, the eastern segment of the Muslim world has an astounding level of diversity. The western segment is equally diverse, from the indigenous tribes of sub-Saharan Africa, to the often blonde and fair-skinned Tatars and Croats of Russia and Eastern Europe, and the beautifully mixed peoples of North Africa. It is virtually impossible to count the number of ethnicities, languages, and cultures represented by the Muslim world, who live in 57 of the 194 countries of the world.

THE MIDDLE EAST

Of the thirteen nation-states that comprise the Middle East, six are currently involved in an armed conflict: Iraq, Syria, Israel, the Palestinian territories, Saudi Arabia, and Yemen. Additionally, both Lebanon and Kuwait have been invaded by a neighbor within the last 40 years and subjected to occupation. Leaving only Jordan, and the Gulf states of Bahrain, Qatar, the United Arab Emirates (UAE), and Oman unscathed.

The primary source of conflict in the Middle East dates only as far back as World Wars I and II—the drawing of arbitrary political boundaries and the creation of nation-states. This has proven to be a recipe for endless unrest in a region containing uncounted tribes and ethnic groups overseen from ancient times only by sheikhs and the law of retribution.

Courtesy of the University of Texas Libraries, The University of Texas at Austin.

Map A1 — The Middle East

SAUDI ARABIA

The holiest places in all of Islam are the two ancient cities of Medina and Mecca, located in the Kingdom of Saudi Arabia. Saudi Arabia was founded by conquest in 1932 and has remained an absolute monarchy since. Its national economy is based almost entirely on oil. As the world's largest oil producer and exporter, they control almost one-fifth of the world's total petroleum reserves according to the US Energy Information Administration.[1]

Politically, Saudi Arabia is a key ally of the United States. However, their record on human rights is disturbing. The ultra-strict Wahhabi version of Islam is the state religion by law, and they are one of the few countries who employ religious police to enforce observance. Gruesome capital punishment is not uncommon.

As of early 2018, the Kingdom has taken significant steps in the right direction. Women are driving and voting. I have high hopes for continuing change.

As far as the rank-and-file Saudi family is concerned, they are under the control of a reigning monarchy that includes approximately seven thousand princes who have all the best positions in the government. They are collectively worth untold billions, while the per capita annual income was recently estimated to be $15,000–$25,000 by the World Bank.[2] The Saudi people are under the watchful eye of the religious police with threat of physical punishment for nonobservance while the royal family lives a life of opulence. It is not difficult to imagine a culture of discontent, especially among the youth in a country where, according to the Wilson Center New Security Beat, over half the population is under 25 years old.[3]

In fact, in an opinion poll published in 2010 by the Washington Institute, the majority of Saudis are concerned with unemployment, government corruption, and the threat of religious extremism.[4]

Saudi Arabia has become the world's largest arms importer according to a March 2015 Reuters story.[5] Donald Trump famously boasted of a $110 billion deal on his visit to Saudi Arabia in May 2017. This weaponry is currently being employed across the border to the south with the Republic of Yemen, which is embroiled in a civil war. Saudi Arabia is supporting one side in the conflict with ongoing military intervention, resulting in a massive humanitarian crisis in Yemen.

YEMEN

The Republic of Yemen is situated directly south of Saudi Arabia, where it shares the southern edge of the Arabian Peninsula with neighboring country Oman. It is the poorest country in the Middle East, with a per capita annual income of only $2,500, according to the CIA factbook.[6] Compared to Saudi Arabia and the Gulf states, its crude oil reserves are meager. It has large proven reserves of natural gas, but Reuters reports that the first liquefied natural gas plant began production only in October 2009.[7]

Civil war continued to rage in Yemen as of mid-2018. The UN Office for the Coordination of Humanitarian Affairs (OCHA) published a long list of heart-rending statistics in March 2018 related to the massive humanitarian crisis taking place. At that time, every ten minutes a child under five was dying of preventable causes. Three million children under five and pregnant or lactating women were acutely malnourished.[8] The list continues relentlessly. An outbreak of cholera affected one million people while safe drinking water was scarce, and hospitals were barely functioning. The colossal humanitarian crisis as a result of the civil war leaves the people of Yemen in precariously dire circumstances.

Yemeni politics have always been a delicate balance between two relatively strong factions. This balance was upset in 2004, when the minority insurgent group, called the Houthis, launched an uprising against the Yemeni government. The Saudis supported the government by executing a nonstop bombing campaign of Houthi areas. Houthi rebels took over the capital of Yemen, Sana'a, in 2014. Al Qaeda, taking advantage of the instability, set up shop in Yemen and as of March 2018, controlled a significant area of Yemen as well.

THE GULF STATES

The remaining states that constitute the Arabian Peninsula are situated along the Persian Gulf and the Gulf of Oman, and are known as the Gulf States: Kuwait, Bahrain, Qatar, Oman, and the United Arab Emirates (UAE), with the famous resort cities of Dubai and Abu Dhabi.

Starting in the early months of 2017, Qatar had fallen out of the good graces of the Saudi kingdom and the other Gulf nations, which are seeking to isolate it. Except for this issue, all of these states remain peaceful and stable, with many positive steps being taken to diversify their economies from dependence on oil revenues and to enhance the well-being of their citizens. Several of these states even have a thriving international tourist sector with ultramodern resorts, hotels, and golf courses, including fantastical manmade islands in the form of a palm tree and a map of the world, in Dubai.

IRAQ

On the landmass of Asia immediately north of the Arabian Peninsula lie the remaining Arabic speaking countries of the Middle East: Iraq, Syria, Lebanon, Jordan, Israel and the Palestinian territories.

Not a soul on American soil is unaware of the nation of Iraq and its capital, Baghdad, having been famously invaded by then president George W. Bush not long after 9/11. Bush invaded under pretenses that Saddam Hussein was developing and hiding away huge stashes of weapons of mass destruction (WMD), which, even more famously, turned out to be false. This unjustified and unnecessary invasion and subsequent political vacuum in huge regions of Iraq led to providing a strong foothold for the Islamic State. Iraqi forces, with US air support, managed to reclaim ISIS-held cities in early 2018.

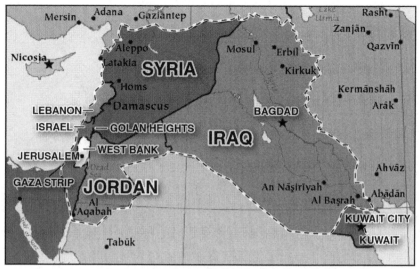

Map A2 — Middle East Close-up

Considered by biblical scholars to be the home of the Garden of Eden—where Adam and Eve were placed by the hand of God, where they were tempted by the serpent, and fell from God as representatives of all mankind—Iraq is surrounded by mystery and mystique as the very cradle of civilization.

Iraq as a nation-state has a unique and complicated religious demographic: Eighty percent of the Arab population is split between Shiites and Sunnis 60/40. All other Muslim majority nations are highly dominated by one or the other. This is further complicated by the fact that another 15 percent of the population is Kurdish, a stateless ethnic group of over 40 million that came up empty when the region was divided up into nation-states. The Kurds in Iraq and other nations, including Syria and Turkey, are in an endless and futile pursuit of their own state, often leading to violence.

SYRIA

Across Iraq's western frontier, ancient Mesopotamia continues into present-day Syria, which has been embroiled in a multifaceted, complex civil war involving outside intervention from Russia, the United States, Iran, and others.

In 2011, inspired by demonstrations and revolts throughout the Arab world commonly known as the Arab Spring, a series of peaceful protests took place in Syria, which were met by a crackdown by President Assad and the Syrian army. Army defectors coalesced into a formal opposition force, and a horrific civil war ensued.

The Wikipedia entry for the "Syrian Civil War" contains 35 pages and 24,000 words, to illustrate the complexity of this conflict. As of 2017, the conflict was ongoing and raging, rendering an accurate and up-to-date status impossible. In summary:

- There are no less than five major factions and dozens of minor factions engaged.

- The US, Britain, and France are supporting the opposition forces, as are Turkey, Qatar, and Saudi Arabia.

- Russia, a long time ally of Syria, and Iran are supporting the Assad government.

- All players claim to be fighting against ISIS.

- There is growing concern of an escalating proxy war between the United States and Russia. US forces claim to have accidentally bombed Syrian troops on September 17, 2016, while the Russian defense ministry threatened to shoot down any US jets engaged in airstrikes against Assad's forces.

- The human toll in Syria since the war broke out in 2011 has been colossal. Reliable data on death tolls is not available, but estimates range up to 475,000,

while a staggering 14 million, over sixty percent
of the entire population are wounded or displaced,
according to the Syrian Observatory for Human
Rights.[9]

LEBANON

Precariously situated between Syria and the Mediterranean Sea with
Israel to the south, Lebanon is the smallest recognized country on
the mainland continent of Asia. Curiously, Lebanon also holds the
distinction of being the most religiously diverse nation of the Middle
East, as pointed out by Richard Dralonge in his book, *Economics and
Geopolitics of the Middle East*. Lebanon's population consists of 54
percent Muslims, 40.5 percent Christians, and 5.6 percent Druze,
with a total representation of seventeen different religious sects.[10]

Established over several years in the 1940s by gaining
independence from France, the Lebanese Republic experienced a
full-scale civil war in 1975, an invasion by Israel in 1982, including
multiple massacres by the Israelis, a Syrian occupation that began in
1976 and did not end until 2005, and a United States Multi-National
Force (USMNF) put in place in Lebanon by Ronald Reagan from
August 1982 to February 1984. US personnel were the targets of
multiple attacks including bombing of the US Embassy in West
Beirut, of the US embassy annex in East Beirut, and of the Marine
barracks located at the Beirut international Airport, where a suicide
attacker was successful in blowing up the barracks, taking the lives of
241 American servicemen in 1983.

Lebanon is the home of some 450,000 Palestinian refugees, many of
whom still live in refugee camps that have been in existence since the late
1940s. A second and third generation of Palestinians has grown up and
lived their entire lives as unwanted guests in one of the twelve refugee

camps in Lebanon. The CIA World Factbook points out that Lebanon is also now home to over one million refugees from neighboring Syria.[11]

Another important player in Lebanon is Hezbollah, a militant political group that formed, with the support of Iran, in response to Israel's 1982 invasion of Lebanon and siege of Beirut. Hezbollah's paramilitary wing is reputed to be stronger than the army of the Lebanese Republic itself, according to Anne Barnard's May 2013 article in The *New York Times*.[12] As of August 2015, Hezbollah, which is recognized as a political party, held twelve seats on the Lebanese Parliament, a significant block of the 126 seats distributed among some twenty-plus parties.

JORDAN

Directly south of Syria and forming the eastern boundary of Israel and Palestine along the Jordan River of biblical notoriety, is the Hashemite Kingdom of Jordan. Jordan is pro-Western and a key ally of the US and the UK. Demographically, 98 percent of the 9.5 million Jordanians are Arab, with 30 percent of these being non-citizens in the form of refugees and illegal immigrants. Palestinians make up over 20 percent of the population, being more than two million strong. These were driven from their homes by the Israeli army in 1948, and subsequently in the Six-Day War of 1967. At the close of 2017, of the two million Palestinians living in Jordan, the United Nations Relief and Works Agency (UNRWA) reports that about 370,000 live in refugee camps. The remainder have had the good fortune of being granted Jordanian citizenship.[13]

The capital of Jordan is Amman, a bustling, modern, upscale city. I have a personal friend who has been living in Amman for a number of years working as the general manager of an electronics tech company. She tells me of Pilates classes, restaurants featuring a wide range of international cuisines and fine wine, and luxurious hotels.

ISRAEL AND THE PALESTINIAN TERRITORIES

Israel and the Palestinian territories are situated on a sliver of land between the Jordan River and the Mediterranean Sea. Today it is called the nation of Israel, but for hundreds of years before that, it was known as Palestine. Many Americans are in the dark about the facts surrounding the creation of the nation of Israel, so this constantly burning cauldron seems an unexplained mystery.

The facts related to the history and current events in this region are of critical importance to our understanding of Muslim radicalization, and why radicals might turn their focus on the US. There is an unambiguous and well-documented history leading to the conflict that brings clarity to our question, "Why do they hate us?"

The land of Palestine was under the control of the British from about 1917 through 1948. In the late 1800s, there were only about 40,000 Jews living in Palestine. They represented only a tiny percentage of the total population and lived in peace with their Arab neighbors. By 1948, this number had swollen to 630,000, roughly a third of the total population, primarily due to emigration from Europe of Zionist devotees and Holocaust survivors. Zionism refers to the nationalist movement for the return of the Jewish people to the land of Palestine and the resumption of Jewish sovereignty there. In both theory and practice, Zionism is exclusive of any other ethnoreligious heritage.

With the beginning of Palestinian land loss and the exponential growth of Jewish settlement inhabitants, the cauldron got too hot for the British, and they handed over control of the region to the newly formed United Nations in 1948. The United Nations General Assembly produced a two-state partition plan that generously offered 56 percent of the land to the newcomers from Europe for the formation of a new nation of Israel. The Jews represented only one third of the population. The balance of 44 percent of the land was to be given to the Palestinians to form their own state. The Palestinian leaders rejected the resolution as grossly unfair—to their people as a whole, and especially to the 438,000 Palestinians living on land that was to become the state of Israel, a state which had open intentions of being ethnically pure.

Upon the Palestinians' rejection of the UN resolution, the Zionists launched a military campaign and systematically took claim to 78 percent of the land of Palestine, driving out over 700,000 Palestinians and depopulating 400 Palestinian villages. The ethnic cleansing operation, known to the Palestinians as "al naqba" or "the cataclysm," and to the Israelis as "plan dalet" (or plan D), ended around the beginning of 1950. The operation left 726,000 Palestinians homeless as forced refugees in other states as well as in their own homeland. The remaining 22 percent of the land not taken over by the Israeli army is broken into two sections known as the West Bank (situated west of the Jordan River) and the Gaza Strip (a small strip of land in the south that touches the Sinai Peninsula of Egypt). Together, these are known as the Palestinian Territories.

Since then, the Palestinian Territories have continued to shrink against the constant influx of new Israeli settlements. The Palestinian territories themselves, now known as "The Occupied Territories," having been invaded and occupied in the Six-Day War of 1967, remain under complete domination and control of the Israeli government. Every meager attempt at resistance is ruthlessly crushed by an Israeli military armed with high-tech US weaponry to the tune of almost $4 billion per year in US military aid. The graphic shown below illustrates Palestinian land loss from 1947 to the present. This map, along with other valuable information, can be found at www. ifamericansknew.org.

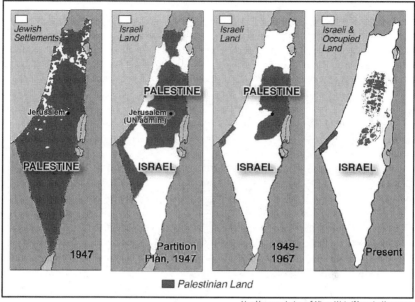

Map A3 — Palestinian Land Loss, 1947-Present

The clear source of the springs of constant conflict in Israel/ Palestine is the Zionist colonization of Palestinian land and the dispossession of over 700,000 Palestinians in 1948–1950.

Several recurring themes emerge related to conflict and radicalization in the Middle East:

- In general, political boundaries between nations were somewhat arbitrarily set by colonial occupiers after World War II. There are many, many tribal and ethnic groups, religious sects, even within Islam, and other factions, many of whose interests were not considered or accommodated in the creation of these political boundaries, nor in the ongoing governing of these nations.

- Most of the nations of the Middle East are either actual or effective monarchies, where a ruling class holds power and maintains a standard of living that can only be classified as royal, while the masses live in poverty or, at best, live with daily concerns of unemployment, low wages, and marginal hopes for a better future.

- Intervention, interference, and/or occupation by foreign powers, often in support of a corrupt ruling class, have been a regular occurrence.

- The creation of the nation of Israel in 1948 resulted in the displacement of over 700,000 Palestinians, whose children and grandchildren remain refugees to the present day. Subsequently, Israel has repeatedly invaded the Sinai Peninsula, the Syrian Golan Heights, Lebanon, and the territories of Palestine, often with full support and empowerment of the United States.

The existence of any one of these issues produces a high potential for unrest. Put them all together in this small region of the world, and it is not difficult to imagine the seething emotions constantly bubbling over in the Middle East.

PERSIAN SPEAKING REGION — IRAN, AFGHANISTAN, TAJIKISTAN

Transitioning eastward from the Middle East, we arrive in neighboring Persia, today known officially as the Islamic Republic of

Iran, which I'll combine with the other Persian-speaking countries of Afghanistan and Tajikistan. Though often lumped together with the Arab countries of the Middle East, from a language and ethnicity standpoint, they are entirely distinct.

Courtesy of the University of Texas Libraries, The University of Texas at Austin.

Map A4 — Persian Speaking

The nations of Iran, Afghanistan, and Tajikistan share a common language family, but could not be more distinct in their recent political history. Tajikistan is the youngest, having achieved statehood only in the early '90s when they declared their independence from the former USSR. Iran has been in existence for over 2,500 years as one of the few remaining ancient civilizations. The events that took place in Iran, beginning with the CIA overthrow of their democratically elected Prime Minister in 1953 and culminating with the so-called Islamic revolution in 1979, represent the opening act of the tragedy that continues to this day in the form of the "war on terror," and were discussed in detail in Chapter Four.

Afghanistan has been at war since 1973, when Soviet troops moved in to support the communist government. After the Soviets left in 1985, the Taliban emerged after years of civil war as the leading faction, but was unable to establish a central government. One month after 9/11, the United States invaded Afghanistan and overthrew the Taliban, but has not been able to establish any sort of stability. US troops are still in Afghanistan as of April 2018.

The presence of Soviet troops in Afghanistan from 1979 to 1989, along with the $3 billion in weapons and training provided to jihadist freedom fighters by the United States during that period, comprise act II in the accelerating drama that would have its horrifying climax on 9/11. In Chapter Four, I covered some details that show how CIA tactics against the USSR during the Cold War led to the creation of Al Qaeda and a sanctuary for Osama bin Laden in Afghanistan.

Afghanistan is surrounded by the historical Persian and Russian empires to the west and north, and the kingdoms of the Indian subcontinent to the east. From ancient times the kingdoms and empires around it have invaded and overrun it. From Darius I of Persia, to Alexander the Great, to its Islamification by the followers of Mohammed, followed by the Mongol invasions of Genghis Khan and Tamerlane, the great central Asian conquerors, Afghanistan has played host to a steady stream of conquering armies for centuries.

Tajikistan is just to the north of Afghanistan and shares a similar history with one profound exception—when the dust of all the invasions settled, it ended up as the southern frontier of the Russian Empire and became a Republic of the Soviet Union.

THE INDIAN SUBCONTINENT — INDIA, PAKISTAN, BANGLADESH

More than 30 percent of all Muslims of the world—almost five hundred million—live in India, Pakistan, and Bangladesh. This represents over one-and-a-half times the entire population of the United States, and almost four times the number of Muslims in the entire Middle East. Both Pakistan and Bangladesh have Muslim majorities in the 90 percent range, while in India Muslims make up only 14 percent of the population.

Courtesy of the University of Texas Libraries, The University of Texas at Austin.

Map A5 — Indian Subcontinent

As in the Middle East, recent history was wholly dominated by British colonization and its effects have overflowed into present-day politics. After almost two centuries of resistance, India gained its independence from Britain with the passage of the Indian Independence Act by the British Parliament in 1947. In the process, Britain partitioned the Indian subcontinent into East and West Pakistan, and India, in a misguided attempt to accommodate the large Muslim populations on the eastern and western reaches of British India. Ian Talbot and Gurharpal, in their book, *The Partition of*

India, estimate that up to two million people were killed in genocidal fighting as a result of the partitioning.[14]. The UNHCR estimates that fourteen million Hindus, Sikhs, and Muslims were displaced, in the largest mass migration in history.[15] In 1971, East Pakistan gained independence as Bangladesh in a bloody liberation war.

The Islamic Republic of Pakistan and the United States have been strong allies since Pakistan's creation. Recent relations have been strained due to the "war on terror" spillover into Pakistan itself as well as numerous US drone strikes in Pakistan. In contrast, relations with Hindu-majority India have been strained due to India's friendly relations with the USSR during the Cold War, and the US generally aligning itself with Pakistan in the unending animosity with India. Current relations with India are as good as they have ever been.

In Muslim-majority Bangladesh, a 2014 Pew Research Center survey revealed that 76 percent of Bangladeshis expressed a favorable view of the United States, one of the highest ratings for the countries surveyed in South Asia.[16]

THE TURKIC SPEAKING WORLD

Directly north of the Middle East, Persia, and the Indian subcontinent, and south of the massive Russian Federation, lies the incredibly exotic Turkic world. Much of the Turkic speaking world was unveiled with the breakup of the Soviet Union in 1992. It consists of Turkey, the native populaces of the former Soviet Central Asian republics of Kazakhstan, Uzbekistan, Turkmenistan, Azerbaijan, and Kyrgyzstan, and several other peoples that do not have the luxury of a national boundary (e.g., the Tatars of Russia and the Uyghurs of northwest China).

With immense mountain ranges linked to the majestic Himalayas and a vast, barely habitable steppe that extends into Siberia, one can hardly imagine a wilder and more exotic region. History—and everyday life—bear witness. Even today, one may encounter Kazakh or Kyrgyz families dwelling in yurts perched high in heavenly summer pastures, where they ascend for the purity of the cool mountain air and the abundance of rich, green grasses. Drinking unfiltered water from glacial streams and subsisting on an abundance of meat from sheep in the summer and horse in the winter, these souls continue to enjoy a simplicity of life completely unknown to those caught up in the complexities of the modern world.

Courtesy of the University of Texas Libraries, The University of Texas at Austin.

Map A6 — Turkic World

The region's peoples are an exotic blend of Mongolian, having been overrun by the Mongol hordes of the descendents of Genghis Khan, and Turkish, from the days of the Ottoman Empire, with some Persian and Arabic ancestry thrown in from earlier times in the Islamic Empire. In the northeast, Kazakhs and Kyrgyz exhibit distinctly Mongolian features, while in the south and west, a more Middle Eastern flavor is the norm, with a continuous transition from northeast to southwest.

With the ancient Silk Road passing through it like a life-giving artery, the major cities of this region have long attracted merchants of dried fruits, spices, fabrics, and rugs. The central bazaars of exotic cities such as Tashkent, Ashgabat, and Istanbul bustle with activity in much the same way they did hundreds of years ago.

From a religious perspective, Soviet-enforced atheism successfully suppressed the practice of Islam. Islam is making a comeback in the independent republics, but the governments are secular and have strong interest in becoming players in the world economy, and thus, using residual Soviet-era tactics, are actively suppressing any tendencies toward radicalization.

There are several other Turkic groups in the region without the good fortune of national homeland, the largest being the Tatars of Russia and the Ukraine, and the Uyghurs of northwest China. The Uyghur territories were assimilated by the People's Republic of China, where an appalling government repression is taking place including the internment of over 1 million Uyghurs and Kazakhs in reeducation camps as of March 2019, and the bulldozing of mosques.

The Turkic world is most renowned for the Ottoman Empire, which was founded at the end of the thirteenth century and lasted through World War I. At its zenith, the empire controlled most of Eastern Europe, Russian territory around the Black Sea, present-day Turkey, key parts of the Middle East—including the holy cities of Islam, Medina and Mecca—and even a large swath along the coastline of North Africa, reaching almost to Spain.

The Ottoman Empire was defeated in World War I and occupied by the Allied forces, ultimately resulting in the partitioning of the territories of the Middle East between Britain and France, while Kazakh, Kyrgyz, Uzbek, Azerbaijani, and Tajik lands went to the Soviet Union. The nation of Turkey emerged after its war of independence with the Allied forces, which ended in 1922.

Turkey has experienced an economic boom in recent decades, impressively, with zero reliance on the export of petroleum. Turkey has been defined as an emerging market economy by the IMF in 2011[17] and is considered a developed country, according to the CIA World Factbook.[18]

Turkey's technical sector includes Turkish Aerospace Industries, which ranks among the top one hundred global players in aerospace and defense, according to the Turkish Armed Forces Foundation.[19]

Sharing almost 600 miles of border with Syria, Turkey is majorly invested in the outcome of the Syrian civil war. They have backed rebel forces fighting against Syrian President Assad, which pits Turkey against Russia, an ally of the Syrian government. Turkey's President Erdogan has faced a battery of accusations of providing support for ISIS in Syria.

Turkey has been on the receiving end of several terrorist bombings as recently as June 2016 when, during an attempted military coup, more than forty people were killed by suicide attackers at Istanbul's Ataturk airport.

SOUTHEAST ASIA AND OCEANIA

Our last stop on our brief tour of the Muslim countries of Asia is the region of Southeast Asia and the island nations to the south known as Oceania. Surprisingly, this corner of Asia contains approximately 232 million Muslim inhabitants. When combined with the number of Muslims in India, Pakistan, and Bangladesh, the total comes to almost 714 million, or almost half of the Muslims in the world—and nearly six times the number of Muslims in the Middle East.

Many are surprised to learn that the largest Muslim nation in the world is Indonesia, with almost 205 million Muslim inhabitants. The Muslim-majority nation of Malaysia, Myanmar (formerly Burma), and interestingly, Thailand and the Philippines contain the bulk of the remaining ten percent.

Indonesia has undergone the perfunctory European colonization since the 1600s, and was occupied by Japan during World War II, during which time some four million people died as a result of famine and forced labor. After Japan surrendered in 1945, Indonesia declared its independence and has remained independent since.

Indonesia has fascinating diversity, including around 300 distinct indigenous ethnic groups and 740 different languages and dialects. Religious freedom is constitutionally guaranteed, and the government formally recognizes the religions of Islam, Protestantism, Roman Catholicism, Hinduism, Buddhism, and Confucianism. That being said, there have been reports since around 2010 of Muslim persecution of Christians in the predominantly Muslim region of Aceh, a region on the northeast tip of the island of Sumatra.

Courtesy of the University of Texas Libraries, The University of Texas at Austin.

Map A7 — Southeast Asia and Oceania

Sharing islands with Indonesia is the nation of Malaysia. With its ultramodern capital city of Kuala Lumpur, home of the Petronas Towers, the tallest twin towers in the world, Malaysia is a prosperous

secular state. Both Indonesia and Malaysia maintain very positive diplomatic relations with the United States, the US being the recipient of substantial exports of petroleum, palm oil, and rubber.

NORTH AFRICA

Separated from the Arabian Peninsula only by the Red Sea, which is only 221 miles across at its widest point, it is not difficult to imagine the spillover of Islam into Africa. In fact, 432 million Muslims (or almost 28 percent of Muslims) dwell on the vast continent of Africa. Africa is divided into two regions: North Africa, and sub-Saharan Africa—the massive Sahara Desert forming a natural boundary as big as an ocean. The Horn of Africa wraps around the Arabian Peninsula to the south.

The nations that make up North Africa include Egypt, the Sudan, Libya, Tunisia, Algeria, Morocco, and Western Sahara. These nations consist primarily of a populace of Berbers, Arabs, and West Africans. The Muslim population of North Africa totals just below 192 million, 12 percent of the world total.

Courtesy of the University of Texas Libraries, The University of Texas at Austin.

Map A8 — North Africa

EGYPT

When we think of Egypt, we cannot help but envision the city of Cairo, the Great Pyramids, and the amazing Nile River. Like Iran, Egypt is not the product of post-World War I and II boundaries drawn up by Europeans. As one of the world's first nation-states, Egypt has been in existence since the tenth millennium BCE.

Demographically, Egypt is more populous than any nation of the Middle East, with a population of eighty-eight million as of 2015. Ninety-one percent of the total population are ethnic Egyptians, with the remaining 9 percent being made up of various minorities, including Bedouin Arab tribes. The national language is Arabic, and Islam is the state religion. Interestingly, 10 percent of the population is Christian, primarily Coptic. The Coptics trace their lineage all the way back to St. Mark and are closely related to Roman Catholicism and Eastern orthodoxy.

Egypt has been caught up in the politics of the Middle East due to part of its territory, the Sinai Peninsula, being adjacent to Palestine. It's been the subject of several Israeli invasions, not without provocation.

From 1956 through 2011, other than ongoing strife with Israel at their common border, Egypt has remained relatively stable under the leadership of presidents Nasser, Sadat, and Mubarak. In 2011 Mubarak was ousted in the midst of the widespread protests of the Arab Spring, with the military stepping in to assume power. Since that time, Egypt has been in a power struggle, mostly between moderates and the reluctantly militant Muslim element called the Muslim Brotherhood. After a short stint with the Islamists in power, the military stepped in and installed an interim government, which instituted a new constitution and, in March 2014, Abdel Fattah el-Sisi, the former head of the Egyptian Armed Forces was elected president by a landslide. According to Hamza Hendawi in an article published in the *Independent* in March 2014, during the transition of power, the Egyptian authorities came down on the Muslim brotherhood, killing hundreds of protesters and jailing thousands more.[20] Since then, The *Washington Post* reported that hundreds associated with the Muslim brotherhood have faced mass trials and death sentences.[21]

Due to its designation as a US ally, Egypt receives significant military aid from the US. The total amount provided in 2015 was $1.3 billion. Current relations are somewhat strained due to recent human rights violations in the bloody crackdown on the Muslim Brotherhood.

LIBYA

Just to the west of Egypt lies Libya, home of Benghazi—of 2016 election fame. In the attack on the US Embassy that resulted in the loss of life of American ambassador Chris Stevens and three CIA employees, political opponents alleged dereliction of duty on the part of then secretary of state Hillary Clinton.

Libya is another story of Western military intervention leading to a power vacuum readily filled by ISIS. Colonel Muammar Qaddafi took control of Libya in 1969 in a military coup and held power for more than forty years. In concert with the Arab Spring movement, which resulted in a change of leadership for two of Libya's neighbors, Tunisia and Egypt, rebels launched a full-scale revolt against Qaddafi's government in 2011. Qaddafi forces were able to resist the revolt militarily until NATO got involved. According to a May 2011 story in The *Guardian*, about 8,000 American soldiers were in the area and at least 3,000 targets were struck.[22] Within a few short months, the government of Qaddafi was toppled, and he was killed.

Since that time, no central government has emerged able to consolidate authority. Multiple regional, tribal, and religious factions continue to fight amongst themselves with armed militias. Forces loyal to ISIS seized control of the cities Derna and Sirte. The top US general in Africa has declared Libya a failed state in a March 2016 article in the *Military Times*.[23]

TUNISIA

Tunisia, sandwiched between Libya and Algeria, is distinguished by being the only fully democratic state in the Arab world, according to Freedom House's "2015 Freedom in the World" report.[24] Occupied by France since 1881, Tunisia attained independence in 1956. In 2011 they experienced a non-violent revolution caused by quality of living issues, including food prices, unemployment, corruption, and lack of individual freedoms. Tunisia's successful revolution and democratization became an inspiration to several other Arab nations, kicking off what became known as the Arab Spring. The new democratically elected government has been clear and directive about maintaining the secular nature of the state.

ALGERIA

Algeria, the largest country in Africa, was a French colony from 1830–1962, at which time they gained their independence in the Algerian War. Hundreds of thousands of Algerians lost their lives in the struggle for independence. Algeria is 99 percent Muslim, but the government is mostly secular. Algeria's economy is primarily driven by oil exports, with oil reserves that are the second largest in Africa. News about Algeria in the US is scarce, primarily because they have historically been an ally of the USSR—now Russia. According to UPI, Algeria has the second-largest military in North Africa,[25] largely supplied by Russia.

MOROCCO

Morocco has a thriving tourism industry, attracting many Europeans to exotic destinations such as the famous port city of Casablanca, ancient Marrakesh, my friend Mohammed's hometown of Agadir, the Atlas Mountains, and, of course, the Sahara Desert for adventures with Bedouin tribes.

Morocco came into existence as such in 789 CE, impressively holding their own against the various conquering empires that rose and fell over the centuries. They stubbornly held off the Ottoman Turks, a feat none of the other North African nations were able to pull off. Morocco is a blend of indigenous Berbers and Arabs, with elements of both cultures and both languages. Morocco is 99 percent Muslim, while the government is a secular monarchy.

THE HORN OF AFRICA

The Horn of Africa is the piece of land that wraps around the southern tip of the Arabian Peninsula and is primarily occupied by the war-torn country of Somalia.

Due to its proximity to the birthplace of Islam on the Arabian Peninsula, Islam took root in Somalia during the same century that Mohammed lived and died, the seventh century CE. Today virtually 100 percent Muslim, Somalia has not escaped the typical regional instabilities of sub-Saharan Africa, mostly involving the painful extraction of European colonial powers after World War II and wars of independence. Frequent unrest is exacerbated by persistent drought conditions.

Somalia disintegrated into a protracted civil war between the years of 1991 and 2006, and both the United States and the UN initiated an unwelcome peacekeeping effort ostensibly to provide a secure environment for humanitarian relief efforts. The capital city,

Mogadishu, was the site of a botched kidnapping attempt by US Special Forces in 1993. Rebels shot down two Black Hawk helicopters and an overnight battle ensued, resulting in the deaths of nineteen US servicemen. The story is told in an Academy Award-winning film produced and directed by Ridley Scott called *Black Hawk Down*.

Courtesy of the University of Texas Libraries, The University of Texas at Austin.

Map A9 — The Horn of Africa

As in the case of Iraq, Syria, Yemen, and Libya, extremist groups have set up shop in the ungoverned regions of Somalia. The Bureau of Investigative Journalism reported in January 2017 that the United States continues to make drone strikes targeting radical leaders in Somalia.[26]

SUB-SAHARAN AFRICA

The vast acreage of the Sahara Desert forms a natural boundary, perhaps even more effective than an ocean, between North Africa and sub-Saharan Africa. Consisting of forty-nine countries divided by political boundaries, real sub-Saharan Africa consists of an unknown number of languages and cultures—some say more than 3,000. In the land of wildlife safaris, jungles, thirty-foot-long snakes, elephants, lions, Swahili and Zulu languages, the great missionary-explorer David Livingstone, and Tarzan, mental images are abundant.

In the last hundred years, huge changes have taken place in this region. According to the Pew Forum, in 1900, the vast majority of people practiced traditional African religions. Today, however, some 57 percent profess Christianity, while 29 percent—over 230 million—are adherents of Islam.[27] Both religions have been highly syncretized, meaning they are combined with traditional rituals and practices.

The most prevalent theory is that Islam reached this region by means of Arab traders. Nigeria has the largest population of Muslims at seventy-eight million, with Ethiopia a distant second at twenty-eight million.

Sub-Saharan Africa is not without terror attacks by those naming Islam as their cause. In September 2013, a Somalia-based, al-Qaeda-affiliated group attacked the Westgate Mall in Nairobi, Kenya, killing dozens. The *New York Times* reported that the group claiming responsibility for the attack cited political, not ideological justification—namely that Kenya had sent troops to Somalia to assist the UN-backed government.[28]

An organization known as Boko Haram has become a significant radical Islamist force in Nigeria, even occupying small regions. The sect began as a religious center and school, attracting poor families from all over Nigeria and the surrounding countries. As is almost universally the case, the driving force was government corruption, and linked to influence from the West.

Boko Haram has continued to grow in numbers and in strength, becoming increasingly violent in the process. Since

2011, they have targeted politicians, religious leaders, security forces, and civilians. The group's boldness in committing acts of terror came to a zenith with the kidnapping of 276 schoolgirls in April 2014.

The group is believed to have begun independently, but at some point there was an alleged link with al-Qaeda. Then, in March 2015, Boko Haram declared itself a member of ISIS, which backfired when ISIS named a new leader for the group in September—the appointment was rejected by the existing leader. This resulted in a split of the group, with fighting between the two factions. Just a month later, the Nigerian government announced they had defeated Boko Haram. Though Boko Haram presently does not occupy any territory in Nigeria, they retain an underground force numbering in the thousands, and Amnesty International reports that, as of March 2018, they still hold over one hundred schoolgirls in captivity.[29]

Sub-Saharan Africa as a whole remains free from the effects of radical Islamist terror. Other than the corner of Nigeria that is home to what's left of Boko Haram, the several ongoing and newly developing conflicts are politically and ethnically driven, including the horrific war in Darfur, where hundreds of thousands have lost their lives.

EUROPE

Europe contains a small but growing proportion of the Muslims of the world, at 2.4 percent as of 2009. The Muslim populations of the top 10 countries are shown in the table on the next page.

Russia	16,482,000
Germany	4,026,000
France	3,554,000
Albania	2,522,000
Kosovo	1,999,000
United Kingdom	1,647,000
Bosnia-Herzegovina	1,522,000
Netherlands	946,000
Bulgaria	920,000
Republic of Macedonia	680,000
Rest of region	3,814,000
Regional Total	38,112,000

Some might find it surprising that 43 percent of all the Muslims in Europe live in Russia. The Russian Empire swallowed up many, many ethnic groups within its vast territorial expansions—and several of them were Muslim. Tatars make up the majority, with most of the balance in the North Caucasus region, where the Chechens are located. The Chechens have been resisting Russian domination since 1785, mostly in guerrilla warfare, and have resorted to terror tactics in recent times. In October 2002 Chechen rebels took 800 hostages in a Moscow theater, where all fifty terrorists and 129 hostages lost their lives. Their key demand was the withdrawal of Russian forces from Chechnya, following the same theme as we saw in the Middle East—resisting the occupation by foreign forces.

Another ten million Muslims, 27 percent of the total in Europe, live in the four Western European nations of Germany, France, the United Kingdom, and the Netherlands. The Muslims of Western Europe have gained a foothold as contributing members of society, several holding positions in the national parliament. Sadiq Khan, former member of the British Parliament, was elected as the mayor of London in 2016, becoming London's first ever ethnic-minority mayor.

The UNHCR reports that almost one million Syrian refugees have requested asylum in Europe as of July 2017,[30] putting more pressure on strained economies as anti-Muslim and anti-refugee sentiment continues to grow.

There are two nations in Europe where the majority of the population is Muslim: Albania and Kosovo, representing about 4.5 million Muslims. Albania was one of the Eastern European satellites of the former Soviet Union, renowned for having perhaps the most oppressive communist anti-religious regime in Eastern Europe. Even though Muslims make up the majority, present-day Albania has a significant percentage of Christians and about a quarter of the population declare themselves to be nonreligious. The government of Albania is wholly secular.

Kosovo came into existence as a nation with the disintegration of Yugoslavia in 1990, followed by years of ethnic violence between the Serbian Christian majority and the Albanian Muslim minority. A campaign of ethnic cleansing against the Albanians was carried out by the Serbs, and NATO intervened with air support for the Kosovo Liberation Army, eventually putting peacekeeping forces on the ground. It was during this period that the term "ethnic cleansing" became part of the legal language in its definition as a crime against humanity under a statute of the International Criminal Court, according to the *Encyclopaedia Britannica*.[31] Kosovo has declared itself an independent nation and has a fully functioning government. It is, however, only recognized by a dozen or so other nations, the United States being one of them.

TO ACE THE FINAL EXAM

- The Middle East contains only 8.4 percent of the Muslims of the world.

- The primary reasons for unrest leading to radicalization in the Middle East are political, related to:

  o arbitrary political boundaries imposed by foreign colonialist governments;

  o foreign support of wealthy and autocratic monarchic rulers;

  o foreign intervention and occupation by foreign troops; and

  o injustices surrounding the displacement of over 700,000 Palestinians during the creation of the state of Israel, and their current status as refugees.

- The Indian subcontinent (India, Pakistan, Bangladesh) contains almost one-third of all the Muslims in the world (482 million), and they have friendly relations with the United States.

- Indonesia is the largest Muslim country in the world, containing 203 million Muslims, also at peace with the United States.

- Egypt is a major non-NATO ally of the United States.

- Libya is a failed state. US/NATO forces took out the Qaddafi regime militarily and no group has emerged in the subsequent leadership vacuum.

- Africa contains over 27 percent of the Muslims of the world (432 million) and is relatively free from radical Islamist attacks.

ACKNOWLEDGEMENTS

I owe a debt of gratitude to my editor, Carly Gelsinger, who took my original and gently massaged it into something better, teaching me how to write in the process. I thank my nephew, Nathan Johnson of Nathan.works for closing his eyes and seeing an amazing cover that he then proceeded to create. Thanks to Teri Rider of Top Reads Publishing for believing in the project and guiding me through the process. I thank Aziz Purmul, founder of the We Love Our Neighbors Project, for his support and tireless efforts to promote friendship and peace. Thank you to Maaz Bajwa, lay imam of the tiny Ahmadi Community of San Diego, for the hours of fellowship and conversation about our dreams. Thank you to the Rev. Joseph Dirbas and his congregation at All Souls' Episcopal Church, who believed in Salaam from the beginning and hosted our first event. I thank Safi and Eman Kaskas for their inspirational leadership in peacemaking and their example of mutual respect and working together as a couple. Thank you to Siddika Jessa, who answered a random Facebook message and has become a colleague and a friend. Last but not least, I acknowledge the humble and hospitable people of Kazakhstan, who showed me a better way.

GLOSSARY

Abdus Salam. A Pakistani theoretical physicist, Abdus Salam (29 January 1926 – 21 November 1996) shared the 1979 Nobel Prize in Physics with Sheldon Glashow and Steven Weinberg for his contribution to the electroweak unification theory. He was the first Pakistani to receive a Nobel Prize in science and the second from an Islamic country to receive any Nobel Prize.

Abu Bakr. A companion and, through his daughter Aisha, a father-in-law of Mohammed, Abu Bakr (573 – 634) is commonly regarded to be the fourth person to have accepted Islam, and he ultimately became the first caliph, or successor to Mohammed.

Abu Talib. Abu Talib ibn 'Abd al-Muttalib (c. 539 – c. 619) was the leader of Banu Hashim, a clan of the Qurayshi tribe of Mecca. He was an uncle of Mohammed and his caretaker after the deaths of Mohammed's father, mother, and grandfather.

Ahmad ibn Taymiyya. Ahmad ibn Taymiyya, one of Islam's most forceful theologians, was born in 1263 in Harran, Mesopotamia, and died on September 26, 1328, in Damascus, Syria. His theology is the source of Wahhabism, the violent and restrictive version of Islam practiced in Saudi Arabia.

Ahmadiyya. The Ahmadiyya Muslim Community is an Islamic revival or messianic movement founded in Punjab, British India, in the late 19th century. It originated with the life and teachings of Mirza Ghulam Ahmad (1835–1908), who claimed to have been divinely appointed as both the promised Mahdi (Guided One) and Messiah expected by Muslims to appear towards the end times and bring about, by peaceful means, the final triumph of Islam.

Ahmed Shah Massoud. An Afghan politician and military leader, Ahmed Shah Massoud was born on September 2, 1953 and was

a powerful guerilla commander during the resistance against
the Soviet occupation between 1979 and 1989. In the 1990s,
he led the government's military wing against rival militias
and, after the Taliban takeover, was the leading opposition
commander against their regime, which he fought against until
his assassination on September 9, 2001.

Ali. Ali ibn Abi Talib (601–661) The cousin and son-in-law of
Mohammed, Ali ruled as the fourth caliph from 656 to 661, but
is regarded as the rightful immediate successor to Mohammed as
an Imam by Shia Muslims.

Al-Amin. Meaning "The Trustworthy One," this informal title
was given to Mohammed by his colleagues during his developing
years in the mercantile world.

Amina. Amina bint Wahb, who died 577 AD, was the mother of
the Islamic prophet Mohammed.

Amir. A regional governor appointed by the caliph. Amirs were
placed throughout the Islamic Empire.

Assad. Syrian President Bashar al-Assad (born 11 September 1965)
inherited power in July 2000, a month after the death of his
father, military strongman Hafez al-Assad. Since March 2011,
his rule over Syria has been under threat, with the country beset
by violence that has killed an estimated 465,000 people and
embroiled regional and world powers. Assad has survived seven
years of war and refuses to step aside.

Ayatollah Ruhollah Khomeini. Khomeini (24 September 1902 – 3
June 1989) was an Iranian politician and marja who founded the
Islamic Republic of Iran and led the 1979 Iranian Revolution
that saw the overthrow of the last Shah of Iran, Mohammad
Reza Pahlavi, and the end of 2,500 years of Persian monarchy.
Following the revolution, Khomeini became the country's

Supreme Leader, a position created in the constitution of the Islamic Republic as the highest-ranking political and religious authority of the nation, which he held until his death.

Banu Qurayza. The Banu Qurayza were a Jewish tribe that lived in northern Arabia, at the oasis of Yathrib, until the 7th century, The tribe joined the alliance forged by Mohammed, but later betrayed the Muslim community by supporting the Quraysh during the Battle of the Trench. In a verdict by the arbitrating sheikh, the 700 men of fighting age in the Banu Quayza were executed in punishment for their betrayal.

Battle of Badr. This was first major battle in which the nascent Muslim community successfully defended itself against the Quraysh army. The battle took place near Medina, where the Muslims had migrated due to the persecution of the Quraysh. Muslims to this day believe that divine intervention gave them the victory.

Battle of Uhud. It was in this battle between the early Muslims and their Qurayshi Meccan enemies in 625 in the Hejazi region of the Arabian Peninsula that many Muslims were killed, and the battle was considered a setback for the Muslims.

Bedouin. The Bedouin or Bedu, singular, are a grouping of nomadic Arab people who have historically inhabited the desert regions in North Africa, the Arabian Peninsula, Iraq, and the Levant.

Byzantine Empire. Also called Byzantium, this was the eastern half of the Roman Empire, based at Constantinople (modern-day Istanbul), that continued on after the western half of the empire collapsed. The empire's territories extended as far as Western Europe and North Africa, after which the Islamic empire pushed them into a portion of western Turkey and Eastern Europe.

Caliph. This title was used for Mohammed's immediate successor and all subsequent leaders of the Muslim community and empire.

fatwa. This is the name of a legal decree usually announced by an Islamic religious leader.

Gulbuddin Hekmatyar. Gulbuddin Hekmatyar (born 1 August 1949) is an Afghan politician and former warlord. He is the founder and current leader of the Hezb-e Islami political party and twice served as Prime Minister of Afghanistan during the 1990s.

Hadith. Hadith in Islam is the record of the words, actions, and silent approval traditionally attributed to the Islamic prophet Mohammed. Within Islam, the authority of hadith as a source for religious law and moral guidance ranks second only to that of the Quran. Quranic verses (such as 24:54, 33:21) enjoin Muslims to emulate Mohammed and obey his judgments, providing scriptural authority for hadith. While the number of verses pertaining to law in the Quran is relatively few, hadiths give direction on everything from details of religious obligations to the correct forms of salutations and the importance of benevolence to slaves. Thus the great bulk of the rules of Sharia (Islamic law) are derived from hadith, rather than the Quran.

Hamid Karzai. An Afghan politician, Hamid Karzai (born 24 December 1957) was the President of Afghanistan from 22 December 2001 to 29 September 2014, originally as an interim leader and then as President for almost ten years, from 7 December 2004 to 2014. After the US invasion, during the December 2001 International Conference on Afghanistan in Germany, Karzai was selected by prominent Afghan political figures to serve a six-month term as Chairman of the Interim Administration. He was then chosen for a two-year term as Interim President during the 2002 loya jirga (grand assembly) that was held in Kabul, Afghanistan. After the 2004 presidential election, Karzai was declared winner and became President of the Islamic Republic of Afghanistan. In the 2009 presidential election, he won a second five-year term, which ended in September 2014.

Hassan al-Turabi. A Sudanese politician, Hassan 'Abd Allah al-Turabi (1 February 1932 – 5 March 2016) was leader of the National Islamic Front (NIF), a political movement that developed considerable political power in Sudan while never obtaining significant popularity among Sudanese voters. It embraced a "top down" approach to Islamization by placing party members in high posts in government and security services. Turabi and the NIF reached the peak of their power from 1989, following a military coup d'état, until 2001. Observers have called Hassan al-Turabi "the power behind the throne," as the head of the only Sunni Islamist movement to take control of a state.

Injil. The Injil refers to the synoptic gospels of the New Testament (Matthew, Mark, and Luke) and is one of the four Scriptures that the Quran records as revealed by Allah—the others being the Zabur, Tawrat, and Quran.

Islamist. A term that came into being in the post-colonial era of nation-states, islamist refers to one who advocates a return to Islamic principles in public and political life, especially in contrast to corrupt and opulent rulers.

Jamal al-Din al-Afghani. A political activist and Islamic ideologist in the Muslim world during the late 19th century, particularly in the Middle East, South Asia and Europe, Jamal al-Din al-Afghani (c. 1838 – 9 March 1897) was one of the founders of Islamic Modernism as well as an advocate of Pan-Islamic unity in Europe and Hindu-Muslim unity in India. He has been described as being less interested in minor differences in Islamic jurisprudence than he was in organizing a united response to Western pressure.

jinn. Jinn, Anglicized as genies, jinn are supernatural creatures in early pre-Islamic Arabian mythology.

Kaaba. Known in English as "The Cube," this building is at the center of Islam's most important mosque, in the city of Mecca, Saudi Arabia, and is the most sacred site in Islam. It is considered by Muslims to be the "House of God" and has a similar role to the Tabernacle and Holy of Holies in Judaism. Its location determines the direction of prayer. Wherever they are in the world, Muslims are expected to face the Kaaba when performing ritual prayers.

Khadija. Khadijah bint Khuwaylid (555–619) was the first wife and first follower of Mohammed. She is commonly regarded by Muslims as the "Mother of the Believers" And thus as one of the most important female figures in Islam. Mohammed was monogamously married to her for 25 years.

Madrasa. The Arabic word for any type of educational institution, secular or religious (of any religion), whether for elementary instruction or higher learning, in the West, the word madrasa usually refers to a specific type of religious school or college for the study of the Islamic religion, though this may not be the only subject studied.

Medina. Originally known as Yathrib, Medina was Mohammed's destination in his migration from Mecca under the persecution of the Quraysh. Medina became the capital of a rapidly increasing Muslim Empire, served as the power base of Islam in its first century, and is where the early Muslim community developed.

Mohammed ibn Saud. Born c. 1880 in Riyadh, Arabia, Mohammed ibn Saud was the tribal and Muslim religious leader who formed the modern state of Saudi Arabia and initiated the exploitation of its oil. He died November 9, 1953, in Al Taif, Saudi Arabia.

Muhammad Mossadegh. Dr. Muhammad Mossadegh (1882– 1967) was a lawyer, professor, author, governor, Parliament member, finance minister, and democratically elected Prime Minister of Iran. Mossadegh fought both internal corruption and foreign interference, enacted social reforms, and nationalized the Iranian oil industry. In 1953 he was overthrown by a British-American coup and was arrested and tried as a traitor in military tribunal court. It was the CIA's first dismantling of a foreign government, and Iran has not known democracy since then.

Mujahadeen. The plural form of mujahid, this is the term for people engaged in jihad (literally, "struggle"). Its widespread use in English began with reference to the guerrilla-type military groups led by the Islamist Afghan fighters in the Soviet-Afghan War and now extends to other jihadist groups in various countries.

Mullah Mohammed Omar. Widely known as Mullah Omar (c. 1960 – 23 April 2013), he was an Afghan mujahideen commander who founded the Islamic Emirate of Afghanistan in 1996 after the Taliban emerged as the victors of the Afghanistan civil war following the Soviet pullout. The Taliban recognized him as the Commander of the Faithful, or the Supreme Leader of the Muslims.

Muslim Brotherhood. The Society of the Muslim Brothers, better known as the Muslim Brotherhood, is a transnational Sunni Islamist organization founded in 1928 in Egypt by Islamic scholar and schoolteacher Hassan al-Banna as a means of resisting a corrupt, post-colonial regime. The organization gained supporters throughout the Arab world and influenced other Islamist groups such as Hamas with its model of political activism combined with Islamic charity work. In 2012, after the January Revolution in 2011, the Muslim Brotherhood sponsored the elected political party in Egypt. However, it faced periodic government crackdowns for alleged terrorist activities, and as of 2015 is considered a terrorist organization by the governments of several Middle Eastern states and Russia. The Brotherhood's stated goal is to instill the Quran and the Sunnah as the sole reference point for ordering the life of the Muslim family, individual, community, and state. It claims to be a peaceful, democratic organization, and that its leader condemns violence and violent acts.

Northern Alliance. The Afghan Northern Alliance, officially known as the United Islamic Front for the Salvation of Afghanistan, was a united military front that formed in late 1996 after the Taliban took over Kabul. The United Front was assembled by key leaders of the Islamic State of Afghanistan, particularly president Burhanuddin Rabbani and former Defense Minister Ahmad Shah Massoud. Initially it included mostly Tajiks; but by 2000, leaders of other ethnic groups had joined the Northern Alliance.

Operation Ajax. The CIA assigned this code name to its operation to overthrow Iran's democratically elected Prime Minister Muhammad Mossadegh.

Pashtun royalists. The Pashtuns are a major ethnic group inhabiting Pakistan and Afghanistan. The royalists favored the return of their last king, who had been ousted by a coup d'etat in 1973, to lead Afghanistan after the US invasion and dismantling of the Taliban government.

President Zia. Muhammad Zia-ul-Haq (12 August 1924 – 17 August 1988) was a Pakistani four-star general who, after declaring martial law in 1977, served as the sixth President of Pakistan from 1978 until his death in 1988. He was the country's longest-serving de-facto head of state.

Quraysh. The Quraysh were a mercantile Arab tribe that historically inhabited and controlled Mecca and its Ka'aba. The Islamic prophet Mohammed was born into the Banu Hashim clan of the Quraysh tribe. The Quraysh staunchly opposed Mohammed until converting to Islam en masse in 630.

Qusayy. Qusayy ibn Kilab ibn Murrah (c. 400 – 480), was a leader of Quraysh tribe and ancestor of the Islamic Prophet Mohammed. He is credited with monopolizing the annual pilgrimage to Mecca, to the huge financial benefit of the Quraysh tribe.

Rumi. Jalal ad-Din Muhammad Rumi (30 September 1207 – 17 December 1273), was a 13th-century Persian poet, jurist, Islamic scholar, theologian, and Sufi mystic.

Salafism. This is a branch of Sunni Islam whose modern-day adherents claim to emulate the first three generations of Muslims. The ideas espoused by these scholars have more or less culminated in the Wahhabi movement.

Sassanid Empire. Named after the House of Sasan, this was the last kingdom of the Persian Empire before the rise of Islam. Succeeding the Parthian Empire, the Sasanian Empire ruled from 224 to 651 and was recognized as one of the leading world powers alongside its neighboring arch-rival, the Roman-Byzantine Empire, for a period of more than 400 years.

SAVAK. Established by Mohammed Reza Shah with the help of the US, SAVAK was the secret police, domestic security, and intelligence service in Iran during the reign of the Pahlavi dynasty.

Sayyid Ahmed Khan. Also known as Sir Syed Ahmad Khan (17 October 1817 – 27 March 1898), he was an Indian Muslim pragmatist, Islamic reformist, philosopher of 19th century British India, and the first who said, regarding the people of India, that Hindus and Muslims are the two communities standing in the same relation to India in which the head and the heart stand in relation to the human body.

Sedentary Arabs. These are city-dwelling Arabs, as compared to the nomadic Bedouins.

Sheikh. This is a title denoting a political or spiritual leader of a community.

Sunnah. This is the body of traditional custom and practice of the Islamic community, both social and legal, based on the verbally transmitted record of the teachings, deeds, sayings, and silent permissions (as recorded in the Hadith) of Mohammed, as well as various reports about Mohammed's companions.

Syncretism. This is the term for the assimilation of cultural practices within the orthodoxies of religions.

Tawhid. Tawhid is the defining doctrine of Islam. It declares absolute monotheism—the unity and uniqueness of God as creator and sustainer of the universe.

Umar. Umar (c. 584 – 3 November 644), also spelled Omar, was a senior companion of the prophet Mohammed. On 23 August 634, he succeeded Abu Bakr as the second caliph of the Rashidun Caliphate.

Umayyad clan. A prominent clan of the Quraysh tribe, the Umayyad clan established themselves as the first dynasty to rule the Islamic empire after the murder of Ali, who was the cousin of Mohammed and the fourth caliph.

Uthman. The third caliph to succeed Mohammed, Uthman ibn Affan (c. 581 – 17 June 656) was assassinated in a rebellion that took place because of his open corruption.

Yathrib. Later renamed as Medina, this was Mohammed's destination of his migration from Mecca under the persecution of the Quraysh, and it became the capital of a rapidly increasing Muslim Empire. It served as the power base of Islam in its first century, where the early Muslim community developed.

Zakat. Zakat is a form of alms-giving treated in Islam as a religious obligation or tax.

Zbigniew Brzezinski. A Polish-American diplomat and political scientist, Brzezinski (March 28, 1928 – May 26, 2017) served as a counselor to President Lyndon B. Johnson from 1966 to 1968 and was President Jimmy Carter's National Security Advisor from 1977 to 1981.

WORKS CONSULTED

"Abbasid dynasty." *Encyclopaedia Britannica.* 2018. https://www.britannica.com/topic/Abbasid-dynasty (accessed December 26, 2018).

"About 465 Thousand Persons Were Killed and 6 Years of the Syrian Revolution and More than 14 Million Were Wounded and Displaced." *SOHR – Syrian Observatory for Human Rights.* March 13, 2017. http://www.syriahr.com/en/?p=62760 (accessed December 26, 2018).

"About 475 Thousand Persons Were Killed in 76 months of the Syrian revolution and More than 14 Million Were Wounded and Displaced." July 16, 2017. http://www.syriahr.com/en/?p=70012 (accessed September 12, 2017).

Abu-Lughod, Lila. *Do Muslim Women Need Saving.* Cambridge: Harvard University Press, 2013.

Ackerman, Spencer. "Obama Restores US Military Aid to Egypt Over Islamic State Concerns." *The Guardian.* March 31, 2015. https://www.theguardian.com/us-news/2015/mar/31/obama-restores-us-military-aid-to-egypt (accessed January 15, 2018).

"Al-Biruni." *Encyclopaedia Britannica.* 2018. https://www.britannica.com/biography/al-Biruni (accessed December 26, 2018).

"Al-Farabi." *Stanford Encyclopedia of Philosophy.* July 15, 2016. https://plato.stanford.edu/entries/al-farabi/ (accessed December 26, 2018).

Algar, Hamid. *Wahhabiism: A Critical Essay.* Oneonta, New York: Islamic Publications International, 2002.

"Algeria's Military Goes on an Arms Spree." *UPI.* March 11, 2013. https://www.upi.com/Business_News/Security-Industry/2013/03/11/Algerias-military-goes-on-an-arms-spree/UPI-89581363031700 (accessed January 11, 2018).

Aljazeera. "The Guantánamo 22." *Uyghur Human Rights Project.* December 7, 2015. https://uhrp.org/news/guantanamo-22 (accessed January 8, 2018).

Al-Rasheed, Madawi. *A History of Saudi Arabia.* Cambridge: Cambridge University Press, 2002.

"Al-Razi." *Encyclopaedia Britannica.* 2018. https://www.britannica.com/biography/al-Razi (accessed December 26, 2018).

Andreopoulos, George J. "Ethnic Cleansing: War Crime." *The Encyclopaedia Britannica.* 2018. https://www.britannica.com/topic/ethnic-cleansing (accessed January 15, 2018).

Armstrong, Karen. *ISLAM, A Short History.* New York: The Modern Library, 2002.

Arnett, Peter. "Transcript of Osama bin Laden Interview by Peter Arnett." *Information Clearing House.* March 1997. http://www.informationclearinghouse.info/article7204.htm (accessed December 27, 2018).

Aslan, Reza. *No god but God.* New York: Random House Trade Paperbacks, 2011.

Atherton, Kelsey D. "Thermobaric Bombs and Other Nightmare Weapons of the Syrian Civil War." *Popular Science.* October 5, 2016. https://www.popsci.com/thermobaric-bombs-and-other-nightmare-weapons-syrian-civil-war (accessed September 12, 2017).

"Averroes." *Encyclopaedia Britannica.* 2018. https://www.britannica.com/biography/Averroes (accessed December 26, 2018).

Bacha, Julia. "How Women Wage Conflict without Violence." *TED: Ideas Worth Spreading.* June 1, 2016. https://www.ted.com/talks/julia_bacha_how_women_wage_conflict_without_violence/transcript?language=en (accessed October 5, 2017).

Ballout, Dana, and Matt Bradley. "5 Things to Know about Lebanon's Government." *The Wall Street Journal.* August 27, 2015. blogs.wsj.com/briefly/2015/08/27/things-to-know-about-lebanons-government (accessed September 15, 2017).

Barnard, Anne and Maxxetti, Mark. "US Admits Airstrike in Syria, Meant to Hit ISIS Killed Syrian Troops." *NYTimes.com.* September 17, 2016. https://www.nytimes.com/2016/09/18/world/middleeast/us-airstrike-syrian-troops-isis-russia.html (accessed September 12, 2017).

Barnard, Anne. "Hezbollah's Role in Syria War Shakes the Lebanese." *New York Times.* May 20, 2013. https://www.nytimes.com/2013/05/21/world/middleeast/syria-developments.html?pagewanted=all&_r=0 (accessed September 15, 2017).

Bowman, Tom. "Afghan Governor Wants Government to Control Poppy Crop." *NPR.* July 6, 2016. https://www.npr.org/2016/07/06/484894669/afghan-governor-wants-government-to-control-poppy-crop (accessed July 10, 2017).

Brown University, Watson Institute for International and Public Affairs. *Costs of War.* January 1, 2018. https://watson.brown.edu/costsofwar/ (accessed March 15, 2017).

Burnham, Gilbert, Shannon Doocy, Elizabeth Dzeng, Riyadh Lafta, and Les Roberts. *The Human Cost of the War in Iraq: A Mortality Study, 2002–2006.* Cambridge: Center for International Studies, Massachusetts Institute of Technology, 2006.

Bush, George W. "Text: President Bush Addresses the Nation." *Washington Post.* September 20, 2001. http://www.washingtonpost.com/wp-srv/nation/specials/attacked/transcripts/bushaddress_092001.html (accessed December 18, 2018).

Cataldi, Rebecca. "Clash of Perceptions: Hostility Perception and the US–Muslim World Relationship." *Journal of Peace, Conflict & Development:* 18 (2011): 27–46.

Chenoweth, Erica, and Maria Stephan. *Why Civil Resistance Works.* New York: Columbia University Press, 2011.

CIA World Factbook. December 3, 2018. https://www.cia.gov/library/publications/the-world-factbook/geos/ym.html (accessed December 23, 2018).

Clapper, Lincoln. "Wahhabiism, ISIS, and the Saudi Connection." *Geopolitical Monitor.* January 31, 2016. https://www.geopoliticalmonitor.com/wahhabism-isis-and-the-saudi-connection/ (accessed December 26, 2018).

Coll, Steve. *Ghost Wars: The Secret History of the CIA, Afghanistan and bin Laden from the Soviet Invasion to September 10, 2001.* New York: Penguin Press, 2004.

Cooper, Anderson. "Donald Trump: 'I Think Islam Hates Us.'" *CNN: Anderson Cooper 360.* March 2016. https://www.cnn.com/videos/politics/2016/03/10/donald-trump-islam-intv-ac-cooper-sot.cnn (accessed December 27, 2018).

Cottam, Richard W. *Human Rights in Iran under the Shah.* 12 Case W. Res. J. Int'l L. 121 (1980): Available at https://scholarlycommons.law.case.edu/jil/vol12/iss1/7.

Cunningham, Erin, and Abigail Hauslohner. "Egypt Sentences 683 to Death in Latest Mass Trial of Dissidents." *Washington Post*. April 28, 2014. https://www.washingtonpost.com/world/middle_east/egypt-sentences-683-to-death-in-latest-mass-trial-of-dissidents/2014/04/28/34e0ca2c-e8eb-4a85-8fa8-a7300ab11687_story.html?utm_term=.ceaf5d0fa6a2 (accessed January 9, 2018).

Curtis, Charlotte. "Tent. City. Awaits Celebration: Shah's 'Greatest Show.'" *New York Times*. October 12, 1971. https://www.nytimes.com/1971/10/12/archives/tent-city-awaits-celebration-shahs-greatest-show.html (accessed March 22, 2018).

Diamond, Jeremy. *Donald Trump: Ban All Muslim Travel to U.S.* December 8, 2015. https://www.cnn.com/2015/12/07/politics/donald-trump-muslim-ban-immigration/index.html (accessed June 30, 2017).

Dralonge, Richard N. *Economics and Geopolitics of the Middle East.* New York: Nova Science Publishers, 2008.

Duff, Michael. "Salam +50: Proceedings of the Conference." London: Imperial College Press, 2008. 85.

Eia. *Saudi Arabia.* October 20, 2017. https://www.eia.gov/beta/international/analysis.php?iso=SAU (accessed November 3, 2017).

"Eleven Facts About the Yemen Crisis." *OHCA – UN Humanitarian*, 2019. https://unocha.exposure.co/eleven-facts-about-the-yemen-crisis (accessed January 6, 2019).

Esposito, John L. *Islam: The Straight Path.* New York/Oxford: Oxford University Press, 1998.

Esposito, John L., and Dalia Mogahed. *Who Speaks for Islam?* New York: Gallup Press, 2007.

Eversley, Melanie, and Victor Kotsev. "41 Killed in Suicide Attack at Istanbul Airport." *USA Today,* June 29, 2016. http://www.usatoday.com/story/news/2016/06/28/reports-least-10-dead-blast-istanbul-airport/86481174 (accessed January 9, 2018).

Evon, Dan. "Pat Robertson Comments on Orlando Shooting." *Snopes.* June 15, 2016. https://www.snopes.com/news/2016/06/15/pat-robertson-orlando-shooting-comments/ (accessed December 26, 2018).

"FACTBOX—Five Facts about Yemen LNG." *Reuters.* October 15, 2009. https://uk.reuters.com/article/lng-yemen-total/factbox-five-facts-about-yemen-lng-idUKL959162220091015 (accessed September 12, 2017).

"Files Reveal US Had Detailed Knowledge of Indonesia's Anti-Communist Purge." *The Guardian.* October 17, 2017. https://www. theguardian.com/world/2017/oct/17/indonesia-anti-communist-killings-us-declassified-files (accessed January 6, 2018).

Ford, Dana. "UAE's First Female Fighter Pilot Led Airstrike against ISIS." *CNN.* October 9, 2014: 13. https://www.cnn. com/2014/09/25/world/meast/uae-female-fighter-pilot/index.html (accessed December 26, 2018).

"Freedom in the World: Tunisia." *Freedom House.* January 1, 2015. https://freedomhouse.org/report/freedom-world/2015/tunisia (accessed July 9, 2018).

Gettleman, Jeffrey, and Nicholas Kulish. "Gunmen Kill Dozens in Terror Attack at Kenyan Mall." *New York Times,* September 21, 2013. https://www.nytimes.com/2013/09/22/world/africa/nairobi-mall-shooting.html (accessed January 9, 2018).

Gibbons-Neff, Thomas, and Joby Warrick. "Army Special Forces Soldiers Killed in Jordan Were Working for the CIA." *Washington Post,* November 12, 2016. https://www.washingtonpost.com/world/national-security/army-special-forces-soldiers-killed-in-jordan-were-working-for-the-cia/2016/11/11/8c6b53de-7b66-40ed-9077-bf954070f2be_story.html?utm_term=.51f8748f1143 (accessed April 10, 2017).

Haass, Richard. "Towards Greater Democracy in the Muslim World." *US Department of State Archive,* December 4, 2002. https://2001-2009.state.gov/s/p/rem/15686.htm (accessed March 16, 2017).

Hamed, Muhammad. "Saudi Arabia Becomes World's Top Arms Importer." *RT.com.* March 9, 2015. https://www.rt.com/news/238881-saudi-arabia-arms-import/ (accessed September 12, 2017).

Hassan, Carma, and Catherine E. Soichet. "Arabic-Speaking Student Kicked Off Southwest Flight." *CNN,* April 18, 2016. https://www. cnn.com/2016/04/17/us/southwest-muslim-passenger-removed/index.html (accessed June 29, 2017).

Hayat, Hayatullah, Tom Bowman, and Dianne Feinstein. "Afghan Governor Wants Government to Control Poppy Crop: Interview." *NPR Morning Edition,* by David Greene (July 6, 2016).

Hazleton, Lesley. *The First Muslim: The Story of Muhammad.* New York: Riverhead Books, 2013.

Hendawi, Hamza. "Abuse Claims Rife as Egypt Admits Jailing 16,000 Islamists in Eight Months." *The Independent.* March 16, 2014. https://www.independent.co.uk/news/world/africa/abuse-claims-rife-as-egypt-admits-jailing-16000-islamists-in-eight-months-9195824.html (accessed March 16, 2018).

Islam: A Religion Based on Terrorism. 2005–2016. http://www.targetofopportunity.com/islam.htm (accessed December 18, 2018).

Kadri, Sadakat. *Heaven on Earth: A Journey Through Shari'a Law from the Deserts of Ancient Arabia to the Streets of the Modern Muslim World.* New York: Farrar, Straus, and Giroux, 2012.

Kamalipou, Yahya. *The US Media and the Middle East: Image and Perception.* Westport: Greenwood Press, 1997.

Kaphle, Anup. "Timeline: How the Benghazi Attack Played Out." *Washington Post,* June 17, 2014. https://www.washingtonpost.com/world/national-security/timeline-how-the-benghazi-attack-played-out/2014/06/17/a5c34e90-f62c-11e3-a3a5-42be35962a52_story.html?utm_term=.c938321bb639 (accessed September 14, 2017).

Keddie, Nikki R. *An Islamic Response to Imperialism.* Berkeley: University of California Press, 1983.

Kinzer, Stephen. *All the Shah's Men: An American Coup and the Roots of Middle East Terror.* Hoboken, NJ: John Wiley & Sons, 2003.

Kister, M. J. "Al-Tahannuth: An inquiry into the meaning of a term." *Bulletin of the School of Oriental and African Studies,* 1968: 223–36.

Lardner, Richard. "U.S. Commander in Africa Says Libya Is a Failed State." *Military Times,* March 8, 2016. https://www.militarytimes.com/news/pentagon-congress/2016/03/08/u-s-commander-in-africa-says-libya-is-a-failed-state (accessed January 9, 2018).

Leung, Rebecca. "Terror in Moscow." *CBS News,* October 24, 2003. https://www.cbsnews.com/news/terror-in-moscow (accessed January 9, 2018).

LeVine, Peter A. *Waking the Tiger: Healing Trauma.* Berkeley: North Atlantic Books, 1997.

Liptak, Kevin. "Trump Lands in Saudi Arabia as Controversies Swirl at Home." *CNN.com,* May 20, 2017. https://www.cnn.

com/2017/05/20/politics/donald-trump-middle-east/index.html (accessed September 12, 2017).

"Living in Indonesia." *Expat.* http://www.expat.or.id/ (accessed January 9, 2018).

Lugo, Luis, and Alan Cooperman. "Tolerance and Tension: Islam and Christianity in Sub-Saharan Africa." *Pew Research Center,* April 15, 2010. http://www.pewforum.org/2010/04/15/executive-summary-islam-and-christianity-in-sub-saharan-africa/ (accessed January 9, 2018).

Mahmood, Iftekhar. *Islam, Beyond Terrorists and Terrorism.* Lanham: University Press of America, 2002.

Massetti, Mark, Jeffrey Gettleman, and Eric Schmitt. "In Somalia, U.S. Escalates a Shadow War." *New York Times,* October 16, 2016. https://www.nytimes.com/2016/10/16/world/africa/obama-somalia-secret-war.html (accessed April 10, 2017).

Mathias, Christopher. "A Pastor Who Said Islam Is 'Evil' Is Speaking at Trump's Inauguration." *Huffpost,* January 18, 2017. https://www.huffingtonpost.com/entry/franklin-graham-islamophobia-trump-inauguration_us_587e3ea5e4b0aaa369429373 (accessed January 5, 2018).

McLeod, Hugh, and a reporter in Syria. "Syria: How It All Began." *PRI,* April 23, 2011. https://www.pri.org/stories/2011-04-23/syria-how-it-all-began (accessed December 26, 2018).

Mearsheimer, John J, and Stephen M. Walt. *The Israel Lobby and U.S. Foreign Policy.* New York: Ferrar, Straus, and Giroux, 2007.

Merdekawaty, Eda. "'Bahasa Indonesia' and Languages of Indonesia." *Wayback Machine,* July 6, 2006. https://web.archive.org/web/20060921074359/http:/www.languagestudies.unibz.it/Bahasa%20Indonesia_Merdekawaty.pdf (accessed January 9, 2018).

Mohammad, Khalid Shaikh. "Letter from the Captive Mujahid Khalid Shaikh Mohammad to the Head of the Snake, Barack Obama." *Miami Herald,* January 8, 2015. https://www.miamiherald.com/latest-news/article131466809.ece/binary/ksmlettertoobama.pdf (accessed December 22, 2018).

"Muhammad: Legacy of a Prophet." *KPBS,* 2002. http://www.pbs.org/muhammad/timeline_html.shtml (accessed December 26, 2018).

Murphy, Caryle. "Saudi Arabia's Youth and the Kingdom's Future." *New Security Beat,* February 7, 2012. https://www.newsecuritybeat.org/2012/02/saudi-arabias-youth-and-the-kingdoms-future/ (accessed September 12, 2017).

"NATO Operations in Libya: Data Journalism Breaks Down Which Country Does What." *The Guardian,* May 22, 2011. https://www.theguardian.com/news/datablog/2011/may/22/nato-libya-data-journalism-operations-country (accessed January 9, 2018).

Nicolle, David. *The Great Islamic Conquests AD 632–750: Essential Histories.* Oxford: Osprey, 2009.

Noorzoy, M. Siddieq. "Afghanistan's Children: The Tragic Victims of Thirty Years of War." *Middle East Institute,* April 20, 2012. https://www.mei.edu/publications/afghanistans-children-tragic-victims-30-years-war (accessed March 15, 2017).

"Off the Charts: Accuracy in Reporting of Israel/Palestine." *if Americans Knew,* December 2004. https://ifamericaknew.org/media/net-report.html#rt (accessed December 27, 2018).

Oliphant, Roland. "Russia Warns It Will Shoot Down Alliance Jets Over Syria if US Launches Airstrikes Against Assad." *The Telegraph,* October 6, 2016. https://www.telegraph.co.uk/news/2016/10/06/russian-air-defence-missiles-would-respond-if-us-launches-air-st/ (accessed September 12, 2017).

Palin, Megan. "'Writhing with Hunger': The Poorest Country in the Middle East on the Brink of a Catastrophic Famine." *news.com.au,* April 26, 2017. https://www.news.com.au/world/middle-east/writhing-with-hunger-the-poorest-country-in-the-middle-east-on-the-brink-of-a-catastrophic-famine/news-story/6809172e7c2cfc4e64a1bef9f7a53447 (accessed September 12, 2017).

Pape, Robert. "The Logic of Suicide Terrorism: An Interview with Robert Pape." By Scott McConnell. *The American Conservative,* July 18, 2005. https://www.theamericanconservative.com/articles/the-logic-of-suicide-terrorism/ (accessed December 27, 2018).

Pappe, Ilan. *The Ethnic Cleansing of Palestine.* London: Oneworld Publications, 2006.

Park, Haeyoun, and Rudy Omri. "US Reaches Goal of Admitting 10,000 Syrian Refugees. Here's Where They Went." *New York Times,* August 31, 2016. https://www.nytimes.com/

interactive/2016/08/30/us/syrian-refugees-in-the-united-states.html (accessed September 15, 2017).

Perci, Lauren. "Landmine Monitor 2015: Casualties and Victim Assistance." *Landmine & Cluster Munition Monitor,* May 1, 2015. http://www.the-monitor.org/en-gb/reports/2015/landmine-monitor-2015/casualties-and-victim-assistance.aspx (accessed April 5, 2017).

Pew Research Center. *Mapping the Global Muslim Population.* October 7, 2009. http://www.pewforum.org/2009/10/07/mapping-the-global-muslim-population/ (accessed December 22, 2018).

Plumer, Brad. "The U. S. Gives Egypt $1.5 Billion a Year in Aid. Here's What It Does." *Washington Post,* July 9, 2013. https://www.washingtonpost.com/news/wonk/wp/2013/07/09/the-u-s-gives-egypt-1-5-billion-a-year-in-aid-heres-what-it-does/?utm_term=.2ff696ac6a9f (accessed January 9, 2018).

Pollock, David. "Saudi Public Opinion: A Rare Look." *The Washington Institute,* January 27, 2010. https://www.washingtoninstitute.org/policy-analysis/view/saudi-public-opinion-a-rare-look (accessed September 12, 2017).

"The Punishment for Theft in the Quran." *True Islam,* 2010. http://www.quran-islam.org/articles/part_4/punishment_of_theft_(P1465).html (accessed September 10, 2017).

Purkiss, Jessica, and Jack Serle. "Obama's Covert Drone War in Numbers: 10 Times More Strikes Than Bush." *Bureau of Investigative Journalism,* January 17, 2017. https://www.thebureauinvestigates.com/stories/2017-01-17/obamas-covert-drone-war-in-numbers-ten-times-more-strikes-than-bush (accessed January 9, 2018).

"Qurra." *Encyclopedia Britannica.* 2018. https://www.britannica.com/topic/qurra (accessed December 26, 2018).

Ramesh, Randeep. "India's Secret History: 'A Holocaust, One Where Millions Disappeared....'" *The Guardian,* August 24, 2007. https://www.theguardian.com/world/2007/aug/24/india.randeepramesh (accessed December 26, 2018).

Razwy, Sayyid Ali Ashgar. "A Restatement of the History of Islam and Muslims, CE 570 to 661." *AlIslam.org,* n.d. https://www.al-islam.org/restatement-history-islam-and-muslims-sayyid-ali-ashgar-razwy (accessed December 26, 2018).

"Report: Nigeria 2017/2018." *Amnesty International.* 2018. https://www.amnesty.org/en/countries/africa/nigeria/report-nigeria (accessed April 2, 2018).

"Rome Statute of the International Criminal Court." *United Nations: Office of Legal Affairs,* July 17, 1998. http://legal.un.org/icc/statute/99_corr/cstatute.htm (accessed December 26, 2018).

Rumi, Jalal al-Din. *Love's Ripening: Rumi on the Heart's Journey.* Translated by Kabir Helminski and Ahamad Reswani. Boston: Shambhala Publications, Inc., 2008.

"Saudi Arabia." *The World Bank: Data,* 2018. https://data.worldbank.org/country/saudi-arabia (accessed December 27, 2018).

Shah, Zia H. "Prophet Muhammad (saw)'s Call to Prophethood." *Muslim Times,* July 26, 2014. https://themuslimtimes.info/2014/07/26/prophet-muhammad-saws-first-call-to-prophethood/ (accessed December 26, 2018).

Shaheen, Jack G. *Reel Bad Arabs: How Hollywood Vilifies a People.* Brooklyn: Olive Branch Press, 2001.

"Sharia (Islamic Law)." *The Religion of Peace, 2002–2018.* https://www.thereligionofpeace.com/pages/articles/sharia.aspx (accessed December 26, 2018).

Slick, Matt. "Islam, the Religion of Peace and Terrorism." *CARM: Christian Apologetics & Research Ministry,* n.d. https://carm.org/islam-religion-peace-and-terrorism (accessed December 26, 2018).

Spencer, Richard. "Tunisia Riots: Reform or Be Overthrown, US Tells Arab States Amid Fresh Riots." *The Telegraph,* January 13, 2011. https://www.telegraph.co.uk/news/worldnews/africaandindianocean/tunisia/8258077/Tunisia-riots-Reform-or-be-overthrown-US-tells-Arab-states-amid-fresh-riots.html (accessed January 9, 2018).

"The State of the World's Refugees 2000: 50 Years of Humanitarian Action." *UNHCR: The UN Refugee Agency,* January 1, 2000. https://www.unhcr.org/en-us/publications/sowr/3ebf9bab0/state-worlds-refugees-2000-fifty-years-humanitarian-action-chapter-3-rupture.html?query=Rupture (accessed September 15, 2017).

Stevens, Joe, and David B. Ottaway. "From U.S., the ABCs of Jihad." *Washington Post,* March 23, 2002. https://www.washingtonpost.com/archive/politics/2002/03/23/from-us-the-

abcs-of-jihad/d079075a-3ed3-4030-9a96-0d48f6355e54/?utm_
term=.425cf198cf88 (accessed December 26, 2018).

Stewart, Richard. *War in the Persian Gulf: Operations Desert Shield
and Desert Storm, August 1990–March 1991.* Washington DC:
Center for Military History, United States Army, 2010.

Stewart, Rory. *The Places in Between.* London: Picador, 2004.

Swangin, Bismarck, and Moohialdin Fuad. "Fathya and the Army
of Volunteers Combating Cholera in Yemen." *UNICEF,* July 5,
2017. https://www.unicef.org/infobycountry/yemen_96592.html
(accessed September 12, 2017).

"Syria Regional Refugee Response." *UNHCR: The UN Refugee
Agency,* December 20, 2018. https://data2.unhcr.org/en/situations/
syria (accessed December 26, 2018).

"Syria: Stories behind Photos of Killed Detainees." *Human Rights
Watch,* December 16, 2015. https://www.hrw.org/news/2015/12/16/
syria-stories-behind-photos-killed-detainees# (accessed
September 15, 2017).

"TAI: Turkish Aerospace Industries." *Turkish Armed Forces
Foundation,* 2018. https://www.tskgv.org.tr/contents/
ortakliklarimiz/31/677 (accessed December 26, 2018).

Talbot, Ian, and Gurharpal Singh. *The Partition of India.* Cambridge:
Cambridge University Press, 2009.

CIA World Factbook. December 3, 2018. https://www.cia.gov/
library/publications/the-world-factbook/geos/ym.html (accessed
December 23, 2018).

"Top 100 Smallest Countries by Area." *Countries-ofthe-World.com.*
https://www.countries-ofthe-world.com/smallest-countries.html
(accessed September 12, 2017).

"Transnational Issues. Middle East: Lebanon." *Central Intelligence
Agency: The World Factbook,* December 17, 2018. https://www.
cia.gov/library/publications/the-world-factbook/geos/le.html
(accessed September 12, 2017).

"Turkey Supports ISIS, Wants to Revive Ottoman Empire: Syria's
UN Envoy." *RT.com,* December 30, 2015. https://www.rt.com/
news/327413-syria-turkey-ottoman-empire/ (accessed January 9,
2018).

Weir, Alison. *Against Our Better Judgment: The Hidden History of How the U.S. Was Used to Create Israel.* Scotts Valley, CA: CreateSpace, 2014.

"What a Downed Black Hawk in Somalia Taught America." *NPR,* October 5, 2013. https://www.npr.org/2013/10/05/229561805/what-a-downed-black-hawk-in-somalia-taught-america (accessed January 9, 2018).

"Where We Work: Jordan." *United Nations Relief and Works Agency,* December 1, 2016. https://www.unrwa.org/where-we-work/jordan (accessed September 15, 2017).

"Where We Work: Lebanon." *United Nations Relief and Works Agency,* July 1, 2014. https://www.unrwa.org/where-we-work/lebanon (accessed September 12, 2017).

"Who Are Nigeria's Boko Haram Islamist Group?" *BBC News,* November 24, 2016. https://www.bbc.com/news/world-africa-13809501 (accessed July 9, 2018).

Wike, Richard. "Global Opposition to U.S. Surveillance and Drones, but Limited Harm to America's Image." *Pew Research Center,* July 14, 2014. http://www.pewglobal.org/2014/07/14/global-opposition-to-u-s-surveillance-and-drones-but-limited-harm-to-americas-image/ (accessed December 12, 2017).

"World Economic Outlook." *International Monetary Fund,* April 1, 2011. http://www.imf.org/external/pubs/ft/weo/2011/01/pdf/text.pdf (accessed January 9, 2018).

Zunes, Stephen, and John Gershman. "The United States and Lebanon: A Meddlesome History." *Foreign Policy in Focus,* April 26, 2006. http://fpif.org/the_united_states_and_lebanon_a_meddlesome_history (accessed April 11, 2017).

INDEX

Thank you for reading!

Dear Reader,

I hope you enjoyed *Why Do they Hate Us? Making Peace with the Muslim World.*

As an author, I appreciate getting feedback. I would enjoy hearing your thoughts and your own stories of your experiences with the Muslim world. You can write me at the addresses below.

Like all authors, I rely on online reviews to encourage future sales. You, the reader, have the power to influence other readers to share your journey with a book you've read. In fact, most readers pick their next book because of a review or on the advice of a friend. So, your opinion is invaluable. Would you take a few moments now to share your assessment of my book on Amazon, Goodreads or any other book review website you prefer? Your opinion will help the book marketplace become more transparent and useful to all.

Thank you so much for reading *Why Do they Hate Us?* And if you are so inclined, please visit the websites below to learn more about how you, too, can help make peace in the world.

Steve Slocum
steve@salaamusa.org
steveslocum.com
whydotheyhateus.org
salaamusa.org

ABOUT THE AUTHOR

STEVE SLOCUM took the adventure of a lifetime when he traveled with his family of five to Kazakhstan to become Christian missionaries. During their five years there, they were often on the receiving end of the iconic Muslim hospitality. It left a lasting impression. Back in the states, Slocum resumed his engineering career, but grew uneasy with the growing levels of animosity towards practicioners of Islam.

In 2018, he founded a nonprofit called *Salaam* whose mission is creating mutual understanding between Muslims, Christians, Jews and other faiths. *Salaam* is religiously unaffiliated, and its first workshop led to the rector of All Souls' Episcopal Church in San Diego, The Rev. Joseph Dirbas, to say "In a world full of division, ignorance and hate, Salaam builds the bridge of peace with education and fellowship as we share our stories and work for the common good."

Slocum is a frequent speaker at churches and civic groups, and creates awareness events, mosque visits, and other connections through Salaam. *Why Do They Hate Us?* is his first book.